Collins Social Studies Atlas for Jamaica

T0328248

In association with

This is a photograph of a classroom. You can see most of the room but not all of it. It shows how the desks and chairs are arranged in rows with the teacher and the whiteboard at the front of the classroom. Look at the plan view below to see what you can't see in the photograph.

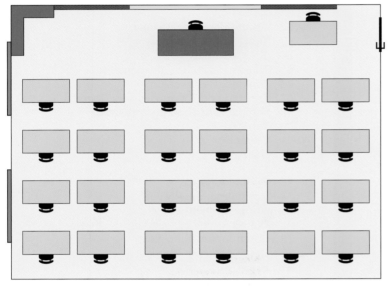

This is a plan of the same classroom. It shows the layout of the room and shows the shapes of the furniture. It is drawn as if you were looking down on it. On a plan we need to use the key to understand what each block of colour means.

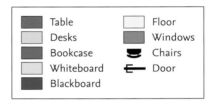

Table		Floor	
Desks		Windows	
Bookcase		Chairs	
Whiteboard		Door	
Blackboard			

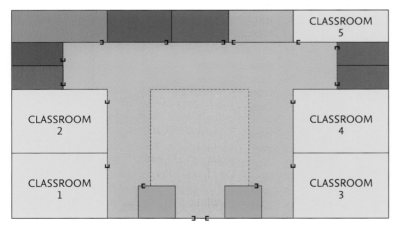

This is a plan of the whole school. It shows all the rooms in the school. Like the plan of the classroom, the key tells you what each block of colour means.

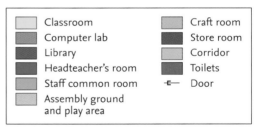

Classroom		Craft room	
Computer lab		Store room	
Library		Corridor	
Headteacher's room		Toilets	
Staff common room		Door	
Assembly ground and play area			

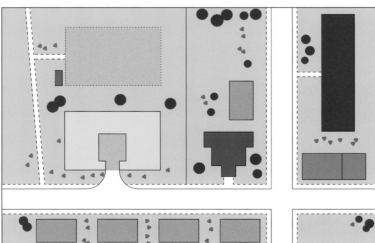

This is a map of the area around the school. It includes a larger area than the plan above and shows houses, a church and shops. The individual buildings here are smaller and less detail is given for each.

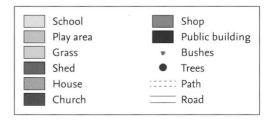

School		Shop	
Play area		Public building	
Grass		Bushes	
Shed		Trees	
House		Path	
Church		Road	

Map types

Many types of map are included in the atlas to show different information. The type of map, its symbols and colours are carefully selected to show the theme of each map and to make them easy to understand. The main types of map used are explained below.

Political maps provide an overview of the size and location of countries in a specific area, such as a continent. Coloured squares indicate national capitals. Coloured circles represent other cities or towns.

Physical or **relief maps** use colour to show oceans, seas, rivers, lakes, and the height of the land. The names and heights of major landforms are also indicated.

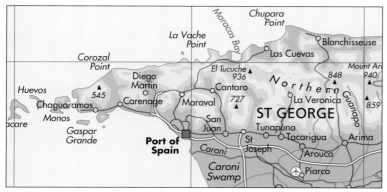

Physical/political maps bring together the information provided in the two types of map described above. They show relief and physical features as well as boundaries, major cities and towns, roads, railways and airports.

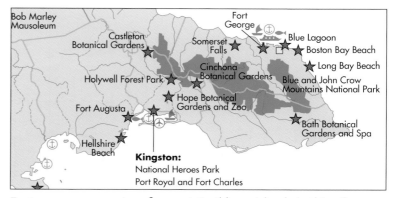

Features maps are given for most Caribbean islands in this atlas. They show points of interest, national parks, main resorts, marinas and important ports for fishing, commerce and cruise ships.

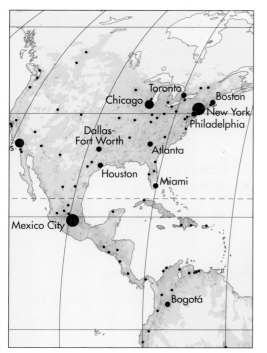

Distribution maps use different colours, symbols, or shading to show the location and distribution of natural or man-made features. In this map, symbols indicate the distribution of the world's largest cities.

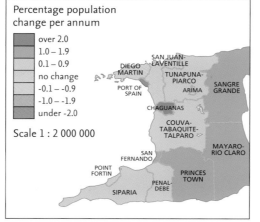

Graduated colour maps use colours or shading to show a topic or theme and a measure of its intensity. Generally, the highest values are shaded with the darkest colours. In this map, colours are used to show the percentage change of the population per year in the different areas of local government in Trinidad. It can be seen from this map that the population is increasing in the east of the island, while it is declining in the northwest.

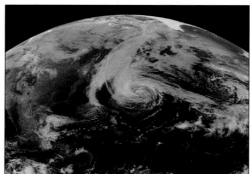

Satellite images are recorded by sensors similar to television cameras which are carried aboard satellites. These satellites orbit 500 km above our planet and beam images back to Earth. This is a natural-colour image of Hurricane Sandy, taken on 28 October 2012.

Maps use **symbols** to show the location of a feature and to give information about it. The symbols used on each map in this atlas are explained in the **key** to each map.

Symbols used on maps can be dots, diagrams, lines or area colours. They vary in colour, size and shape. The numbered captions to the map below help explain some of the symbols used on the maps in this atlas.

Different styles of type are also used to show differences between features, for example, country names are shown in large bold capital letters, small water features, rivers and lakes in small italics.

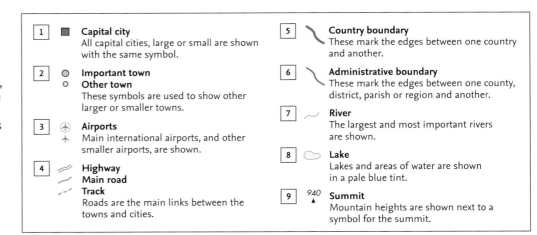

1 Capital city
All capital cities, large or small are shown with the same symbol.

2 Important town
Other town
These symbols are used to show other larger or smaller towns.

3 Airports
Main international airports, and other smaller airports, are shown.

4 Highway
Main road
Track
Roads are the main links between the towns and cities.

5 Country boundary
These mark the edges between one country and another.

6 Administrative boundary
These mark the edges between one county, district, parish or region and another.

7 River
The largest and most important rivers are shown.

8 Lake
Lakes and areas of water are shown in a pale blue tint.

9 940 Summit
Mountain heights are shown next to a symbol for the summit.

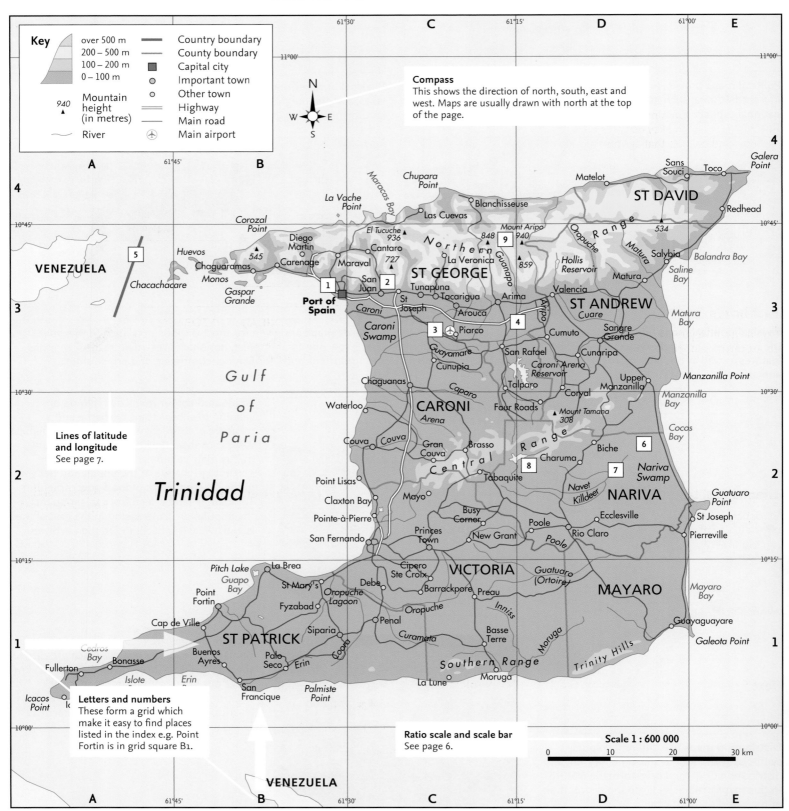

Key
over 500 m
200 – 500 m
100 – 200 m
0 – 100 m

940 Mountain height (in metres)

River

Country boundary
County boundary
Capital city
Important town
Other town
Highway
Main road
Main airport

Compass
This shows the direction of north, south, east and west. Maps are usually drawn with north at the top of the page.

Lines of latitude and longitude
See page 7.

Letters and numbers
These form a grid which make it easy to find places listed in the index e.g. Point Fortin is in grid square B1.

Ratio scale and scale bar
See page 6.

Scale 1 : 600 000

0   10   20   30 km

Location maps

These appear on most pages of the atlas. The little map shows you where the area mapped on that page is located in the world.

Photographs

There are many photographs in the atlas. Photos show you what places look like. Some photos show cities and relate to people. Other photos may relate to nature and the landscape.

Map keys

All maps have a key. A map key is a little box next to the map. The key explains all the symbols and colours that are on the map.

Mining

△ Asphalt
△ Gypsum
✕ Limestone
▭ Oilfield
▭ Gasfield
— Oil pipeline
— Gas pipeline

Scale 1 : 1 250 000

Manufacturing

▭ Factories zone
⊟ Cement works
◢ Chemicals
🏛 Oil refinery
♉ Metal
🗑 Food processing
⛏ Clothing/textiles
♀ Electrical goods
🏭 Other light industries

Features

● National park
★ Point of interest
▢ Major resort
⊕ Port
⛴ Cruise ships
⚓ Major marina
🐟 Fishing port
🗼 Lighthouse

Fact boxes

Fact boxes give you extra information about the map or region mapped on the page.

Caribbean islands facts

 Population
41 303 029

 Largest country
Cuba 110 860 sq km

 Country with most people
Cuba 11 167 325

 Largest city
Port-au-Prince (Haiti) 2 481 000

TRINIDAD AND TOBAGO

Population *(2011)*	1 328 019
Capital city	Port of Spain
Area	5128 sq km
Languages	English, creole, Hindi
National flower	Wild Poinsettia (Chaconia)
National bird *(Trinidad)*	Scarlet Ibis
National bird *(Tobago)*	Chachalaca (Cocrico)

Graphs and tables

Statistical information is shown through a variety of different kinds of graphs (histograms, line graphs and pie charts) and tables.

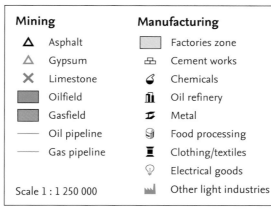

Average rainfall — Georgetown

Population increase, 1851–2011

Urban/rural population, 2011

48% 52%

▶ Urban
▶ Rural

Text

Bulleted text and photo captions give more detailed information on particular topics of interest for the area featured.

Mud volcanoes

- Mud volcanoes are a mixture of gas, mud and hot water
- The gas most associated with Trinidad's mud volcanoes is methane
- They are mainly found in the southern half of Trinidad near oil reserves
- There is no eruption of lava but the volcanoes bubble most of the time and generally form a cone of mud and clay

Island	Area (sq km)	Population (2011)	Pop. density (per sq km)
Trinidad	4828	1 267 145	262
Tobago	300	60 874	203

Using scale

The **scale** of each map in this atlas is shown in two ways:

1. The ratio scale is written, for example, as 1 : 1 000 000. This means that one unit of measurement on the map represents 1 000 000 of the same unit on the ground.

e.g. **Scale 1 : 1 000 000**

2. The line or **bar scale** shows the scale as a line with the distance on the ground marked at intervals along the line.

Different scales

The three maps below cover the same area of the page but are at different scales. Map A is a large scale map which shows a small area in detail. Map C is a small scale map which means it shows a larger area in the same space as Map A, however in much less detail. The area of Map A is highlighted on maps B and C. As the scale ratio increases the map becomes smaller.

Map A

Scale 1 : 3 500 000

Measuring distance

The scale of a map can also be used to work out how far it is between two places. In the example below, the straight line distance between Caracas and St George's on the map is 6 cm. The scale of the map is 1 : 10 000 000. Therefore 6 cm on the map represents 6 x 10 000 000 cm or 60 000 000 cm on the ground. Converted to kilometres this is 600 km. The real distance between Caracas and St George's is therefore 600 km on the ground.

Scale 1 : 10 000 000

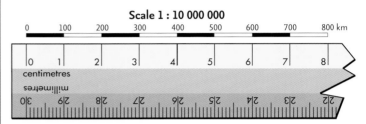

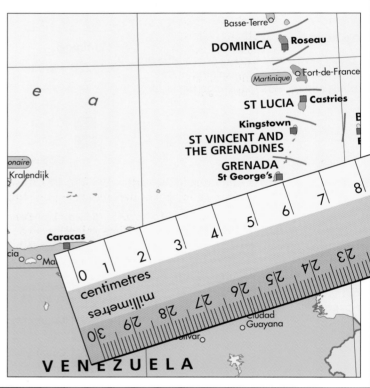

Map B

Scale 1 : 10 000 000

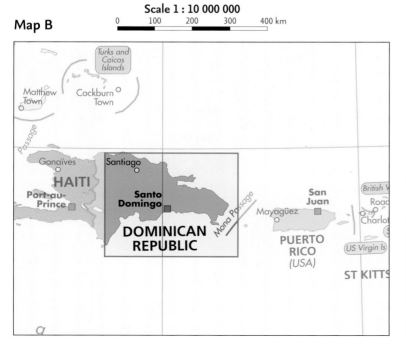

Map C

Scale 1 : 80 000 000

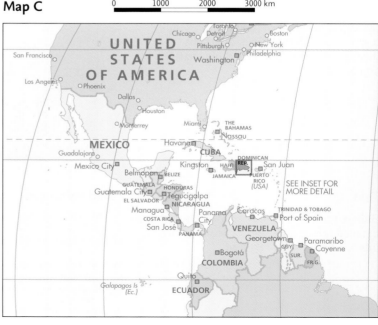

Latitude and longitude

Lines of latitude are imaginary lines which run in an east-west direction around the globe. They run parallel to each other and are measured in degrees, written as °. The most important line of latitude is the Equator, 0°. All other lines of latitude have a value between 0° and 90° north or south of the Equator. 90° north is the North Pole and, 90° south, the South Pole.

Lines of longitude are imaginary lines which run in a north-south direction between the North Pole and the South Pole. The most important line of longitude is 0°, the Greenwich Meridian, which runs through the Greenwich Observatory in London. Exactly opposite the Greenwich Meridian on the other side of the world, is the 180° line of longitude. All other lines of longitude are measured in degrees east or west of 0°.

When both lines of latitude and longitude are drawn on a map they form a grid. It is easy to find a place on the map if the latitude and longitude values are known. The point of intersection of the line of latitude and the line of longitude locates the place exactly.

The Equator can be used to divide the globe into two halves. Land north of the Equator is the Northern Hemisphere. Land south of the Equator is the Southern Hemisphere. The 0° and 180° lines of longitude can also be used to divide the globe into two halves, the Western and Eastern Hemispheres. Together, the Equator and 0° and 180°, divide the world into four areas, for example, North America is in the Northern Hemisphere and the Western Hemisphere.

1 The globe

2 Lines of latitude

North Pole (90°N)
75°N
Arctic Circle
60°N
45°N
30°N
Tropic of Cancer
15°N
Equator
15°S
Tropic of Capricorn
South Pole (90°S)

3 Lines of longitude

North Pole
40°W
30°W
Greenwich Meridian
60°E
90°E
30°E
South Pole

4 Lines of latitude and longitude

North Pole
South Pole

Time zones

Time varies around the world due to the earth's rotation. This causes different parts of the world to be in light or darkness at any one time.

To account for this, the world is divided into 24 Standard Time Zones based on 15° intervals of longitude (1 hour of time). All places in a time zone have the same time of day. The shapes of some zones have been adjusted so that all of the country or region lies in the same zone.

There is one hour difference between each zone – one hour in the day earlier to the west, one hour later to the east. The local time in another city can be found by counting the number of hours earlier or later than the local time in your own country.

The time at 0° is known as Greenwich Mean Time (GMT) because the line passes through Greenwich in London. Most countries of the Caribbean are either 4 or 5 hours behind GMT.

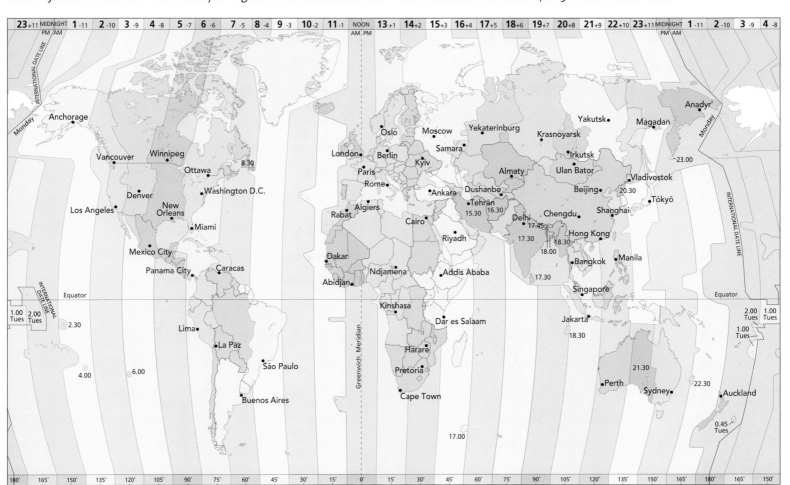

The Solar System

The Solar System is the Sun and the many objects that orbit it. These objects include eight planets, at least five dwarf planets and countless asteroids, meteoroids and comets. Orbiting some of the planets and dwarf planets are over 160 moons. The Sun keeps its surrounding objects in its orbit by its pull of gravity which has an influence for many millions of kilometres.

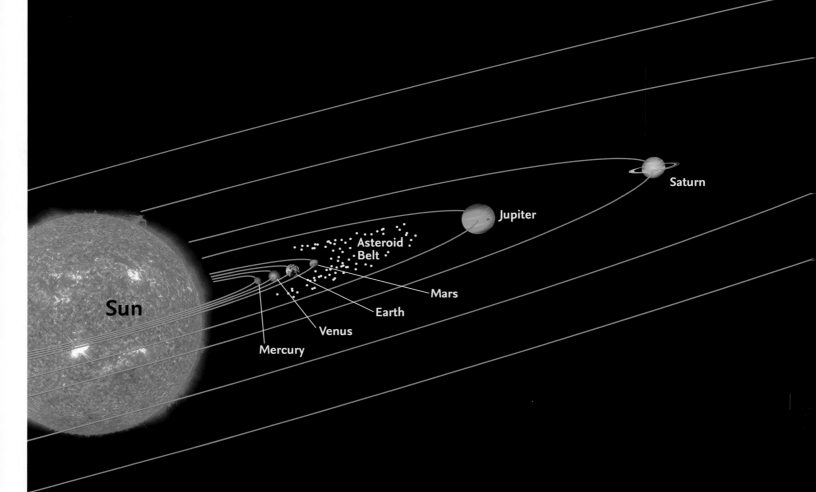

Saturn
Jupiter
Asteroid Belt
Mars
Earth
Venus
Mercury
Sun

The Sun

Diameter
1 391 016 km
Circumference
4 370 000 km
Average temperature
5504 °C
Rotation about axis
(measured at its equator)
25 Earth days 9 hours

The Planets

	Mercury	Venus	Earth	Mars
Diameter	4900 km	12 100 km	12 700 km	6779 km
Circumference	15 300 km	38 000 km	40 000 km	21 300 km
Distance from Sun	58 million km	108 million km	150 million km	228 million km
Length of year	88 Earth days	244 Earth days 17 hours	365 days 6 hours	687 Earth days
Length of day	59 Earth days	243 Earth days	23 hours 56 minutes	24 hours 37 minutes

	Jupiter	Saturn	Uranus	Neptune
Diameter	143 000 km	116 500 km	50 700 km	49 200 km
Circumference	450 000 km	366 000 km	159 000 km	154 700 km
Distance from Sun	778 million km	1427 million km	2871 million km	4498 million km
Length of year	11 Earth years 314 days	29 Earth years	84 Earth years	165 Earth years
Length of day	9 hours 55 minutes	10 hours 39 minutes	17 hours 14 minutes	16 hours 7 minutes

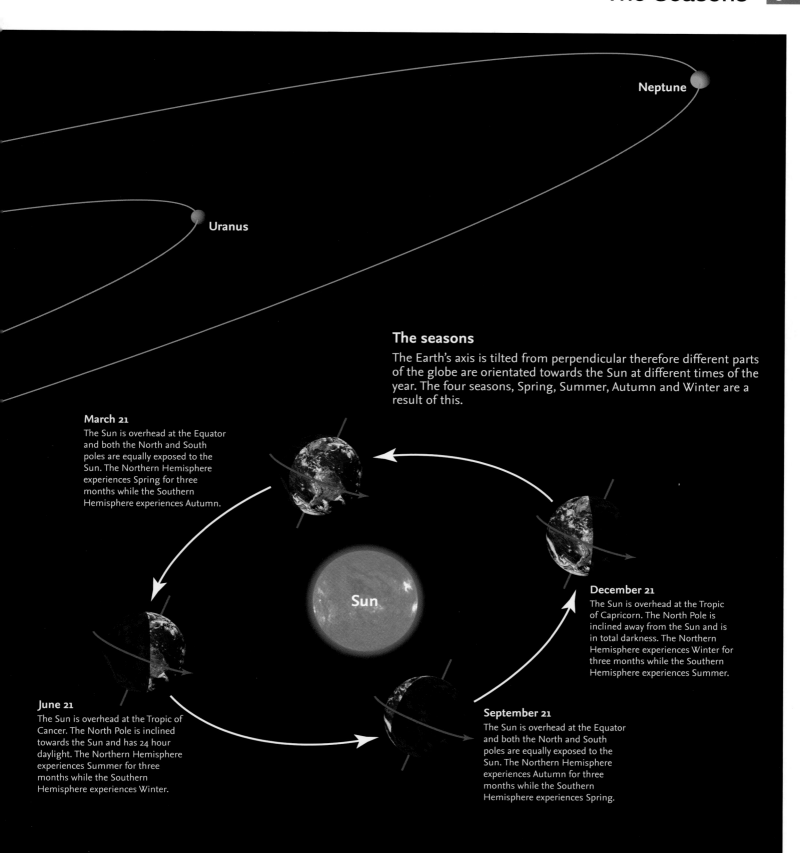

Neptune

Uranus

The seasons

The Earth's axis is tilted from perpendicular therefore different parts of the globe are orientated towards the Sun at different times of the year. The four seasons, Spring, Summer, Autumn and Winter are a result of this.

March 21
The Sun is overhead at the Equator and both the North and South poles are equally exposed to the Sun. The Northern Hemisphere experiences Spring for three months while the Southern Hemisphere experiences Autumn.

Sun

December 21
The Sun is overhead at the Tropic of Capricorn. The North Pole is inclined away from the Sun and is in total darkness. The Northern Hemisphere experiences Winter for three months while the Southern Hemisphere experiences Summer.

June 21
The Sun is overhead at the Tropic of Cancer. The North Pole is inclined towards the Sun and has 24 hour daylight. The Northern Hemisphere experiences Summer for three months while the Southern Hemisphere experiences Winter.

September 21
The Sun is overhead at the Equator and both the North and South poles are equally exposed to the Sun. The Northern Hemisphere experiences Autumn for three months while the Southern Hemisphere experiences Spring.

Day and night

The Earth turns round on its axis every 23 hours 56 minutes and it is this rotation that is responsible for the daily cycles of day and night. At any one moment in time, one half of the Earth is in sunlight, while the other half, facing away from the Sun, is in darkness. As the Earth rotates it also creates the apparent movement of the Sun from east to west across the sky.

Direction of rotation

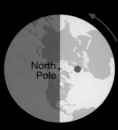
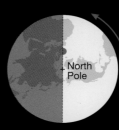

Dawn in the UK   **Midday in the UK**   **Dusk in the UK**   **Midnight in the UK**

A   90°W   B   85°W   C   80°W   D   75°W

Caribbean islands facts

Population
41 303 029

Largest country
Cuba 110 860 sq km

Country with most people
Cuba 11 167 325

Largest city
Port-au-Prince (Haiti) 2 481 000

Gulf of Mexico

U.S.A.

Freeport City

Nassau

Andros Town

THE BAHAMA

Tropic of Cancer

Straits of Florida

Havana

Cienfuegos

C U B A

Bayamo

Guantánamo

Yucatan Channel

Cayman Is

George Town

Montego Bay

Jamaica Channel

Win

JAMAICA

Kingston

Bahía de Campeche

MEXICO

Belize City

Belmopan

Flores

BELIZE

Gulf of Honduras

C a r i b b

San Pedro Sula

HONDURAS

GUATEMALA

Guatemala City

Santa Ana

Tegucigalpa

San Salvador

EL SALVADOR

Puerto Cabezas

NICARAGUA

León

Managua

Liberia

Barranquilla

Cartagena

COSTA RICA

San José

Colón

David

Panama City

PANAMA

Medellín

PACIFIC OCEAN

Manizales

Bogotá

N W E S

1 2 3 4 5

20°N
15°N
10°N
5°N

Buenaventura

Cali

Scale 1 : 10 000 000

0 100 200 300 km

A   90°W   B   85°W   C   80°W   D   75°W

Country/territory	Last coloniser	Independence/Current status	Country/territory	Last coloniser	Independence/Current status
Anguilla	UK	British Overseas Territory	Haiti	USA	1934
Antigua and Barbuda	UK	1981	Jamaica	UK	1962
Aruba	Netherlands	Self-governing Territory	Martinique	France	Department of France
The Bahamas	UK	1973	Montserrat	UK	British Overseas Territory
Barbados	UK	1966	Puerto Rico	USA	US Commonwealth
Belize	UK	1981	Saba	Netherlands	Special Municipality
Bonaire	Netherlands	Special Municipality	St-Barthélemy	France	Overseas Collectivity
British Virgin Islands	UK	British Overseas Territory	St Eustatius	Netherlands	Special Municipality
Cayman Islands	UK/Jamaica	British Overseas Territory	St Kitts and Nevis	UK	1983
Cuba	USA	1902	St Lucia	UK	1979
Curaçao	Netherlands	Self-governing Territory	St-Martin	France	Overseas Collectivity
Dominica	UK	1978	Sint Maarten	Netherlands	Self-governing Territory
Dominican Republic	Haiti/Spain	1844/1865	St Vincent and the Grenadines	UK	1979
Grenada	UK	1974	Suriname	Netherlands	1975
Guadeloupe	France	Department of France	Trinidad and Tobago	UK	1962
Guyana	UK	1966	Turks and Caicos Islands	UK	British Overseas Territory
			US Virgin Islands	USA	Unincorporated Territory

Key

- —— Country boundary
- – – Disputed boundary
- ■ Capital city
- ○ Important city / town

Territories
- France
- Netherlands
- United Kingdom
- United States

Lambert Conformal Conic projection

Caribbean islands facts

Area	234 765 sq km
Highest peak	Pico Duarte (Dom. Rep.) 3175 m
Longest river	Cauto (Cuba) 370 km
Largest lake	Lago de Enriquillo (Dom. Rep.) 265 sq km

Mangroves are common in and around the Caribbean Sea. These red mangrove roots are providing a nursery and shelter for young fish that will later populate the deeper waters.

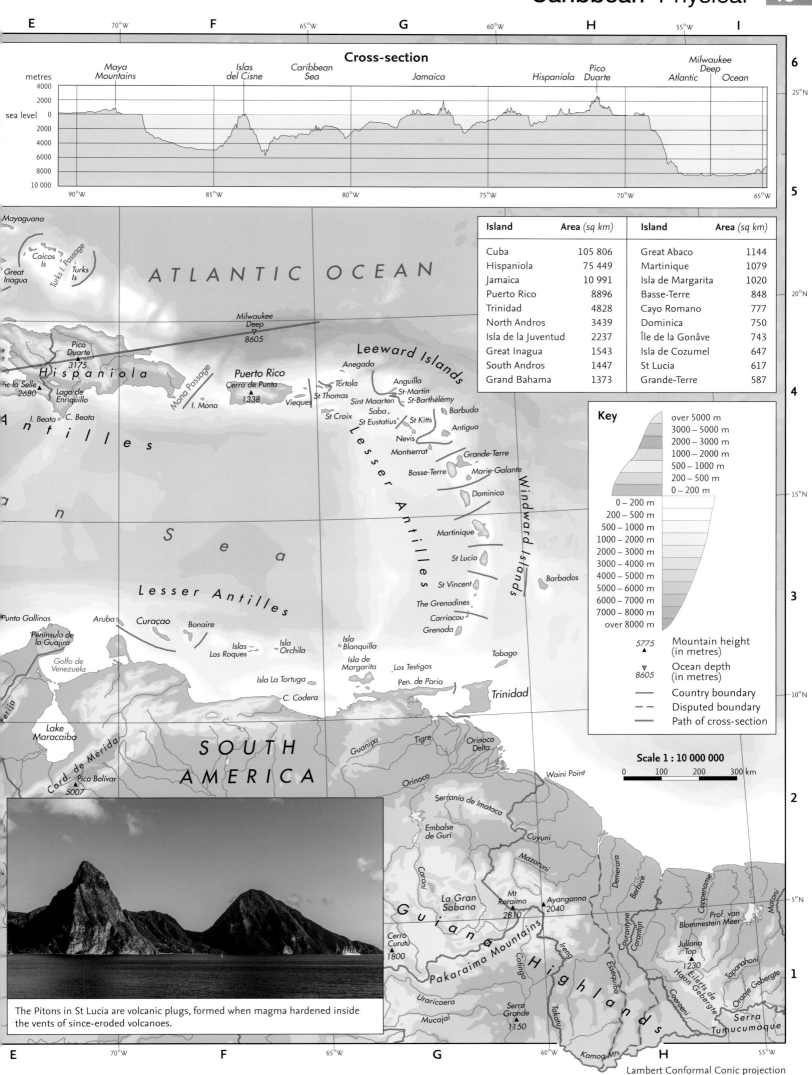

E   70°W   F   65°W   G   60°W   H   55°W   I

Cross-section

metres
4000
2000
sea level 0
2000
4000
6000
8000
10 000

Maya Mountains | Islas del Cisne | Caribbean Sea | Jamaica | Hispaniola | Pico Duarte | Milwaukee Deep | Atlantic | Ocean

90°W   85°W   80°W   75°W   70°W   65°W

25°N

6

5

Mayaguana

ATLANTIC OCEAN

Caicos Is
Turks Is
Turks I. Passage
Great Inagua

Milwaukee Deep
8605

Pico Duarte
3175
H i s p a n i o l a
Pic la Selle
2680
Lago de Enriquillo
I. Beata   C. Beata

Mona Passage
I. Mona

Puerto Rico
Cerro de Punta
1338
Vieques

Leeward Islands
Anegada
Tortola
St Thomas
St Croix
Anguilla
St-Martin
Sint Maarten   St-Barthélémy
Saba
St Eustatius   St Kitts
Nevis
Montserrat
Barbuda
Antigua

A n t i l l e s

Grande-Terre
Basse-Terre
Marie-Galante

Dominica

Windward Islands

L e s s e r   A n t i l l e s

Martinique

St Lucia

St Vincent

The Grenadines
Carriacou
Grenada

Barbados

20°N

15°N

n   S e a

L e s s e r   A n t i l l e s

Punta Gallinas
Aruba
Curaçao
Bonaire
Islas Los Roques
Isla Orchila

Isla Blanquilla
Isla de Margarita
Los Testigos

Tobago

10°N

Península de la Guajira
Golfo de Venezuela
Perijá
Lake Maracaibo

Isla La Tortuga
C. Codera

Pen. de Paria

Trinidad

S O U T H
A M E R I C A

Cord. de Mérida
Pico Bolívar
5007

Guanipa   Tigre   Orinoco Delta

Orinoco

Waini Point

Island / Area (sq km)

Island	Area (sq km)	Island	Area (sq km)
Cuba	105 806	Great Abaco	1144
Hispaniola	75 449	Martinique	1079
Jamaica	10 991	Isla de Margarita	1020
Puerto Rico	8896	Basse-Terre	848
Trinidad	4828	Cayo Romano	777
North Andros	3439	Dominica	750
Isla de la Juventud	2237	Île de la Gonâve	743
Great Inagua	1543	Isla de Cozumel	647
South Andros	1447	St Lucia	617
Grand Bahama	1373	Grande-Terre	587

Key

over 5000 m
3000 – 5000 m
2000 – 3000 m
1000 – 2000 m
500 – 1000 m
200 – 500 m
0 – 200 m

0 – 200 m
200 – 500 m
500 – 1000 m
1000 – 2000 m
2000 – 3000 m
3000 – 4000 m
4000 – 5000 m
5000 – 6000 m
6000 – 7000 m
7000 – 8000 m
over 8000 m

▲ 5775   Mountain height (in metres)
▽ 8605   Ocean depth (in metres)
———   Country boundary
- - -   Disputed boundary
———   Path of cross-section

Scale 1 : 10 000 000

0   100   200   300 km

Serranía de Imataca
Embalse de Guri
Cuyuni
Mazaruni
Caroni
La Gran Sabana
Mt Roraima
2810
Ayanganna
2040
Cerro Curutú
1800
G u i a n a
P a k a r a i m a   M o u n t a i n s
Colingo
Urcaricoera
Serra Grande
1150
Mucajaí
Takutu
Kamoa Mts
Ireng
Essequibo
Courantyne
Corantijn
Coppename
Demerara
Berbice
H i g h l a n d s
Prof. van Blommestein Meer
Juliana Top
1230
Eilerts de Haan Gebergte
Saramacca
Oranje Gebergte
Tapanahoni
Maroni
Serra Tumucumaque

The Pitons in St Lucia are volcanic plugs, formed when magma hardened inside the vents of since-eroded volcanoes.

E   70°W   F   65°W   G   60°W   H   55°W

Lambert Conformal Conic projection

Rainfall, winds and currents

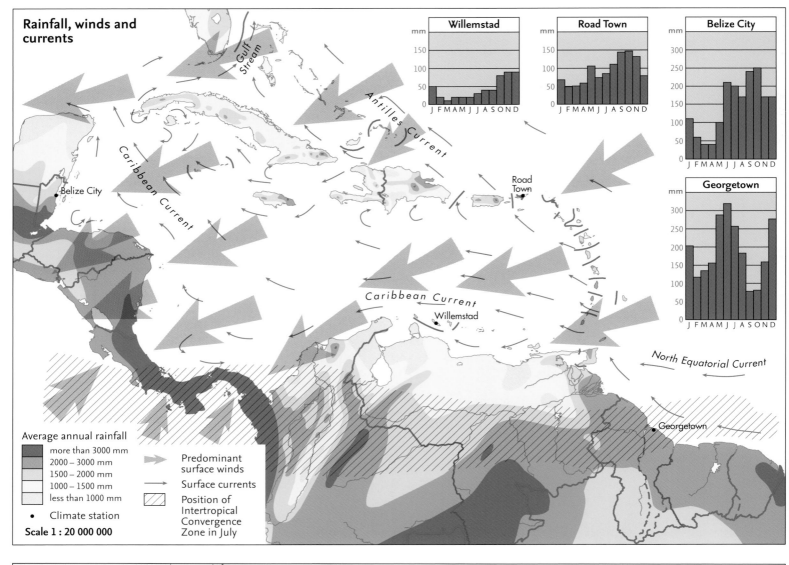

Willemstad

Road Town

Belize City

Georgetown

Average annual rainfall

- more than 3000 mm
- 2000 – 3000 mm
- 1500 – 2000 mm
- 1000 – 1500 mm
- less than 1000 mm

- Climate station

Scale 1 : 20 000 000

Predominant surface winds

Surface currents

Position of Intertropical Convergence Zone in July

Gulf Stream

Antilles Current

Caribbean Current

Caribbean Current

North Equatorial Current

Belize City

Road Town

Willemstad

Georgetown

Climate regions

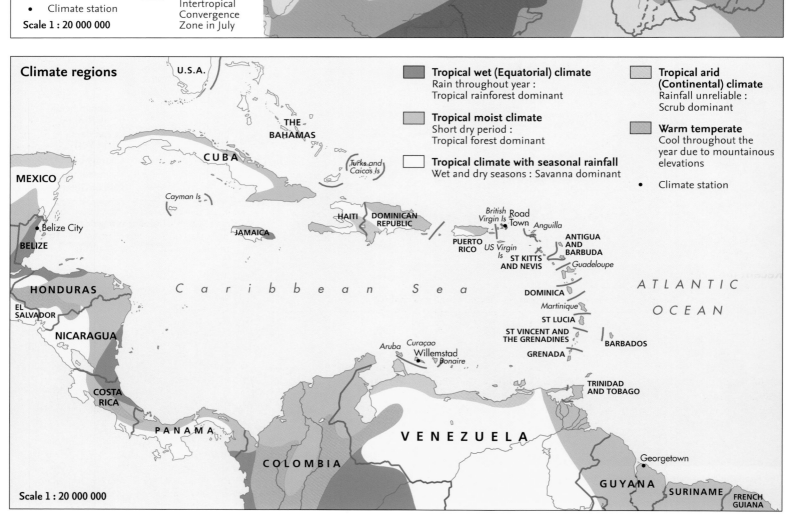

Tropical wet (Equatorial) climate
Rain throughout year :
Tropical rainforest dominant

Tropical moist climate
Short dry period :
Tropical forest dominant

Tropical climate with seasonal rainfall
Wet and dry seasons : Savanna dominant

Tropical arid (Continental) climate
Rainfall unreliable :
Scrub dominant

Warm temperate
Cool throughout the year due to mountainous elevations

- Climate station

U.S.A.

THE BAHAMAS

CUBA

MEXICO

Turks and Caicos Is

Cayman Is

Belize City

BELIZE

JAMAICA

HAITI

DOMINICAN REPUBLIC

British Virgin Is

Road Town

Anguilla

PUERTO RICO

US Virgin Is

ST KITTS AND NEVIS

ANTIGUA AND BARBUDA

Guadeloupe

HONDURAS

DOMINICA

EL SALVADOR

Martinique

ST LUCIA

NICARAGUA

ST VINCENT AND THE GRENADINES

BARBADOS

Aruba

Curaçao

Willemstad

Bonaire

GRENADA

COSTA RICA

C a r i b b e a n   S e a

A T L A N T I C

O C E A N

TRINIDAD AND TOBAGO

PANAMA

VENEZUELA

COLOMBIA

Georgetown

GUYANA

SURINAME

FRENCH GUIANA

Scale 1 : 20 000 000

Hurricanes affecting the Caribbean originate over the warm waters of the Atlantic Ocean or Caribbean Sea. They rotate anticlockwise and always try to move north, but are often forced to travel west or northwest before they can turn. The tracks on the map below show how they do this. Their wind strength declines rapidly once they reach land, but they may still be very wet and cause extensive flooding.

- The most deaths usually occur in the poorest communities
- Heavy rainfall during a hurricane may be more damaging than the wind or storm surge
- Mountainous islands are vulnerable to severe flooding, mudslides and landslides
- Flatter islands suffer much damage from storm surges and coastal flooding
- Many islands are hit by major hurricanes, but those with good preparations and a sound building code rarely have any deaths
- The extent and cost of damage can be excessive even if there are no deaths

Hurricane risk

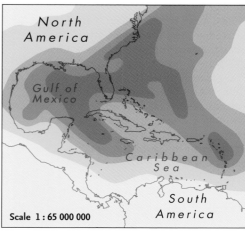

Scale 1 : 65 000 000

Chance of a hurricane during one year

less than 5% | 5 – 35% | 35 – 55% | 55 – 65% | 65 – 90%

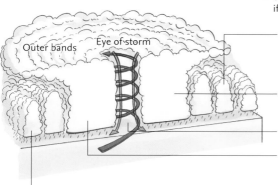

As the hurricane passes, wind speeds and rainfall decrease and the outer bands bring sunny intervals

After the eye has passed, hurricane-force winds begin immediately from the opposite direction, often accompanied by heavy rain

In the eye of the storm, winds are light and the sky is clear with little rain

Closer to the centre, wind speeds increase to over 100 km/hr, and there may be torrential rain (more than 200 mm/day)

As the hurricane approaches, clouds form and the wind speed increases. The outer bands bring alternate rain showers and sunny intervals

Total number of recorded storms for each month over a century

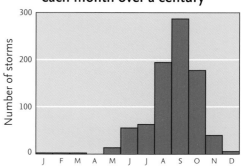

Hurricane tracks

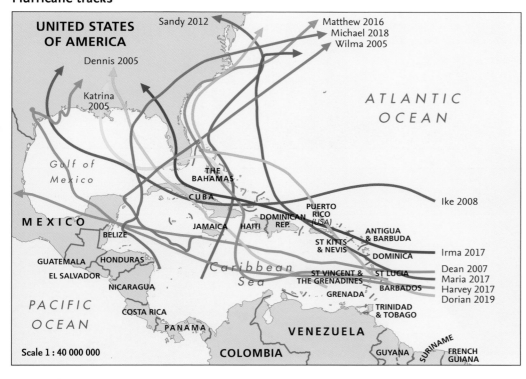

Scale 1 : 40 000 000

Hurricane Sandy extended over 1000 km and moved very slowly, staying over Cuba, Haiti and The Bahamas for many days and causing much damage.

Recent hurricanes

Year	Name	Category	Main countries/territories affected (number of deaths)
2005	Dennis	4	Haiti (56), Jamaica (1), Cuba (16), USA (15)
2005	Katrina	5	USA (>1200)
2005	Wilma	4	Haiti (12), Jamaica (1), Cuba (4), Mexico (8), USA (61)
2007	Dean	5	Martinique (3), Dominica (2), Haiti (14), Jamaica (3), Belize, Mexico (13)
2008	Ike	4	Turks & Caicos Is, The Bahamas, Dom. Rep. (2), Haiti (74), Cuba (7), USA (113)
2012	Sandy	3	Jamaica (2), Cuba (11), Haiti (54), Dom. Rep. (2), The Bahamas (2), USA (157)
2016	Matthew	5	Haiti (>500), Dom. Rep. (4), Cuba (4), The Bahamas, USA (47)
2017	Harvey	4	Suriname, Guyana (1), Barbados, St Vincent & Grenadines, USA (76)
2017	Irma	5	Antigua & Barbuda (3), St-Martin/St-Barthélemy (11), Sint Maarten (4), British Virgin Is (4), US Virgin Is (4), Puerto Rico (3), Cuba (10), USA (88)
2017	Maria	5	Dominica (65), Guadeloupe (2), Puerto Rico (2975), Dom. Rep. (5), USA (4)
2018	Michael	5	Honduras (8), Nicaragua (4), El Salvador (3), USA (59)
2019	Dorian	5	The Bahamas (74), Puerto Rico (1), USA (9)

The Red Cross distributes supplies in Port-au-Prince, Haiti, in the aftermath of Hurricane Sandy.

The world's major earthquakes occur most frequently at the boundaries of the crustal plates. As all the Caribbean islands are located around the edge of the Caribbean plate they are vulnerable to earthquakes as this plate moves relative to its neighbours. The greatest movement is in the west in Central America, which has the worst earthquakes. Next in severity is the northern boundary, which includes Jamaica and Hispaniola, and the least pressure is exerted in the Eastern Caribbean, which has smaller earthquakes.

The Caribbean islands have around 20 – 30 minor earthquakes a year; they are more common than hurricanes.

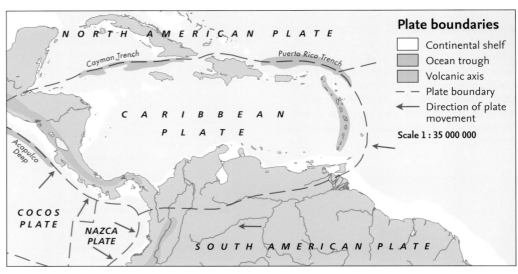

Plate boundaries

- Continental shelf
- Ocean trough
- Volcanic axis
- – – Plate boundary
- ← Direction of plate movement

Scale 1 : 35 000 000

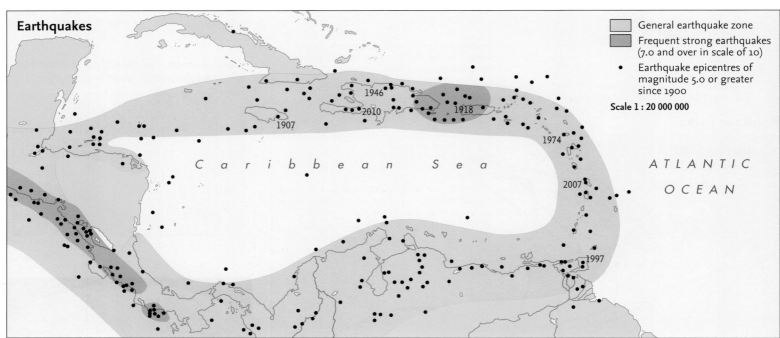

Earthquakes

- General earthquake zone
- Frequent strong earthquakes (7.0 and over in scale of 10)
- • Earthquake epicentres of magnitude 5.0 or greater since 1900

Scale 1 : 20 000 000

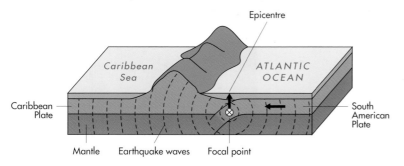

Major earthquakes

Year	Location	Magnitude (Richter scale)	
1692	Port Royal, Jamaica	7.5	2000 dead; also minor earthquakes in 1907 and 1993
1842	Cap-Haïtien, Haiti	8.1	5000 dead
1843	near Guadeloupe	8.0 – 8.5	2000 – 3000 dead on Guadeloupe; English Harbour on Antigua submerged
1907	Kingston, Jamaica	6.5	800 – 1000 dead
1918	western Puerto Rico	7.5	118 dead
1946	El Cibao, Dom. Rep.	8.1	75 dead
1974	near Antigua	7.5	many islands affected; epicentre in Venezuela
1997	Trinidad and Tobago	6.5	81 dead in Venezuela
2007	Martinique	7.4	6 dead
2010	Port-au-Prince, Haiti	7.0	230 000 dead

Transitional shelter homes being built in large numbers near Port-au-Prince, Haiti, in the aftermath of the devastating earthquake of 2010.

Like earthquakes, volcanoes occur mainly along plate boundaries and the Caribbean is no exception. One difference is that they do not occur along the northern edge of the plate as this is not a collision zone, but they do occur in the west and east. For the same reason that Central America has the largest earthquakes it also has the largest number of volcanoes, and the most active ones. The Eastern Caribbean is a less active plate margin, but the few active volcanoes it does have are extremely dangerous and these, and older dormant volcanoes, are what formed many of the islands.

- Most Caribbean volcanoes are dormant but may erupt in the future
- Volcanic activity, such as sulphur springs and fumaroles, is common on many islands (e.g. Dominica, St Lucia, St Kitts, Montserrat)

Scale 1 : 15 000 000

Volcanoes

▲ Currently active   ▲ Dormant   ▲ Extinct

1 Saba, 1640
2 The Quill, St Eustatius, 250 AD ± 150 years
3 Mount Liamuiga, St Kitts and Nevis, 160 AD ± 200 years
4 Nevis Peak, St Kitts and Nevis
5 Soufrière Hills, Montserrat, 1995 – 2011, 2012
6 Bouillante Chain, Guadeloupe
7 La Soufrière, Guadeloupe, 1977
8 Morne Aux Diables, Dominica
9 Morne Diablotins, Dominica
10 Morne Trois Pitons, Dominica, 920 AD ± 50 years
11 Morne Watt, Dominica, 1997
12 Morne Plat Pays, Dominica, 1270 ± 50 years
13 Montagne Pelée, Martinique, 1932
14 Qualibou, St Lucia, 1766
15 Soufrière, St Vincent and the Grenadines, 1979
16 Kick 'em Jenny, Grenada, 2001
17 Mount St Catherine, Grenada

List gives year of last eruption

Volcanic eruptions

Year	Volcano	Location		
1902 (and 1979, minor)	Soufrière	St Vincent	2000 dead	
1902 (and 1932, minor)	Montagne Pelée	Martinique	30 000 dead	
1939 – present	Kick 'em Jenny	off the coast of Grenada		
1977	La Soufrière	Basse-Terre, Guadeloupe	evacuated, no deaths	
1995 – present	Soufrière Hills	Montserrat	southern two-thirds of the island abandoned	

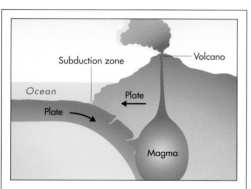

Formation of Caribbean volcanoes

Wherever two tectonic plates collide a destructive margin is formed. One of these plates will be forced under the other in an area called the subduction zone. Friction (and the increase in temperature as the crust moves downwards) causes the crust to melt and some of the newly formed magma may be forced to the surface to form volcanoes.

The structure of a typical volcano formed in this way is shown below. The increase in pressure as the plate is forced downwards can also trigger severe earthquakes.

Montserrat

- In 1995 there were minor eruptions at the summit of Soufrière Hills, and then later in the year more severe eruptions covered parts of Plymouth in ash
- It was decided to evacuate Plymouth at the end of 1995 and although there were attempts to resettle the town, a major eruption in September 1996 destroyed much of the southern half of the island
- In 1997 a further eruption destroyed the rest of Plymouth and the airport, killing 26 people who had not left the area. Ash and sediment covered much of Plymouth
- As volcanic activity has continued to this day, the southern two-thirds of the island has been abandoned and new settlements, and an airport, set up in the northern sector
- The larger part of Montserrat will remain uninhabitable for the foreseeable future. A permanent volcanic observatory monitors the situation around the clock
- The population has declined from about 10 000 in 1995 to about 5000 today

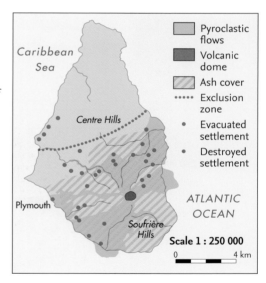

Pyroclastic flows

Volcanic dome

Ash cover

Exclusion zone

Evacuated settlement

Destroyed settlement

Scale 1 : 250 000

0   4 km

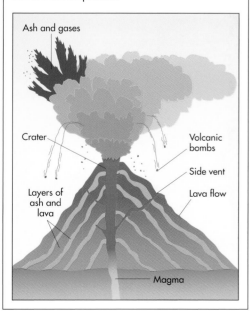

A view of the buried town of Plymouth from the sea. In the foreground the ash and sediment has reached the sea. The Soufrière Hills are in the centre background, and the highest point, Chances Peak, is on the right covered in cloud. The South Soufrière Hills are on the far right.

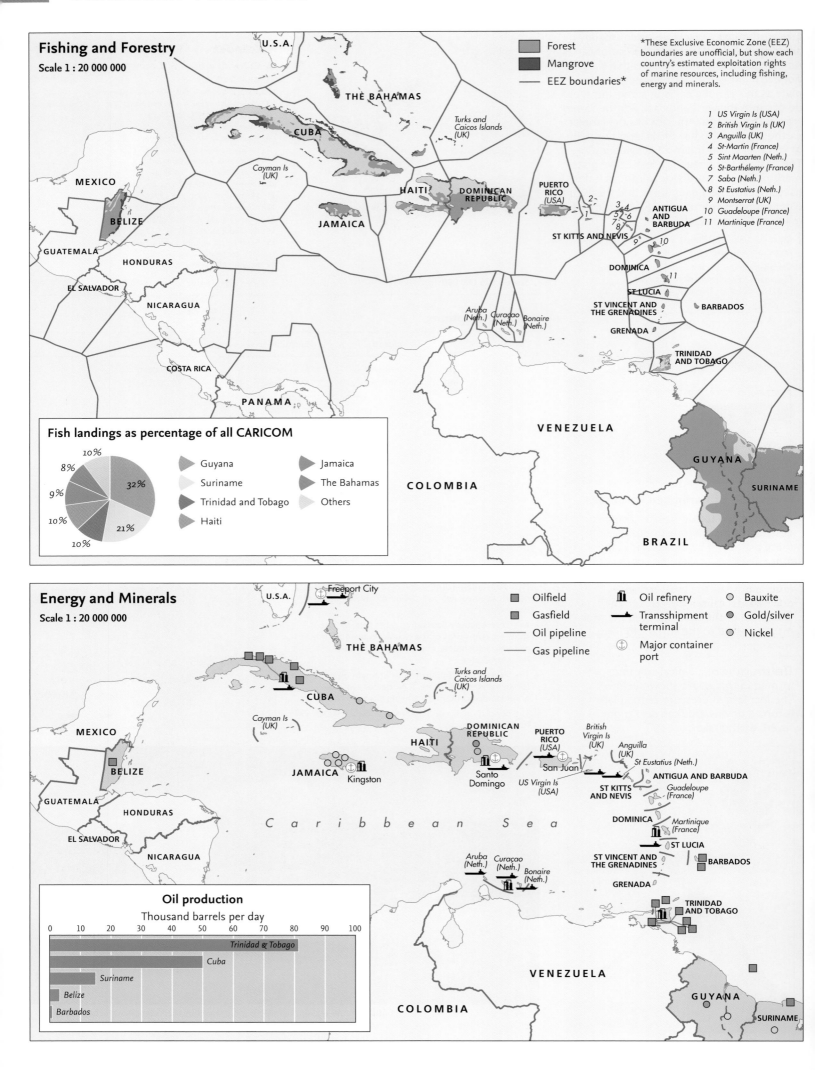

Fishing and Forestry

Scale 1 : 20 000 000

Forest
Mangrove
EEZ boundaries*

*These Exclusive Economic Zone (EEZ) boundaries are unofficial, but show each country's estimated exploitation rights of marine resources, including fishing, energy and minerals.

1 US Virgin Is (USA)
2 British Virgin Is (UK)
3 Anguilla (UK)
4 St-Martin (France)
5 Sint Maarten (Neth.)
6 St-Barthélemy (France)
7 Saba (Neth.)
8 St Eustatius (Neth.)
9 Montserrat (UK)
10 Guadeloupe (France)
11 Martinique (France)

U.S.A.
THE BAHAMAS
Turks and Caicos Islands (UK)
CUBA
Cayman Is (UK)
MEXICO
BELIZE
GUATEMALA
HONDURAS
EL SALVADOR
NICARAGUA
COSTA RICA
PANAMA
HAITI
DOMINICAN REPUBLIC
JAMAICA
PUERTO RICO (USA)
ANTIGUA AND BARBUDA
ST KITTS AND NEVIS
DOMINICA
ST LUCIA
ST VINCENT AND THE GRENADINES
BARBADOS
GRENADA
Aruba (Neth.)
Curaçao (Neth.)
Bonaire (Neth.)
TRINIDAD AND TOBAGO
VENEZUELA
COLOMBIA
GUYANA
SURINAME
BRAZIL

Fish landings as percentage of all CARICOM

10%
8%
9%
10%
10%
21%
32%

Guyana
Suriname
Trinidad and Tobago
Haiti
Jamaica
The Bahamas
Others

Energy and Minerals

Scale 1 : 20 000 000

Oilfield
Gasfield
Oil pipeline
Gas pipeline

Oil refinery
Transshipment terminal
Major container port

Bauxite
Gold/silver
Nickel

Freeport City
U.S.A.
THE BAHAMAS
Turks and Caicos Islands (UK)
CUBA
Cayman Is (UK)
MEXICO
BELIZE
GUATEMALA
HONDURAS
EL SALVADOR
NICARAGUA
HAITI
DOMINICAN REPUBLIC
Santo Domingo
JAMAICA
Kingston
PUERTO RICO (USA)
San Juan
British Virgin Is (UK)
US Virgin Is (USA)
Anguilla (UK)
St Eustatius (Neth.)
ANTIGUA AND BARBUDA
ST KITTS AND NEVIS
Guadeloupe (France)
DOMINICA
Martinique (France)
ST LUCIA
ST VINCENT AND THE GRENADINES
BARBADOS
GRENADA
Aruba (Neth.)
Curaçao (Neth.)
Bonaire (Neth.)
TRINIDAD AND TOBAGO
Caribbean Sea
VENEZUELA
COLOMBIA
GUYANA
SURINAME

Oil production

Thousand barrels per day

0 10 20 30 40 50 60 70 80 90 100

Trinidad & Tobago
Cuba
Suriname
Belize
Barbados

Population and Language

Scale 1 : 20 000 000

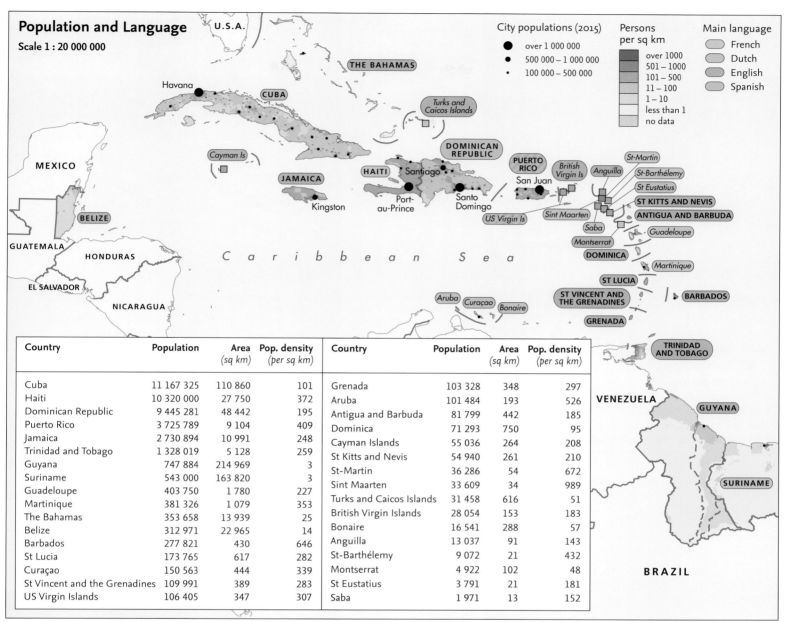

Country	Population	Area (sq km)	Pop. density (per sq km)
Cuba	11 167 325	110 860	101
Haiti	10 320 000	27 750	372
Dominican Republic	9 445 281	48 442	195
Puerto Rico	3 725 789	9 104	409
Jamaica	2 730 894	10 991	248
Trinidad and Tobago	1 328 019	5 128	259
Guyana	747 884	214 969	3
Suriname	543 000	163 820	3
Guadeloupe	403 750	1 780	227
Martinique	381 326	1 079	353
The Bahamas	353 658	13 939	25
Belize	312 971	22 965	14
Barbados	277 821	430	646
St Lucia	173 765	617	282
Curaçao	150 563	444	339
St Vincent and the Grenadines	109 991	389	283
US Virgin Islands	106 405	347	307

Country	Population	Area (sq km)	Pop. density (per sq km)
Grenada	103 328	348	297
Aruba	101 484	193	526
Antigua and Barbuda	81 799	442	185
Dominica	71 293	750	95
Cayman Islands	55 036	264	208
St Kitts and Nevis	54 940	261	210
St-Martin	36 286	54	672
Sint Maarten	33 609	34	989
Turks and Caicos Islands	31 458	616	51
British Virgin Islands	28 054	153	183
Bonaire	16 541	288	57
Anguilla	13 037	91	143
St-Barthélemy	9 072	21	432
Montserrat	4 922	102	48
St Eustatius	3 791	21	181
Saba	1 971	13	152

Tourism

Scale 1 : 22 500 000

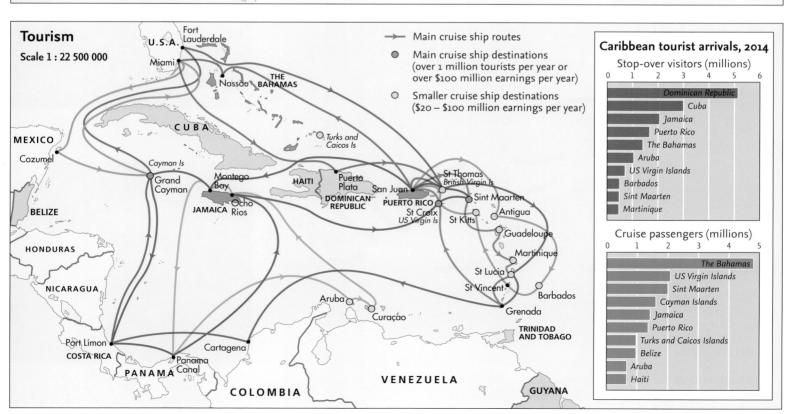

Caribbean tourist arrivals, 2014
Stop-over visitors (millions)
Cruise passengers (millions)

Amerindian civilisations, 1000 BC – AD 1500

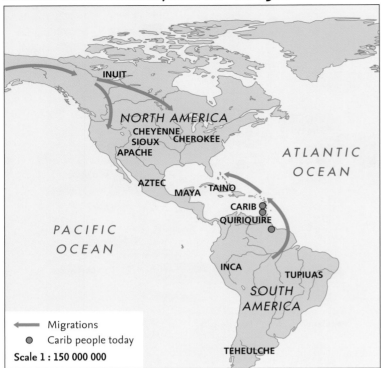

Migrations
Carib people today
Scale 1 : 150 000 000

European exploration westwards, up to AD 1500

Early Norse explorers
First voyage of Columbus 1492 – 1493
Scale 1 : 150 000 000

The migration of people from Asia to America across the Bering Strait began about 13 000 years ago. These people, today known as Amerindians, moved southwards from Alaska establishing great civilisations throughout the Americas. Carib and Taino peoples migrated northwards from South America to Jamaica, Cuba and The Bahamas. Caribs who survived the European invasions are now mainly concentrated in Dominica where some 3000 live, with a few hundred spread throughout the other Eastern Caribbean islands. Many Amerindian tribes, including Caribs, survive today in parts of Guyana, Suriname and French Guiana. Belize's present day population includes people descended from the Maya civilisation.

There is evidence to suggest that there was European exploration of North America before Columbus. According to Icelandic Sagas, Vikings first settled in Greenland in the 980s. The only known site of a Viking village in North America outside Greenland is L'Anse aux Meadows in Newfoundland which may be connected with an attempt by Leif Ericson to establish the colony of Vinland around 1003. In 1492 Christopher Columbus set sail westwards from Europe and explored the Greater Antilles. He first landed in The Bahamas and went on to sight and name many of the islands in the Caribbean. He was to make four voyages of discovery and opened up the New World.

Enslavement of Africans, 1500 – 1870

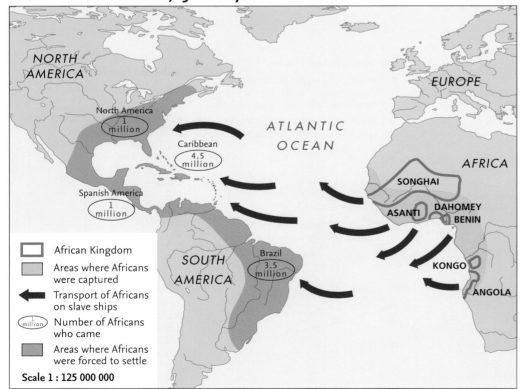

African Kingdom
Areas where Africans were captured
Transport of Africans on slave ships
Number of Africans who came
Areas where Africans were forced to settle
Scale 1 : 125 000 000

The El Castillo ruin in the ancient Mayan city of Xunantunich in Belize. El Castillo was probably built around AD 800.

Christopher Columbus (1451–1506) was Italian, but his great voyages were undertaken for the king and queen of Spain, which ensured the influence of Spain in the region for ever afterward.

At the beginning of the 16th century Africans were captured and transported across the Atlantic in ships to work as slaves in the Americas. Many died on the three-month voyage but 10 million Africans did arrive with 4.5 million forced to settle in the Caribbean.

Migration of peoples to the Caribbean, 1830s – 1920s

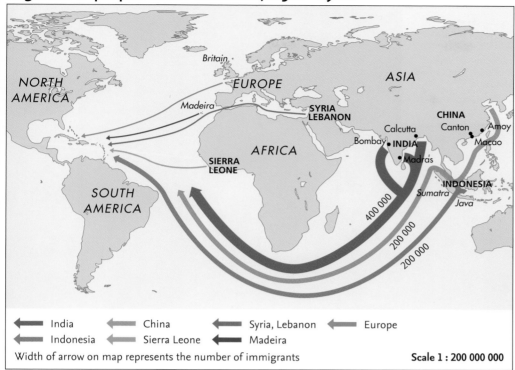

India
China
Syria, Lebanon
Europe
Indonesia
Sierra Leone
Madeira

Width of arrow on map represents the number of immigrants

Scale 1 : 200 000 000

Some peoples migrated to the Caribbean of their own free will from Africa, Europe and Asia – the greatest numbers coming from India, Indonesia and China. The Caribbean is now a multicultural area as different groups have brought their own languages, religions and cultures to the region and integrated with existing communities.

Colonies that recruited immigrants

Indians
Indonesians
Chinese
Madeirans

Scale 1 : 40 000 000

The Syrian community in Martinique is about 1000-strong and has become fully integrated.

Emigration from the English-speaking Caribbean, 1850s – today

Migrations
Caribbean member of the Commonwealth

Scale 1 : 80 000 000

As well as people migrating to the Caribbean, large numbers of Caribbean people have emigrated from the region. From the 1850s to the 1930s migrants from the former British Caribbean colonies moved to Latin America where developments such as the opening of oilfields in Venezuela and building of the Panama Canal created new opportunities. Caribbean people also migrated northwards to the USA and Canada from 1900 onwards in search of a better life. Serious labour shortages in Britain after the Second World War resulted in government recruitment schemes aimed at encouraging Colonial workers to fill this gap. Nearly a million people crossed the Atlantic from the West Indies to take up new employment in Britain, the main migration taking place between 1945 and 1962.

Patricia Scotland was born in Dominica but her family migrated to the UK, where she was made a Baroness. She is the first woman to become Secretary-General of the Commonwealth of Nations.

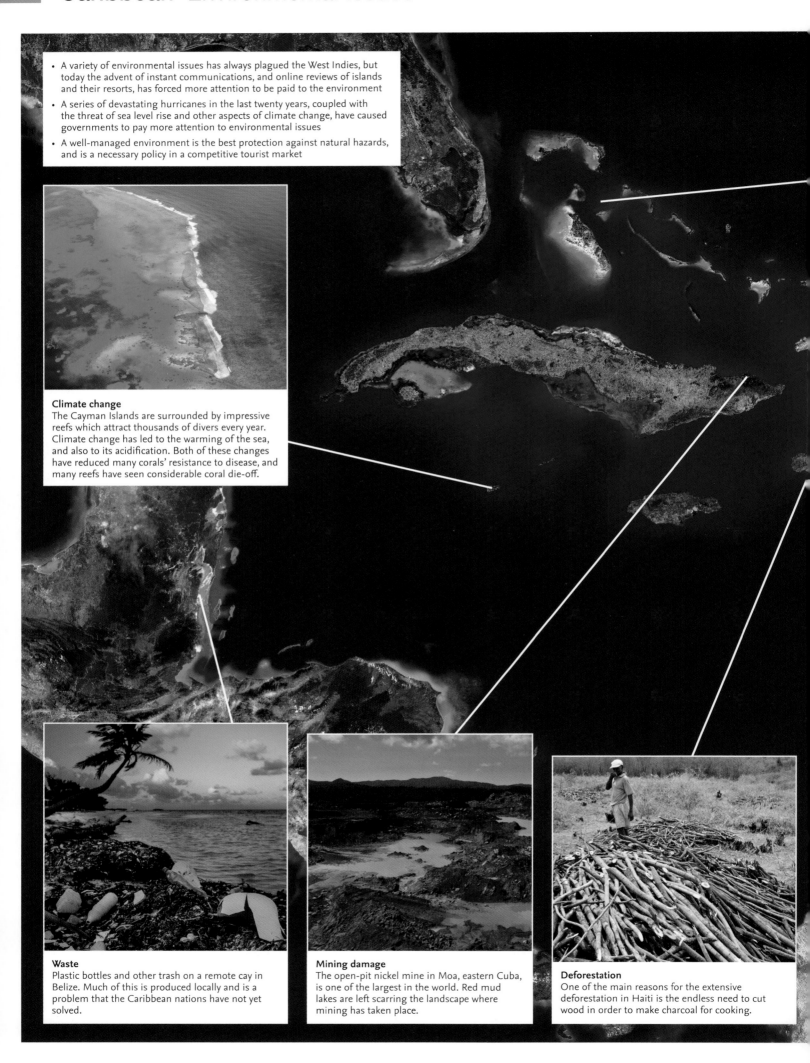

- A variety of environmental issues has always plagued the West Indies, but today the advent of instant communications, and online reviews of islands and their resorts, has forced more attention to be paid to the environment
- A series of devastating hurricanes in the last twenty years, coupled with the threat of sea level rise and other aspects of climate change, have caused governments to pay more attention to environmental issues
- A well-managed environment is the best protection against natural hazards, and is a necessary policy in a competitive tourist market

Climate change
The Cayman Islands are surrounded by impressive reefs which attract thousands of divers every year. Climate change has led to the warming of the sea, and also to its acidification. Both of these changes have reduced many corals' resistance to disease, and many reefs have seen considerable coral die-off.

Waste
Plastic bottles and other trash on a remote cay in Belize. Much of this is produced locally and is a problem that the Caribbean nations have not yet solved.

Mining damage
The open-pit nickel mine in Moa, eastern Cuba, is one of the largest in the world. Red mud lakes are left scarring the landscape where mining has taken place.

Deforestation
One of the main reasons for the extensive deforestation in Haiti is the endless need to cut wood in order to make charcoal for cooking.

Invasive species

The **cane toad** is a native of South America, but was introduced into the Eastern Caribbean as long ago as the 19th century. It is an omnivore and will eat small animals, as well as being poisonous (including its tadpoles). As recently as 2013 it had invaded The Bahamas.

The **casuarina** (commonly called the Australian pine) is widespread in the Caribbean, where it suppresses the native vegetation and can cause beach erosion. This stand on Paradise Island in The Bahamas has since been removed.

The **lionfish** is an Indo-Pacific species that is a voracious carnivore with poisonous spines. It has invaded the entire Caribbean, probably starting from the US coast, where some are believed to have escaped from an aquarium, then spreading south through The Bahamas. It can be eaten and this is one way of reducing its numbers.

Endangered species
Whale-watching is a popular tourist attraction on many Caribbean islands from the Turks and Caicos to Dominica and St Lucia. Unfortunately many whales, like this humpback, are endangered.

Wind power
Aruba is blessed with strong winds throughout the year. Power from wind turbines has reduced its energy costs and dependence on oil.

Coral reef damage
Coral bleaching is the effect of any disease causing the coral to die and leave a white patch on its skeleton, as seen by this example from Curaçao. This has seriously affected all the Caribbean reefs and the dive tourist industry.

Carbon dioxide emissions
Trinidad and Tobago has one of the highest amounts of CO_2 emissions per person in the Caribbean – 25 tonnes per person in 2014, compared to the global average of 5. The former Netherlands Antilles is another high emitter; both areas have large oil refineries.

Flag

The colours of the national flag symbolize different aspects of the island. **Gold** represents the country's wealth and sunshine, **green** reflects the island's rich vegetation and **black** stands for the creativity and strength of the people.

Coat of Arms

Jamaica's history and natural wealth are symbolized in each part of the Coat of Arms. The two figures on either side of the shield represent the first inhabitants of Jamaica, the **Taino** tribe. The **crocodile** on top of the royal helmet of the British monarchy and the **pineapples** on the shield represent the indigenous animals and fruits of the island. The motto, **"Out of Many, One People"**, is a tribute to the unity of the multicultural nation.

Anthem

Eternal Father bless our land,
Guard us with Thy Mighty Hand,
Keep us free from evil powers,
Be our light through countless hours.
To our Leaders, Great Defender,
Grant true wisdom from above.
Justice, Truth be ours forever,
Jamaica, land we love.
Jamaica, Jamaica, Jamaica land we love.

Teach us true respect for all,
Stir response to duty's call,
Strengthen us the weak to cherish,
Give us vision lest we perish.
Knowledge send us Heavenly Father,
Grant true wisdom from above.
Justice, Truth be ours forever,
Jamaica, land we love.
Jamaica, Jamaica, Jamaica land we love.

Bird

The national bird is the Red-billed Streamertail or Doctor Bird, a species of humming bird, which lives only in Jamaica and is endangered.

Tree

The national tree is the indigenous Blue Mahoe which grows rapidly and is often used for reforestation. Due to the beauty and durability of the wood it is widely used in cabinet-making and for carving decorative objects.

Pledge

Before God and all mankind, I pledge the love and loyalty of my heart, the wisdom and courage of my mind, the strength and vigour of my body in the service of my fellow citizens; I promise to stand up for Justice, Brotherhood and Peace, to work diligently and creatively, to think generously and honestly, so that Jamaica may, under God, increase in beauty, fellowship and prosperity, and play her part in advancing the welfare of the whole human race.

Flower

The attractive blue blossom of the Lignum Vitae, or "Wood of Life", is the national flower. Various parts of the plant are used for a variety of purposes including medicinal remedies.

Fruit

The ackee, the national fruit, was originally from West Africa and was probably brought over on a slave ship. The ackee tree now grows abundantly on the island and produces large quantities of fruit.

Government structure

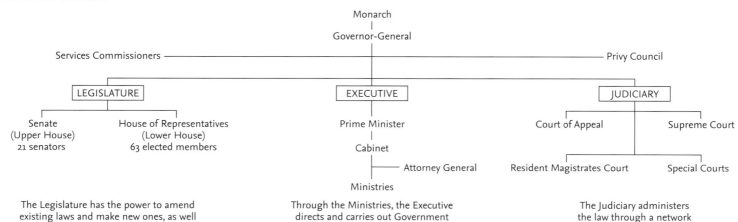

Monarch
Governor-General

Services Commissioners — Privy Council

LEGISLATURE   **EXECUTIVE**   **JUDICIARY**

Senate (Upper House) 21 senators   House of Representatives (Lower House) 63 elected members   Prime Minister   Court of Appeal   Supreme Court

Cabinet

Attorney General   Resident Magistrates Court   Special Courts

Ministries

The Legislature has the power to amend existing laws and make new ones, as well as controlling Government finances

Through the Ministries, the Executive directs and carries out Government policies and programmes

The Judiciary administers the law through a network of courts

The Cockpit Country

The Cockpit Country is an area of severely weathered limestone creating a wilderness of conical hills and deep hollows. It remains largely inaccessible today. Due to its difficult access it is still heavily forested and contains the largest area of rainforest in Jamaica.

Coastal plains

The widest stretches of the flat coastal plains are found in the southwest. On the southern coast dark-coloured sand beaches line small stretches of plains. Behind many of the white sand beaches of the northern coast is a narrow strip of plains formed from raised coral reefs.

Central uplands

The central mountain chains, formed by igneous and metamorphic rocks, stretch across the island from west to east. Nearly half of Jamaica's land area is 300 m above sea level. The Blue Mountains in the east are the highest and most rugged mountainous area.

The Cockpit Country

Falmouth

The Blue Mountains

Wetlands

The most common wetlands of Jamaica are the mangroves and morasses of the coastal zone. They represent less than 2% of the country's land area but are very important for protecting the shoreline from erosion, reducing the effects of flooding and providing a rich wildlife habitat.

Rivers and valleys

Many rivers flowing southwards from the central plateau have formed flat-bottomed valleys filled with rich soils giving some of the most productive agricultural land in the country. In contrast, as the north-flowing rivers have cut in to the steep mountain sides they have formed deep-sided valleys with magnificent waterfalls.

Urban

The Kingston urban area is the largest in Jamaica. It is a sprawl of diverse neighbourhoods from the historic downtown area overlooking the natural harbour to the commercial and financial district of New Kingston and the affluent northern suburbs. To its west lie the island's other main urban areas of Portmore and Spanish Town.

Mangrove forest on the Black River

Rio Minho

Kingston

Counties and parishes

— County boundary
— Parish boundary
o Parish capital

Scale 1 : 2 000 000

Constituencies

Jamaica is divided into 63 constituencies, for the purposes of electing members to the House of Representatives.

Number of constituencies per parish

Clarendon 6	St Catherine 11
Hanover 2	St Elizabeth 4
Kingston 3	St James 5
Manchester 4	St Mary 3
Portland 2	St Thomas 2
St Andrew 12	Trelawny 2
St Ann 4	Westmoreland 3

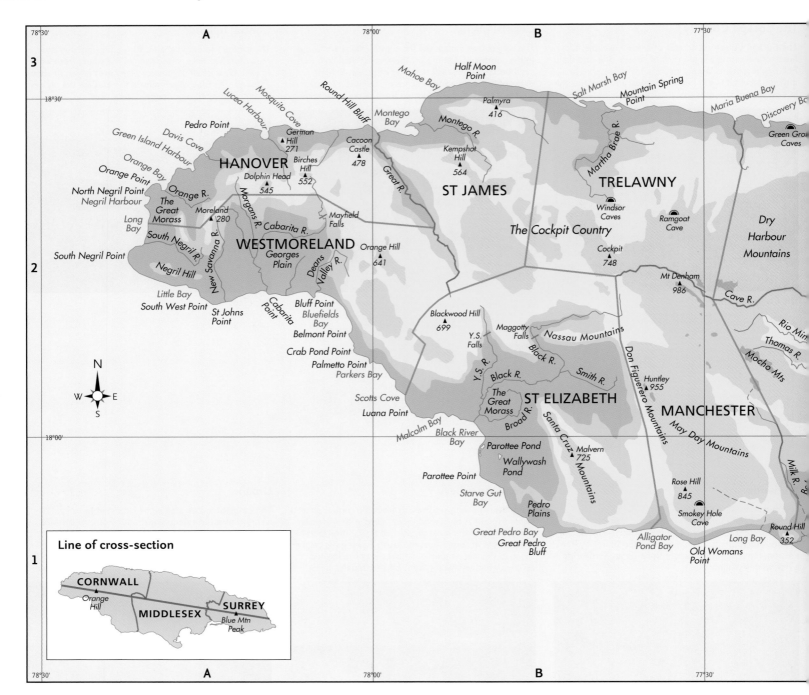

Cross-section

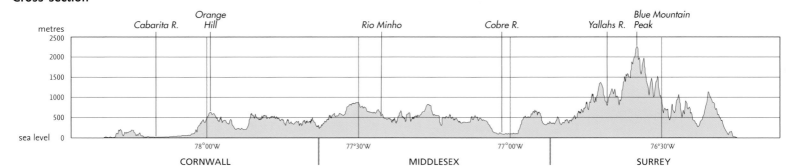

Physical statistics

Highest peak	Blue Mountain Peak, 2256 m		**Length of coastline**	1022 km
Longest river	Rio Minho, Clarendon Parish, 92.8 km		**Most westerly point**	South Negril Point
Widest river	Black River, St Elizabeth Parish, navigable for 28 km		**Most northerly point**	Half Moon Point
Largest freshwater lake	Wallywash Pond, St Elizabeth Parish, 1 km long		**Most easterly point**	Morant Point
Highest terraced waterfall	Dunns River Falls, St Ann Parish, 55 m high and 180 m long		**Most southerly point**	Portland Point
Deepest cave	Smokey Hole Cave, Manchester Parish, 194 m			

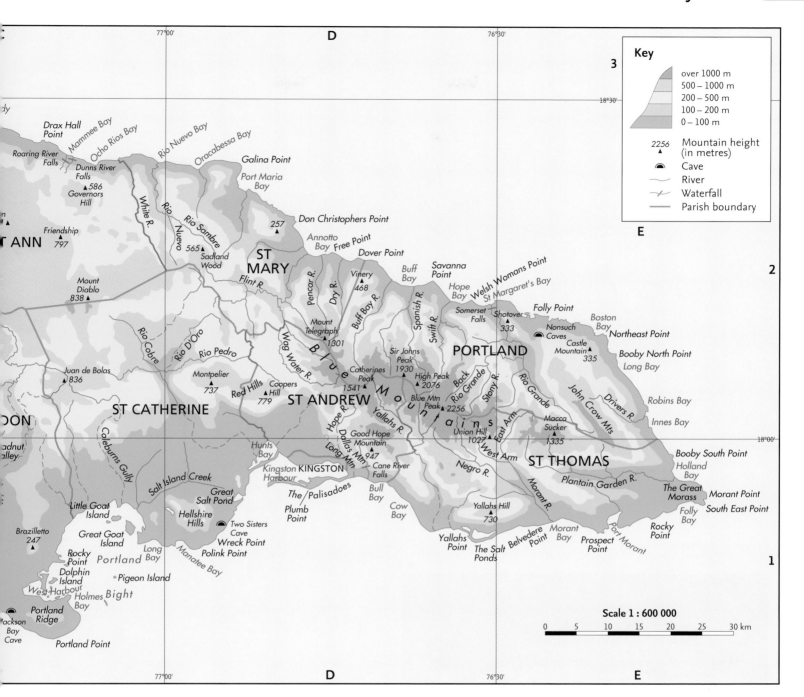

Key

- over 1000 m
- 500 – 1000 m
- 200 – 500 m
- 100 – 200 m
- 0 – 100 m

2256 ▲ Mountain height (in metres)

◖ Cave

~~~ River

⤳ Waterfall

—— Parish boundary

3

18°30'

2

18°00'

1

ST ANN
Drax Hall Point
Mammee Bay
Ocho Rios Bay
Roaring River Falls
Dunns River Falls
▲ 586 Governors Hill
Friendship 797
Mount Diablo 838 ▲
Rio Nuevo Bay
Oracabessa Bay
White R.
Rio Nuevo
Rio Sambre
565▲
Sadland Wood
Galina Point
Port Maria Bay
Don Christophers Point
Annotto Bay
Free Point
Dover Point
257
ST MARY
Flint R.
Pencar R.
Dry R.
Vinery 468
Buff Bay R.
Mount Telegraph 1301
Buff Bay
Savanna Point
Hope Bay
Welsh Womans Point
St Margaret's Bay
Somerset Falls
Shotover 333
Folly Point
Boston Bay
Nonsuch Caves
Castle Mountain 335
Northeast Point
Booby North Point
Long Bay

Rio D'Oro
Rio Cobre
Rio Pedro
Juan de Bolas 836 ▲
Montpelier 737
Red Hills
Coopers Hill 779
Blue
Spanish R.
Swift R.
Sir Johns Peak 1930
Catherines Peak 1541
High Peak 2076
Blue Mtn Peak 2256
PORTLAND
Back
Rio Grande
Stony R.
Rio Grande
East Arm
West Arm
John Crow Mts
Drivers R.
Robins Bay
Innes Bay
Macca Sucker 1335
Booby South Point

ST CATHERINE
Wog Water R.
ST ANDREW
Hope R.
Yallahs R.
Mountains
Union Hill 1027
ST THOMAS
Holland Bay

Coleburns Gully
Hunts Bay
Dallas Mtn
Good Hope Mountain 947
Long Mtn
Cane River Falls
Negro R.
Yallahs Hill 730
Plantain Garden R.
The Great Morass
Morant Point
South East Point

Salt Island Creek
Kingston Harbour
KINGSTON
The Palisadoes
Plumb Point
Bull Bay
Cow Bay
Morant R.
Rocky Point
Folly Bay

Little Goat Island
Great Salt Pond
Hellshire Hills
Two Sisters Cave
Wreck Point
Polink Point
Yallahs Point
The Salt Ponds
Belvedere Point
Morant Bay
Prospect Point
Port Morant

Brazilletto 247
Great Goat Island
Long Bay
Manatee Bay
Portland
Bight
Holmes Bay
Pigeon Island
West Harbour
Dolphin Island
Rocky Point

Jackson Bay Cave
Portland Ridge
Portland Point

Scale 1 : 600 000

0 5 10 15 20 25 30 km

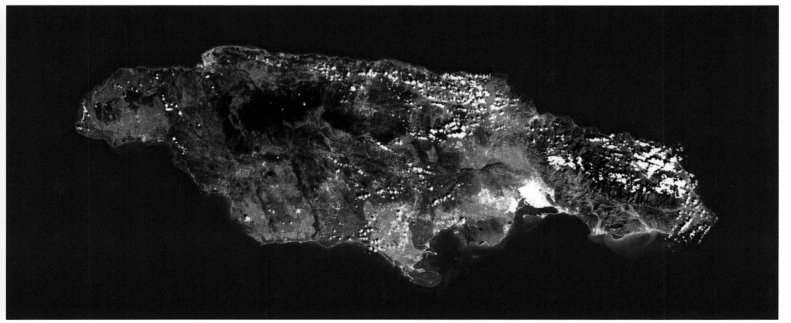

This satellite image shows Kingston and nearby Spanish Town as bright white areas, while the red patches are the bauxite workings in the interior. To the far east the rugged Blue Mountains can be seen, and in the west the very dark green represents the forests of The Cockpit Country. Note the clouds along the north coast, the wetter side of Jamaica as opposed to the drier south coast.

Jamaica West

N · W · E · S

18°30'N

78°15'W · 78°00'W

4

Half Moon Point
Mahoe Bay
Umbrella Point
Sangster International Airport
Coral Gardens
Ironshore
Barrett To
Salt Spring
Spot V
Flower Hill
Palm
41

Round Hill Bluff
Montego Bay
Montego Bay
Montego Bay
Bogue
Tucker
Granville
Sign
Orange
Ae

Pedro Point
Lances Bay
Lucea Harbour
Paradise
German Hill ▲ 271
Kew
Jericho
Mosquito Cove
Sandy Bay
Flint River
Old Pen
Hopewell
Reading
Wiltshire
Anchovy
Mount Carey
ST JAMES
Johns Hall
Kempshot Hill ▲ 564
Roehamton
Hopeton
Spring Mount
Sunderland

Lucea
Johnson Town
Cousins Cove
Davis Cove
Davis Cove
Middlesex
Cacoon
Dias
HANOVER
Harvey River
Maryland
Mosquito Cove
Great Valley
Cacoon Castle ▲ 478
Haddington
Great R.
Chigwell
Thompson Hill
Lethe
Copse
Montpelier
Bickersteth
Kensington
Poin

Green Island Harbour
Green Island
Prospect
Salt Spring
Kingsvale
Grange
Cessnock
Askenish
Dolphin Head ▲ 545
Cash Hill
Birches Hill ▲ 552
Miles Town
Shettlewood
Seven Rivers
Mount Horeb
Maroon Te
Flamstead
Garle

3

Orange Bay
Orange Point
North Negril Point
Negril Harbour
Orange Bay
Santoy
Orange R.
Rock Spring
March Town
Glasgow
Morgans R.
Georges Plain Mountain
Axe and Adze
Alexandria
Williamsfield
Grange
Ramble
Haughton Grove
Chester Castle
Greenwich
Duckets
Cambridge
Bruce Hall
Mocho
Catodupa

Logwood
Cave Valley
Moreland ▲ 280
Mint
Kings Valley
Town Head
Mount Grace
Truro Gate
Mayfield Falls
Locust Tree
Mackfield
Haddo
Fort William
Friendship Cross
Bethel Town
Orange Hill ▲ 641
Struie
Rat Trap
Lambs River
Marchmont

Long Bay
The Great Morass
Moreland Hill
Grange Hill
Alma
Paul Island
Delve Bridge
WESTMORELAND
Cabarita R.
Banbury
Petersfield
Whithorn
CORNWALL
Woodstock
Seaford Town
Chesterfield
Elder

South Negril R.
Negril
South Negril Point
Springfield
Albany
Georges Plain
Georges Plain
Amity Cross
Galloway
Darliston
Three Roads
Dundee
Leamington
Mulgrave
Ginger Hill
Ipswich

Sheffield
Negril Spots
New Hope
Little London
Torrington
Deans Valley R.
Cairn Curran
Content
Lenox
New Roads
Pisgah
Blackwood Hill ▲ 699
Newmarket
Springfield
Four Path
Y.S.

Mount Airy
Orange Hill
Retreat
Negril Hill
Brighton
Bay Road
Old Hope
Savanna-la-Mar
Wakefield
Ferris Cross
Lenox Bigwoods
Mearnsville
Lenox
Beeston Spring
Brighton
Happy Grove
Y.S.
Y.S. R.

Little Bay
South West Point
New Broughton
St Johns Point
Cabarita Point
Bluff Point
Cave
Bluefields Bay
Bluefields
Hopeton
Kilmarnoch
Whitehall
Middle Quarters
Baptist
Ne
Ho
Black

2

Belmont Point
Belmont
Crab Pond Point
Auchindown
Culloden
Luana
Speculation
Luana
Frenchmar

Palmetto Point
Parkers Bay
Whitehouse
Brompton
Sandy Ground
Hodges
The
M

Scotts Cove
Luana Point
Crawford
Y.S. R.
Blac

Malcolm Bay
Black River
Fullerswood

18°00'N

Black River Bay
Parottee Pond
Parottee Beach
Parottee
Hill

Scale 1 : 320 000

0 · 5 · 10 · 15 · 20 km

Parottee Point

78°00'W

Starve G
Bay

The Falmouth Courthouse in Trelawny.

Peeling ginger in Manchester in the early 1900s.

Key

2256 ▲ Mountain height (in metres)	■ Capital city
◠ Cave	● Parish capital
⌇ River	◉ Important town
⌇ Seasonal river	○ Other town
↯ Waterfall	═══ Highway
⌇ Swamp	─── Main road
⌇ Reef	─── Other road
━━━ County boundary	─── Railway
─── Parish boundary	✈ Main airport
	✈ Other airport

1

C

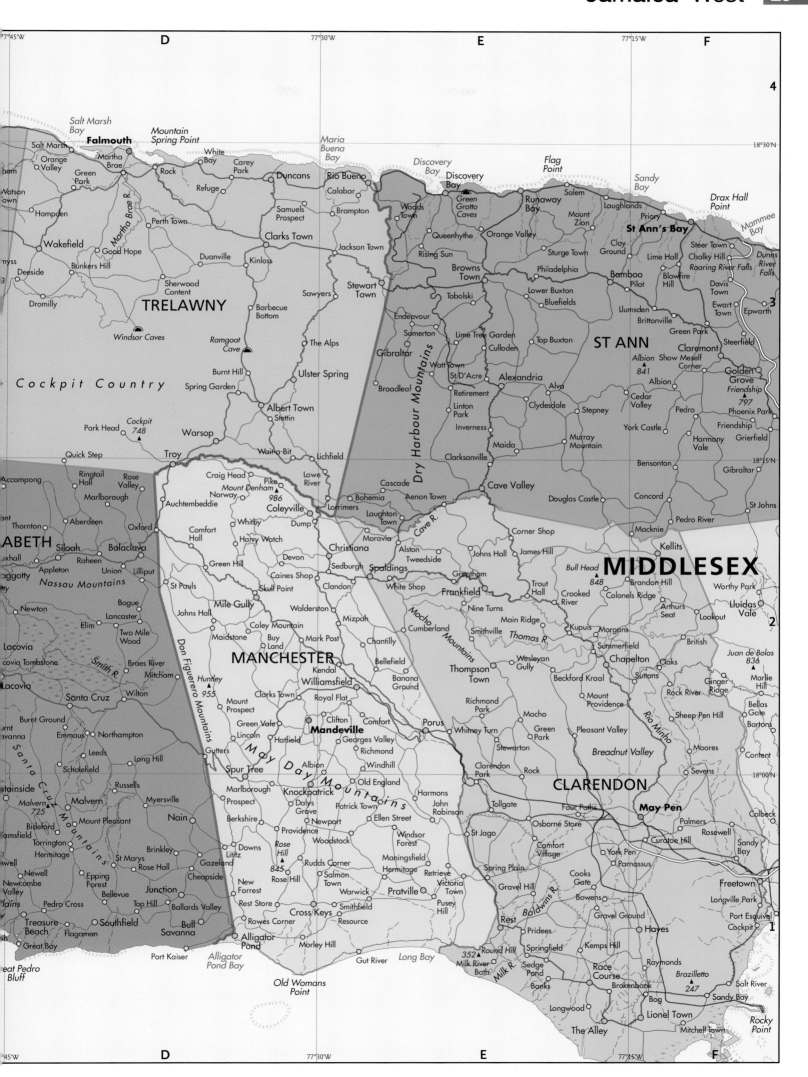

TRELAWNY

Salt Marsh Bay
Salt Marsh
Orange Valley
Martha Brae
Falmouth
Green Park
Rock
Watson
Hampden
own
Wakefield
Perth Town
Good Hope
Bunkers Hill
yss
Deeside
Dromilly
Sherwood Content

Mountain Spring Point
White Bay
Carey Park
Duncans
Refuge
Samuels Prospect
Brampton
Clarks Town
Duanville
Kinloss
Jackson Town
Sawyers
Barbecue Bottom
The Alps

Maria Buena Bay
Rio Bueno
Calabar
Stewart Town

Cockpit Country

Windsor Caves
Ramgoat Cave
Burnt Hill
Spring Garden
Albert Town
Stettin

Park Head
Cockpit 748
Warsop
Troy
Wait-a-Bit
Lichfield
Quick Step

Discovery Bay
Discovery Bay
Green Grotto Caves
Woods Town
Queenhythe
Rising Sun
Browns Town
Tobolski
Endeavour
Somerton
Lime Tree Garden
Gibraltar
Watt Town
St D'Acre
Broadleaf
Retirement
Linton Park
Inverness
Maida
Clarksonville

Flag Point
Salem
Runaway Bay
Mount Zion
Orange Valley
Sturge Town
Philadelphia
Lower Buxton
Bluefields
Culloden
Top Buxton
Alexandria
Alva
Clydesdale
Stepney
Murray Mountain

Sandy Bay
Laughlands
Priory
St Ann's Bay
Clay Ground
Lime Hall
Bamboo
Pilot
Llumsden
Brittonville
Green Park

Drax Hall Point
Mammee Bay
Steer Town
Chalky Hill
Roaring River Falls
Blowfire Hill
Davis Town
Ewart Town
Epworth

ST ANN

Claremont
Steerfield
Albion 841
Show Meself Corner
Albion
Cedar Valley
Pedro
York Castle
Concord
Macknie
Pedro River

Golden Grove
Friendship 797
Phoenix Park
Friendship
Harmony Vale
Grierfield
Gibraltar
St Johns

Dry Harbour Mountains

Cascade
Bohemia
Aenon Town
Cave R.
Laughton Town
Moravia
Alston
Tweedside
Corner Shop
Bull Head 848
Cave Valley
Douglas Castle
Bensonton

MIDDLESEX

Craig Head
Lowe River
Mount Denham Pike 986
Coleyville
Lorrimers
Dump
Whitby
Christiana
Sedburgh
Spaldings
White Shop
Grantham
James Hill
Brandon Hill
Worthy Park
Kellits
Auchtembeddie
Comfort Hall
Harry Watch
Devon
Caines Shop
Clandon
Frankfield
Nine Turns
Trout Hall
Crooked River
Colonels Ridge
Arthurs Seat
Lookout
Lluidas Vale
Oxford
St Pauls
Green Hill
Mile Gully
Johns Hall
Skull Point
Walderston
Mizpah
Chantilly
Bellefield
Smithville
Main Ridge
Thomas R.
Kupuis
Morgans
British
Coley Mountain
Mark Post
Buy Land
Maidstone
Banana Ground
Wesleyan Gully
Summerfield
Chapelton
Oaks
Suttons
Juan de Bolas 836
Marlie Hill
MANCHESTER
Kendal
Williamsfield
Clarks Town
Royal Flat
Clifton
Comfort
Porus
Thompson Town
Richmond Park
Mocho
Green Park
Beckford Kraal
Mount Providence
Rock River
Ginger Ridge
Mandeville
Mount Prospect
Green Vale
Lincoln
Hatfield
Georges Valley
Richmond
Windhill
Old England
Whitney Turn
Pleasant Valley
Sheep Pen Hill
Bellas Gate
Bartons
Mocho Mountains
Stewarton
Clarendon Park
Rock
Rio Minho
Breadnut Valley
Moores
Content
Sevens
Harmons
John Robinson
Tollgate
Four Paths
CLARENDON
May Pen
Colbeck
May Day Mountains
Marlborough
Prospect
Knockpatrick
Dalys Grove
Patrick Town
Newport
Ellen Street
Osborne Store
Palmers
Curatoe Hill
Rosewell
Berkshire
Providence
Woodstock
Windsor Forest
St Jago
Comfort Village
York Pen
Parnassus
Sandy Bay
Downs
Lititz
Rose Hill 845
Rudds Corner
Maningsfield
Hermitage
Spring Plain
Cooks Gate
Bowens
Freetown
Gazeland
Cheapside
Salmon Town
Pratville
Retrieve
Victoria Town
Gravel Hill
Gravel Ground
Longville Park
New Forrest
Rose Hill
Warwick
Smithfield
Pusey Hill
Rest
Pridees
Hayes
Port Esquivel
Cockpit
Rest Store
Cross Keys
Resource
Rowes Corner
Morley Hill
Springfield
Kemps Hill
Raymonds
Salt River
Alligator Pond
Gut River
Long Bay
Round Hill 352
Milk River Bath
Sedge Pond
Race Course
Brazilletto 247
Alligator Pond Bay
Old Womans Point
Milk R.
Banks
Brokenbank
Bog
Sandy Bay
Longwood
Lionel Town
Mitchell Town
The Alley
Rocky Point

St ELIZABETH (ABETH)
Accompong
Ringtail Hall
Rose Valley
Marlborough
Thornton
Aberdeen
Siloah
Raheen
Appleton
Union
Lilliput
Nassau Mountains
aggotty
Balaclava
Bogue
Lancaster
Newton
Elim
Two Mile Wood
Lacovia
Tombstone
Smith R.
Braes River
Mitcham
Wilton
Santa Cruz
Burnt Ground
Emmaus
Northampton
Leeds
Scholefield
Long Hill
Russells
Myersville
Malvern 725
Malvern
Mount Pleasant
Nain
Bideford
Torrington
Hermitage
St Marys
Rose Hall
Brinkley
Santa Cruz Mountains
Newell
Newcombe Valley
Epping Forest
Bellevue
Junction
Top Hill
Ballards Valley
Bull Savanna
Pedro Cross
Southfield
Treasure Beach
Flagaman
Great Bay
eat Pedro Bluff
Port Kaiser

Don Figuerero Mountains
Huntley 955
Mount Prospect
Gutters
Spur Tree

77°45'W 77°30'W 77°15'W
18°30'N 18°15'N 18°00'N

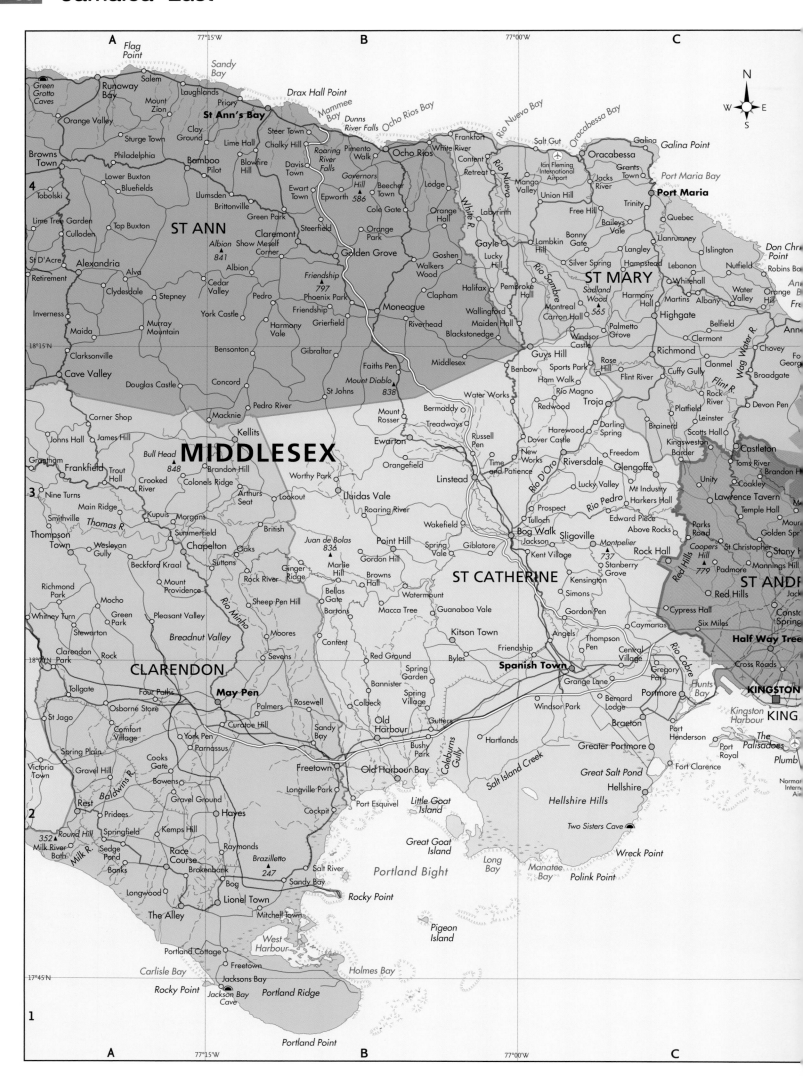

A   77°15'W   B   77°00'W   C

N
W • E
S

Flag Point
Sandy Bay
Green Grotto Caves
Salem
Runaway Bay
Laughlands
Priory
Drax Hall Point
Mammee Bay
Ocho Rios Bay
Mount Zion
St Ann's Bay
Steer Town
Orange Valley
Clay Ground
Chalky Hill
Dunns River Falls
Pimento Walk
Frankfort
Rio Nuevo Bay
Salt Gut
Oracabessa Bay
Galina
Galina Point
Browns Town
Philadelphia
Lime Hall
Davis Town
Roaring River Falls
White River
Content
Ocho Rios
Retreat
Rio Nuevo
Mango Valley
Ian Fleming International Airport
Oracabessa
Grants Town
Jacks River
Port Maria Bay
Port Maria
Bamboo
Pilot
Blowfire Hill
Ewart Town
Governors Hill
Epworth ▲ 586
Beecher Town
Lodge
Orange Hall
Union Hill
Free Hill
Trinity
Baileys Vale
Quebec
Lower Buxton
Bluefields
Llumsden
Brittonville
Green Park
Cole Gate
White R.
Labyrinth
Lambkin Hill
Bonny Gate
Silver Spring
Langley
Llanrumney
Islington
Don Chr Point
Robins Ba

4

Tobolski
Lime Tree Garden
Culloden
Steerfield
Claremont
Show Meself Corner
Orange Park
Goshen
Lucky Hill
Gayle
Hampstead
Lebanon
Whitehall
Water Valley
Orange Hill
Ann
Fre

St D'Acre
Alexandria
Alva
Albion ▲ 841
Albion
Cedar Valley
Pedro
Friendship 797
Walkers Wood
Clapham
Halifax
Pembroke Hall
Rio Sambre
Montreal
Carron Hall
Windsor Castle
Palmetto Grove
Harmony Hall
Martins
Albany
Highgate
Belfield
Clermont
Ann

18°15'N
Retirement
Inverness
Clydesdale
Stepney
Phoenix Park
Friendship
York Castle
Moneague
Riverhead
Wallingford
Maiden Hall
Blackstonedge
Sadland Wood ▲ 565
Richmond
Clonmel
Wag Water R.
Chovey
St George

Maida
Clarksonville
Mutray Mountain
Harmony Vale
Grierfield
Benbow
Sports Park
Ham Walk
Guys Hill
Rose Hill
Flint River
Cuffy Gully
Flint R.
Broadgate
Devon Pen

Cave Valley
Bensonton
Gibraltar
Faiths Pen
Middlesex
Water Works
Rio Magno
Troja
Redwood
Harewood
Platfield
Leinster
Rock River
Scotts Hall

Douglas Castle
Concord
Mount Diablo ▲ 838
St Johns
Bermaddy
Treadways
Darling Spring
Freedom
Brainerd
Kingsweston Border
Castleton
Toms River
Brandon H

Corner Shop
Pedro River
Macknie
Mount Rosser
Russell Pen
New Works
Riversdale
Glengoffe
Unity
Coakley
Brandon H

Johns Hall
James Hill
Kellits
Ewarton
Orangefield
Time and Patience
Lucky Valley
Mt Industry
Harkers Hall
Lawrence Tavern
Temple Hall
Moura

Grantham
Frankfield
Trout Hall
Bull Head ▲ 848
Brandon Hill
MIDDLESEX
Worthy Park
Dover Castle
Prospect
Edward Piece
Above Rocks
Parks Road
Golden Spr
St Christopher
Stony H

3
Nine Turns
Main Ridge
Crooked River
Colonels Ridge
Lookout
Linstead
Rio Pedro
Tulloch
Wakefield
Bog Walk
Jackson
Sligoville
Montpelier ▲ 737
Rock Hall
Coopers Hill ▲ 779
Padmore
Mannings Hill

Smithville
Thompson Town
Thomas R.
Kupuis
Morgans
Summerfield
Arthurs Seat
British
Roaring River
Point Hill
Spring Vale
Giblatore
Kent Village
Stanbery Grove
Red Hills
ST ANDR
Jack

Wesleyan Gully
Chapelton
Oaks
Juan de Bolas ▲ 836
Marlie Hill
Gordon Hill
Browns Hall
Kensington
Simons
Red Hills

Richmond Park
Mocho
Beckford Kraal
Suttons
Ginger Ridge
Bellas Gate
Bartons
Watermount
Guanaboa Vale
ST CATHERINE
Gordon Pen
Cypress Hall
Caymanas
Six Miles
Half Way Tree

Whitney Turn
Green Park
Mount Providence
Pleasant Valley
Sheep Pen Hill
Macca Tree
Kitson Town
Angels
Thompson Pen
Central Village
Gregory Park
Rio Cobre
Constant Spring

18°00'N
Clarendon Park
Rock
Rio Minho
Breadnut Valley
Moores
Sevens
Content
Red Ground
Byles
Friendship
Spanish Town
Grange Lane
Windsor Park
Bernard Lodge
Portmore
Braeton
Cross Roads
KINGSTON
KING

CLARENDON
Tollgate
Four Paths
May Pen
Rosewell
Bannister
Spring Garden
Spring Village
Colbeck
Hartlands
Greater Portmore
Part Henderson
Kingston Harbour

Osborne Store
Palmers
Gutters
Bushy Park
Old Harbour
Coleburns Gully
Salt Island Creek
Hellshire
Fort Clarence
Port Royal
The Palisadoes
Plumb

St Jago
Comfort Village
Curatoe Hill
Sandy Bay
Old Harbour Bay
Great Salt Pond
Hellshire Hills
Norman Internat Air

Spring Plain
Gravel Hill
Cooks Gate
York Pen
Parnassus
Freetown
Longville Park
Port Esquivel
Little Goat Island
Two Sisters Cave

Victoria Town
Gravel Ground
Cockpit
Great Goat Island
Long Bay
Manatee Bay
Wreck Point
Polink Point

2
Rest
Pridees
Hayes
Kemps Hill
Raymonds
Portland Bight

▲ 352
Milk River Bath
Springfield
Sedge Pond
Banks
Race Course
Brokenbank
Brazilletto ▲ 247
Salt River
Sandy Bay
Rocky Point
Pigeon Island

Milk R.
Baldwins
Bog
Longwood
Lionel Town
The Alley
Mitchell Town
West Harbour
Holmes Bay

17°45'N
Portland Cottage
Freetown
Jacksons Bay
Carlisle Bay
Rocky Point
Jackson Bay Cave
Portland Ridge

1
Portland Point

A   77°15'W   B   77°00'W   C

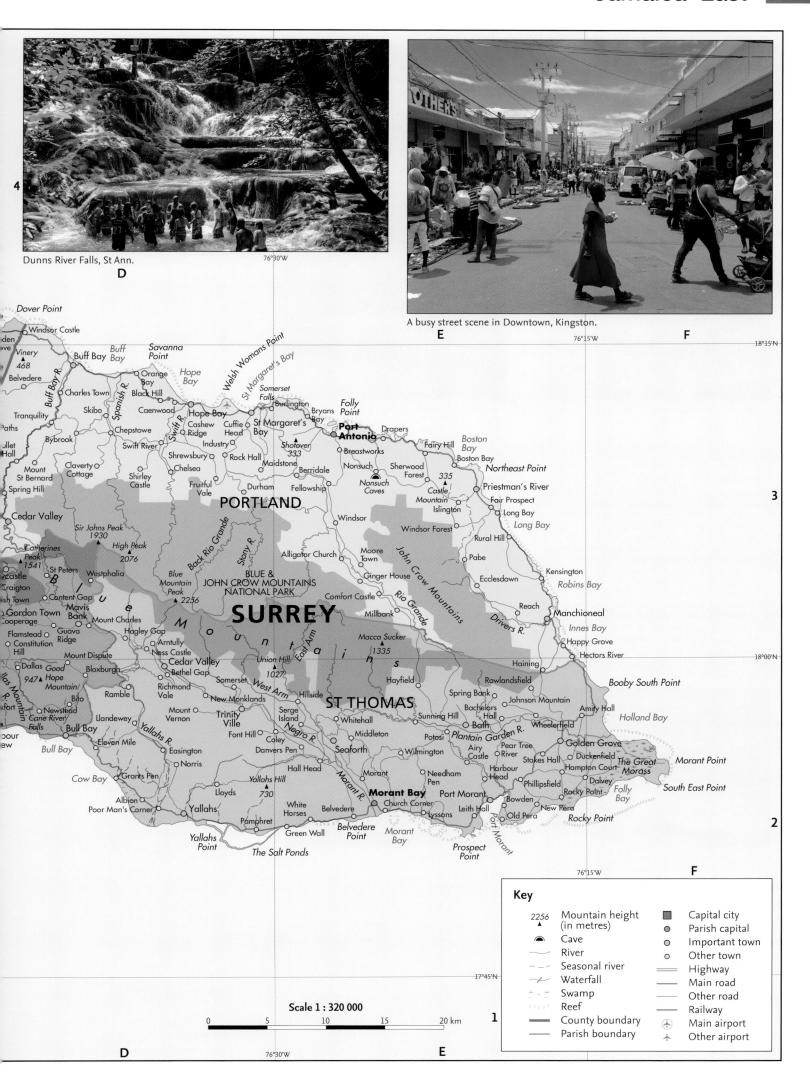

Dunns River Falls, St Ann.

D

76°30'W

A busy street scene in Downtown, Kingston.

E   76°15'W   **F**   18°15'N

Dover Point

Windsor Castle

Buff Bay   *Savanna Point*   Welsh Womans Point   *St Margaret's Bay*

Vinery ▲ 468   Buff Bay   *Bay*   *Hope Bay*   Somerset Falls   Bryans Bay   *Folly Point*

Belvedere

Orange Bay   Black Hill   Burlington   **Port Antonia**   Drapers

Tranquility   Charles Town   Caenwood   Hope Bay   St Margaret's Bay   *Boston Bay*

Skibo   Cashew Ridge   Cuffie Head   Fairy Hill   Boston Bay

Paths   Bybrook   Chepstowe   Industry   Breastworks   *Northeast Point*

Swift River   Shrewsbury   Rock Hall   Maidstone   Nonsuch   Sherwood Forest   335 ▲   Priestman's River

Mount St Bernard   Claverty Cottage   Chelsea   Fruitful Vale   Durham   Fellowship   Nonsuch Caves   Castle Mountain   Fair Prospect

Spring Hill   Shirley Castle   Berridale   **PORTLAND**   Islington   Long Bay

Cedar Valley   Windsor   Windsor Forest   *Long Bay*

Sir Johns Peak 1930 ▲   Rural Hill   **3**

Catherines Peak ▲ 1541   High Peak 2076 ▲   Alligator Church   Moore Town   Pabe   *Robins Bay*

St Peters   Blue Mountain Peak   **BLUE & JOHN CROW MOUNTAINS NATIONAL PARK**   Ginger House   Ecclesdown   Kensington

Westphalia   ▲ 2256   Comfort Castle   Reach   Manchioneal

Content Gap   **SURREY**   Millbank   *Innes Bay*

Gordon Town   Mavis Bank   Mount Charles   Hagley Gap   Macca Sucker 1335 ▲   Drivers R.   Happy Grove

Flamstead   Guava Ridge   Arntully   East Arm   Haining   Hectors River   18°00'N

Constitution Hill   Ness Castle   Union Hill 1027 ▲   West Arm   Rowlandsfield   *Booby South Point*

Mount Dispute   Cedar Valley   Hayfield   Spring Bank   Johnson Mountain   Amity Hall

Dallas *Good Hope Mountain*   Bloxburgh   Bethel Gap   Hillside   Bachelors Hall   Wheelerfield   *Holland Bay*

947 ▲   Somerset   Sunning Hill   Bath   Golden Grove

Bito   Richmond Vale   New Monklands   **ST THOMAS**   Potosi   Plantain Garden R.   Duckenfield   *The Great Morass*   *Morant Point*

Newstead   Ramble   Mount Vernon   Serge Island   Whitehall   Airy Castle   Pear Tree River   Stokes Hall   Hampton Court   Dalvey

Cane River Falls   Llandewey   Trinity Ville   Middleton   Wilmington   Harbour Head   Phillipsfield   Rocky Point   *South East Point*

Bull Bay   Eleven Mile   Font Hill   Caley   Seaforth   Needham Pen   Leith Hall   Bowden   New Pera   *Rocky Point*

Bull Bay   Easington   Danvers Pen   Morant   **Morant Bay**   Port Morant   Old Pera   *Folly Bay*

Cow Bay   Norris   Hall Head   Morant R.   Church Corner   Lyssons   **2**

Grants Pen   Yallahs Hill   White Horses   Belvedere   *Port Morant*

Albion   Lloyds   730   Belvedere Point   *Morant Bay*

Poor Man's Corner   Yallahs   Pamphret   Green Wall   *Prospect Point*

Yallahs Point   *The Salt Ponds*

76°15'W   **F**

17°45'N

Scale 1 : 320 000

0   5   10   15   20 km

1

76°30'W   **E**

Key

2256 ▲	Mountain height (in metres)
⌂	Cave
~~	River
–·–·–	Seasonal river
⤳	Waterfall
Swamp	Swamp
Reef	Reef
━━	County boundary
──	Parish boundary

▪	Capital city
●	Parish capital
●	Important town
○	Other town
═══	Highway
──	Main road
──	Other road
──	Railway
✈	Main airport
✈	Other airport

Hanover

Population *(2016)*   70 374
Capital city   Lucea
Area   451 sq km

The parish capital, Lucea, was once the centre of an important sugar-growing area and one of the busiest ports in Jamaica. Today, Hanover is known for producing crops such as sugar cane, yams, ginger, pimento and breadfruits. Cattle-rearing is important in the hilly southern region of the parish. Although it is not one of Jamaica's major tourist areas, there are now several resorts at Negril Harbour in the southwest of the parish.

A rocky shoreline near Lucea.

Westmoreland

Population *(2016)*   145 854
Capital city   Savanna-la-Mar
Area   785 sq km

The parish capital, Savanna-la-Mar, dates back to around 1730 when it developed as a port for the export of sugar. It is an important regional centre for administration and commerce. The fertile soils, abundant rainfall and low-lying plains of Westmoreland make it ideal for growing a variety of crops – primarily sugar cane but also coffee, cocoa, ginger and pimentos. Cattle-rearing is also important. Manufactured products include sugar, food and drink, textiles, animal feeds and tobacco. The fastest growing sector in the parish is tourism. Negril, on the west coast, is one of Jamaica's major tourist destinations with hotels and resorts fringing its sandy beaches.

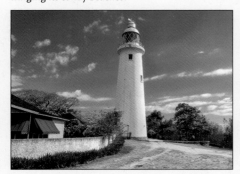

Negril lighthouse.

St James

Population *(2016)*   185 985
Capital city   Montego Bay
Area   591 sq km

Montego Bay was officially named Jamaica's second city in 1981. It is an important centre for commerce, industry and tourism. The Montego Free Zone is the location for many manufacturing and technological industries. To the north of the bay along the coast is the tourist area with the international airport and cruise ship terminal bringing many thousands of tourists annually to the region. Manufacturing activities in the south are mainly involved in food processing, woodwork and garments whilst agriculture production includes sugar cane and forestry.

A cruise ship in Montego Bay.

St Elizabeth

Population *(2016)*   152 074
Capital city   Black River
Area   1211 sq km

Since the 1960s, St Elizabeth has been a major producer of bauxite. It is refined at the alumina plant at Nain and taken by rail to the deep-water terminal at Port Kaiser, in the southeast of the parish, for export. St Elizabeth is also one of Jamaica's largest producers of sugar and other agricultural products include cassava, onions, tomatoes, corn and beef cattle. Tourism has been growing in importance since the 1990s, especially on the Black and YS rivers and the large wetland area of the Great Morass in the southwest. Black River, the parish capital, developed in the 18th and 19th centuries as a busy seaport for the export of sugar, rum and logwood. Today it is a centre for eco-tourism.

The Nassau Mountains.

Trelawny

Population *(2016)*   76 099
Capital city   Falmouth
Area   874 sq km

Trelawny is famous for its sugar estates and mills. Falmouth, the parish capital, developed as a thriving seaport for the export of sugar. It is known for its well-preserved Georgian buildings. The main manufacturing activities are sugar, rum and textiles. As well as sugar cane, other crops grown include yams, coffee, bananas, coconuts and vegetables. Tourism is also important to the local economy with a cruise ship terminal at Falmouth and hotel developments along the north coast. The southern part of the parish is covered by The Cockpit Country, an uninhabited area of rainforest.

— County boundary
— Parish boundary
∘ Parish capital

Manchester

Population *(2016)*   192 178
Capital city   Mandeville
Area   828 sq km

Manchester has one of the largest deposits of bauxite in Jamaica. The growth of the bauxite and alumina industries led to the fast development of the parish and in particular the capital, Mandeville, which became the centre of operations. The town's situation at high altitude resulting in a cool climate, attracted British expatriates to settle there as well as Jamaicans, drawn by the higher wages offered by the bauxite mining companies. Mandeville continues to grow today and is one of the most affluent urban areas in the country, an important centre for education and medical services. Due to its hilly terrain farming is not practised on a large scale in Manchester but oranges and grapefruits are produced for export and other crops such as coffee, ginger and pimentos are grown.

Parish evolution

1664

Scale 1 : 2 500 000

1738

Scale 1 : 2 500 000

St Ann

Population *(2016)*   174 473
Capital city   St Ann's Bay
Area   1210 sq km

The earliest inhabitants of Jamaica, the Arawak or Taino peoples, are thought to have settled first in St Ann. Christopher Columbus arrived in Jamaica in 1494 at Discovery Bay and the first Spanish town was established at what is now called Seville. St Ann's Bay gradually developed as a fishing port and was made capital mainly due to its large harbour and port which acted as a hub for the export of goods such as bauxite and bananas. In recent years Ocho Rios has grown rapidly to become the main centre for commerce and tourism. St Ann is one of Jamaica's major tourist destinations with its cruise ship terminal at Ocho Rios, many fine beaches and numerous hotels and resorts extending right along the coast. Agricultural products include bananas, citrus fruit, sisal and coconuts as well as livestock farming of beef and dairy cattle.

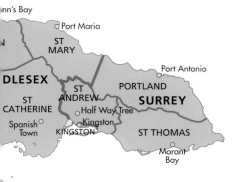

Scale 1 : 1 700 000

Clarendon

Population *(2016)*   248 087
Capital city   May Pen
Area   1193 sq km

Sugar is the dominant crop grown in the low-lying lands in the south of this largely agricultural parish with bananas, coffee, cocoa and citrus fruits produced in the higher ground to the north. The parish capital, May Pen, is considered one of Jamaica's main agricultural towns and is important as a citrus packing centre. The largest agricultural show in the Caribbean is held annually at Denbigh on the outskirts of the town. Sugar refineries and rum distilleries are located to the south. Bauxite mining is well established in Clarendon and the mineral is exported from Port Esquivel (in St Catherine) and Rocky Point on Portland Bight.

New Yarmouth Sugar Estate Rum Distillery.

St Mary

Population *(2016)*   115 045
Capital city   Port Maria
Area   611 sq km

A good variety of agricultural products are grown in St Mary such as bananas, cocoa, coconuts, citrus fruit, sugar cane and vegetables. The recent investment in infrastructure, including a new international airport and highway, has boosted the economy by encouraging tourism, particularly the development of luxury resorts along the coast. In Port Maria, the capital of the parish, several old buildings survive from its time as a busy port.

	St Andrew	**Kingston**
Population *(2016)*	580 626	90 184
Capital city	Half Way Tree	Kingston
Area	435 sq km	23 sq km

St Andrew was one of the first Jamaican parishes to be established by law in 1867. In 1923 the two parishes of St Andrew and Kingston were merged to be administered jointly as the Kingston and St Andrew Corporation with an elected council and mayor. Kingston, the national capital and largest city, refers to the whole urban area, most of which lies in the parish of St Andrew. As well as being the heart of government it is also the commercial, financial, industrial, cultural and educational centre of the nation. Kingston Harbour is one of the largest natural harbours in the world and Jamaica's largest port. Suburbs such as Half Way Tree, Constant Spring and New Kingston, considered the financial capital of the island, are important commercial centres. An industrial estate has been established bordering on Western Kingston to encourage industries to move from the business areas of the city. St Andrew is also home to some of Jamaica's top higher education establishments such as the University of the West Indies and the University of Technology. Much of the northern part of St Andrew is an important agricultural area producing crops such as coffee, cocoa, sugar, peas and beans.

St Catherine

Population *(2016)*   522 057
Capital city   Spanish Town
Area   1191 sq km

From 1534 to 1872, the capital of St Catherine, Spanish Town, was the capital of Jamaica. It has some fine historical buildings and holds the country's archives. To the southeast, Portmore developed as a residential new town in the 1960s to house the overspill from densely populated Kingston and has now become the largest urban area in the parish. St Catherine is the fastest growing parish with the biggest economy due to its many resources. Agriculture dominates the hillier northern area. Main crops include bananas, coffee, sugar cane, peppers and citrus fruits. A variety of industrial activities make St Catherine second only to Kingston as a centre of industry. Factories in the Old Harbour and Spanish Town areas produce goods such as sugar, rum, pharmaceuticals, salt, cigarettes and plastics and there is an alumina factory in the north.

Rodney memorial in Spanish Town.

St Mary Parish Church in Port Maria.

Portland

Population *(2016)*   82 771
Capital city   Port Antonio
Area   814 sq km

Port Antonio is regarded as the birthplace of Jamaica's tourist industry having been the first place to accommodate visitors to the country. Recently it has increased in importance as a cultural and economic centre. Portland is renowned for its natural beauty. The Blue Mountains, clothed in lush vegetation, run along its southern border and there are beautiful beaches, caves, waterfalls and rivers. The rich soils of the coastal areas are suitable for growing a variety of crops and it is a leading producer of bananas, coffee, coconuts, breadfruits and ackee.

Turtle Bay, near Manchioneal.

St Thomas

Population *(2016)*   95 087
Capital city   Morant Bay
Area   742 sq km

The first Spanish settlers in St Thomas established cattle ranches at Morant Bay and Yallahs and livestock farming is still important in the lowlands of St Thomas today. Agriculture is of great importance to the economy. Finest-quality coffee is grown in the Blue Mountains region in the north of the parish and bananas and sugar are also important export crops. There are many food processing factories and gypsum is produced in the Bull Bay area to the west of the parish.

A banana plantation in St Thomas parish

Rainfall

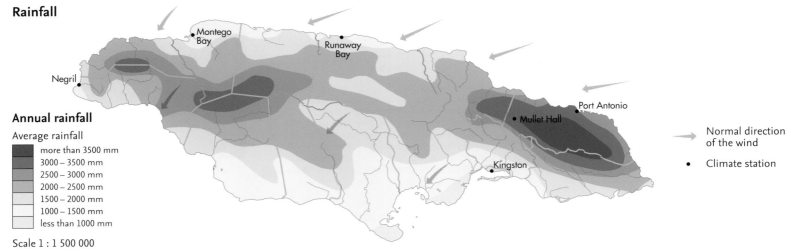

Annual rainfall

Average rainfall

- more than 3500 mm
- 3000 – 3500 mm
- 2500 – 3000 mm
- 2000 – 2500 mm
- 1500 – 2000 mm
- 1000 – 1500 mm
- less than 1000 mm

Scale 1 : 1 500 000

→ Normal direction of the wind

• Climate station

Seasonal rainfall, March

Average rainfall

- more than 300 mm
- 250 – 300 mm
- 200 – 250 mm
- 150 – 200 mm
- 100 – 150 mm
- 75 – 100 mm
- 50 – 75 mm
- less than 50 mm

Scale 1 : 2 500 000

Seasonal rainfall, October

Average rainfall

- more than 300 mm
- 250 – 300 mm
- 200 – 250 mm
- 150 – 200 mm
- less than 150 mm

Scale 1 : 2 500 000

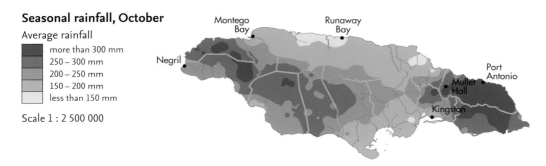

October is the rainiest month in most parts of Jamaica.

Average rainfall graphs

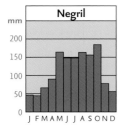

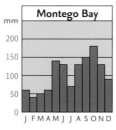

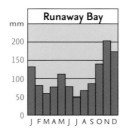

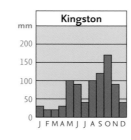

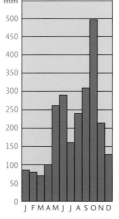

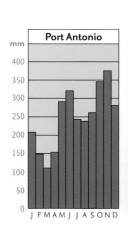

Average temperature graphs

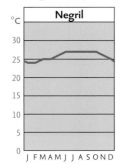

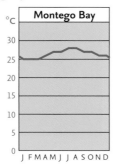

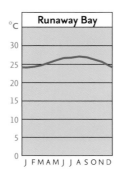

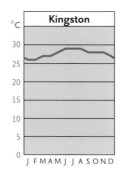

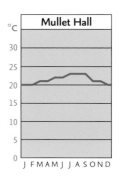

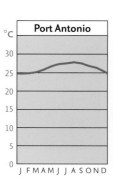

Weather definitions

Weather is the condition of the air at a given time. The different elements that go to make up weather include temperature, rainfall, wind direction and speed, cloud cover, sunshine, air pressure and humidity.

The typical weather that a place experiences over a longer period of time is known as **climate**. Elements of the weather such as rainfall and temperature are averaged out over about 30 years to give a picture of what the weather is usually like in different places around the world.

Jamaica lies within the tropics and has a **tropical maritime** climate. The prevailing winds are from the east and northeast. These bring rain throughout the year with the greatest rainfall in the mountains facing the north and east. In contrast, the southwest of the island, protected in the lee of the mountains, has a semi-arid climate. Temperatures vary very little during the year but the height of the land above sea level has an influence on temperature causing the mountains to be cooler than the lowlands.

Weather instruments and measuring

Weather is measured and recorded by **meteorologists** at weather stations which consist of various instruments.

Stevenson screen

In order to measure the true temperature of the air, thermometers are kept in a Stevenson screen which has louvered sides and an insulated roof to protect instruments from sun, rain and wind.

Maximum-minimum thermometer

This thermometer is specially designed to record the maximum and minimum temperatures in a 24-hour period.

Rain gauge

Rainfall is measured using a rain gauge. It must be located in the open, away from water dropping from buildings or vegetation.

Anemometer and wind vane

Two different sets of data are recorded for wind: direction and speed. A wind vane is used to record direction with the arrow pointing to the direction from which the wind is blowing. An anemometer measures wind speed. The movement of the air rotates the instrument and the number of rotations is recorded and converted to km per hour.

Aneroid barometer

Variations in air pressure are measured using an aneroid barometer.

Hurricanes

Due to its location in the Atlantic hurricane belt, Jamaica is regularly hit by hurricanes and tropical storms which occur between June and November. A mountainous island such as Jamaica is vulnerable to severe flooding and landslides resulting from the heavy rains during a hurricane which often cause more damage than the winds and storm surge. After floods devastated parts of western Jamaica in 1979, the government established the Office of Disaster Preparedness and Emergency Management to raise awareness of and help deal with natural disasters such as hurricanes.

Recent major hurricanes

Year	Name	Deaths	Damage
1988	Gilbert	45	US$ 800 million – 20% of houses destroyed or severely damaged
2004	Ivan	17	US$ 689 000 – 18 000 homeless
2005	Dennis/Emily	7	US$ 97 million – majority of damage to roads and bridges
2007	Dean	3	US$ 330 000 – 2854 houses destroyed
2008	Gustav	10	US$ 214 million – 450 000 people directly affected
2012	Sandy	2	US$ 107 million – 17 000 households affected, 807 houses destroyed

Coastal homes devastated by Hurricane Ivan on the south coast of Jamaica. It was a Category 4 hurricane when it made landfall on 10 September 2004 and developed to Category 5 by 11 September. Over 360 000 people were directly affected and 17 people were killed. There was a great deal of damage to roads and buildings due to flooding and mudslides.

Tropical Storm Gustav hit Jamaica on 28–29 August 2008. The satellite image shows the tropical storm directly over the island having passed across Haiti and the Dominican Republic to the east. Some areas were badly hit by floods and landslides, 10 people died and 70–85% of the banana crop was destroyed.

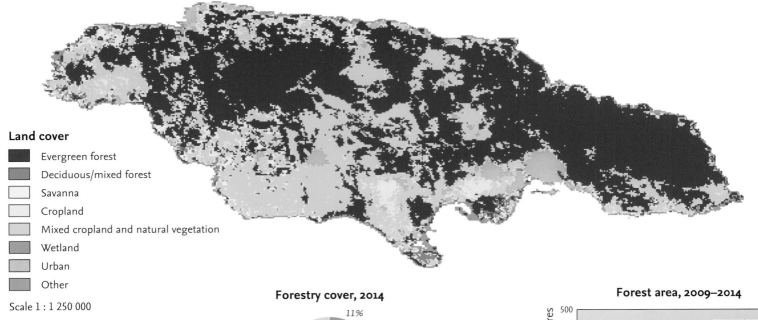

Land cover

- Evergreen forest
- Deciduous/mixed forest
- Savanna
- Cropland
- Mixed cropland and natural vegetation
- Wetland
- Urban
- Other

Scale 1 : 1 250 000

Forestry cover, 2014

11%

29%

60%

- Protected forest area
- Other forest area
- Other land

Forest area, 2009–2014

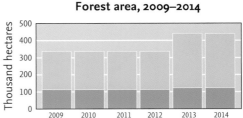

Thousand hectares

500
400
300
200
100
0

2009 2010 2011 2012 2013 2014

Environmental issues

In addition to the issues below, other threats to the environment in Jamaica include air pollution, coral bleaching and the loss of areas of natural vegetation for houses, factories and roads.

Water pollution

Water pollution is a major environmental problem. Coastal areas are polluted by industrial waste, sewage and oil spills. The mining and refining of bauxite has led to the contamination of ground water. In Jamaica's urban areas such as Kingston and Montego Bay, waterways are polluted by sewage and trash, particularly plastics which do not biodegrade.

Montego Bay

Deforestation

Between 1990 and 2010, Jamaica lost about 8000 hectares of forest, 2.3% of its total forest cover. Although there has been an increase recently in the total forest area, from 337 100 hectares in 2010 to 438 800 hectares in 2014, deforestation is still a major issue with pressure from mining, illegal logging, clearance for crop cultivation and expansion of urban areas for housing and tourism.

Mining damage

After the excavation of bauxite, red sludge waste is produced during the refining process; red mud lakes now cover many areas of Jamaica where alumina refining has taken place.

Endangered species

Jamaica has over 3300 species of plants and around 400 species of birds, mammals, reptiles and amphibians, over 20% of which are endemic. However, 28 species are on the endangered list including 7 birds, 8 reptiles and 5 mammals. The adult population of the Jamaican iguana is thought to be below 200 and is now critically endangered. Their natural habitat has been destroyed by the clearing of forests for charcoal and they are under threat from the introduction of other animals, particularly the mongoose.

Jamaican iguana

Agriculture

▨	Livestock farming
▧	Crop cultivation
🥥	Coconuts
🍌	Bananas
🍊	Citrus fruits
🥥	Cocoa
☕	Coffee
Ψ	Sugar cane

Scale 1 : 1 250 000

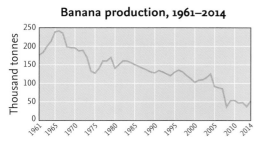

Banana production, 1961–2014

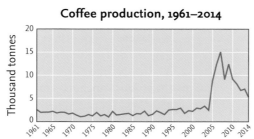

Coffee production, 1961–2014

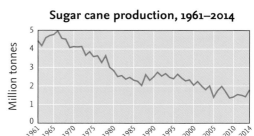

Sugar cane production, 1961–2014

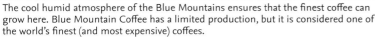

The cool humid atmosphere of the Blue Mountains ensures that the finest coffee can grow here. Blue Mountain Coffee has a limited production, but it is considered one of the world's finest (and most expensive) coffees.

Casting nets in Portland Bight. This protected area is one of the main fishing grounds in Jamaica.

Fishing grounds

▢	Island shelf
▨	Banks
●	Main landing sites
·	Other landing sites

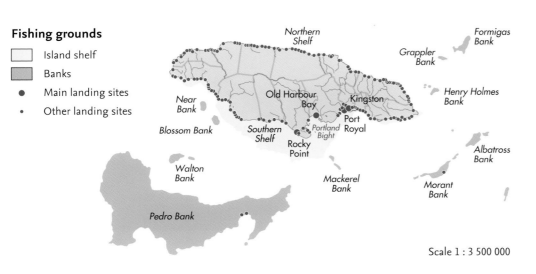

Northern Shelf · Formigas Bank · Grappler Bank · Old Harbour Bay · Kingston · Henry Holmes Bank · Near Bank · Blossom Bank · Southern Shelf · Portland Bight · Port Royal · Rocky Point · Walton Bank · Mackerel Bank · Morant Bank · Albatross Bank · Pedro Bank

Scale 1 : 3 500 000

Fish production, 1995–2015

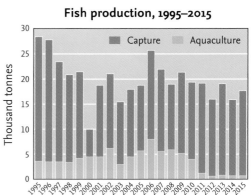

Capture   Aquaculture

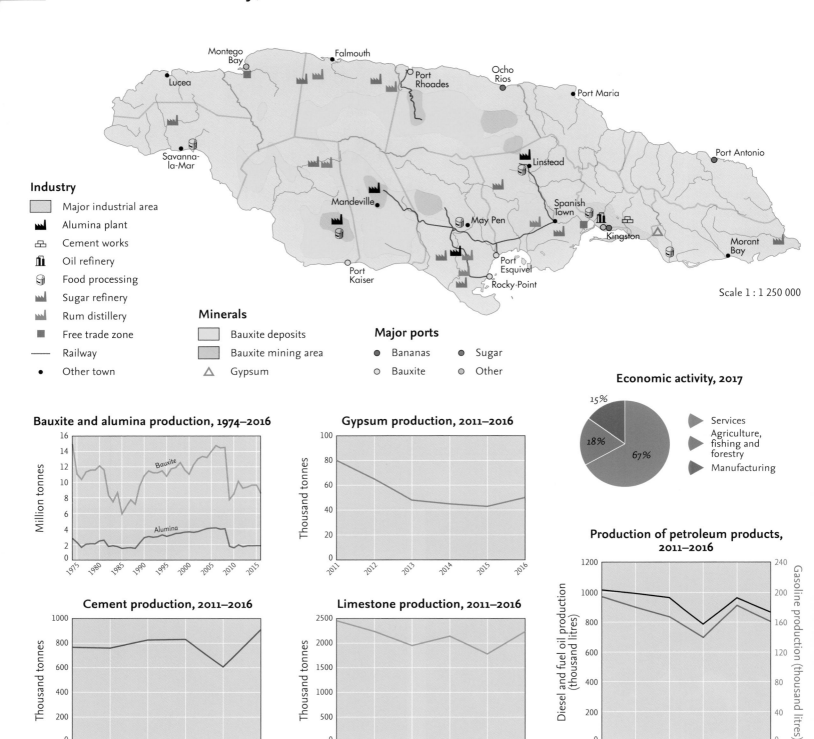

Industry

- ▨ Major industrial area
- ⚒ Alumina plant
- ⚒ Cement works
- 🏭 Oil refinery
- 🥫 Food processing
- ⚒ Sugar refinery
- ⚒ Rum distillery
- ■ Free trade zone
- — Railway
- • Other town

Minerals

- ▨ Bauxite deposits
- ▨ Bauxite mining area
- △ Gypsum

Major ports

- ● Bananas
- ● Bauxite
- ● Sugar
- ● Other

Scale 1 : 1 250 000

Economic activity, 2017

- ▶ Services
- ▶ Agriculture, fishing and forestry
- ▶ Manufacturing

15%
18%
67%

Bauxite and alumina production, 1974–2016

Million tonnes

Bauxite
Alumina

1975 1980 1985 1990 1995 2000 2005 2010 2015

Gypsum production, 2011–2016

Thousand tonnes

2011 2012 2013 2014 2015 2016

Cement production, 2011–2016

Thousand tonnes

2011 2012 2013 2014 2015 2016

Limestone production, 2011–2016

Thousand tonnes

2011 2012 2013 2014 2015 2016

Production of petroleum products, 2011–2016

Diesel and fuel oil production (thousand litres)

Gasoline production (thousand litres)

2011 2012 2013 2014 2015 2016

Port Kaiser is the export point for bauxite and alumina being shipped from Alpart's mines at Nain. The port was re-opened in 2015, the first exports going to Ukraine.

The Appleton rum distillery in St Elizabeth Parish. The site is also now a major tourist attraction, with tours of the estate available.

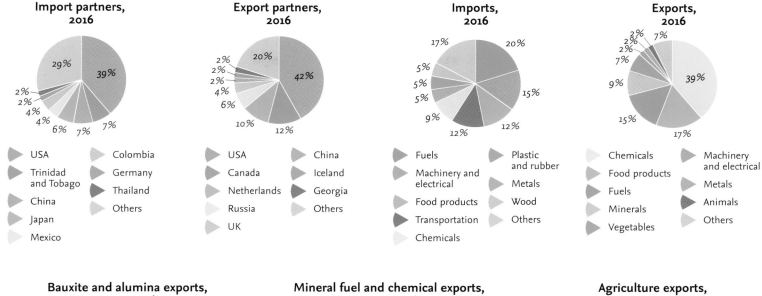

Import partners, 2016

- USA 39%
- 29%
- 2%
- 2%
- 4%
- 4%
- 6%
- 7%
- 7%

USA · Colombia · Trinidad and Tobago · Germany · Thailand · China · Japan · Others · Mexico

Export partners, 2016

- USA 42%
- 20%
- 2%
- 2%
- 2%
- 4%
- 6%
- 10%
- 12%

USA · China · Canada · Iceland · Netherlands · Georgia · Russia · Others · UK

Imports, 2016

- 20%
- 17%
- 15%
- 12%
- 12%
- 9%
- 5%
- 5%
- 5%

Fuels · Plastic and rubber · Machinery and electrical · Metals · Food products · Wood · Transportation · Others · Chemicals

Exports, 2016

- 39%
- 17%
- 15%
- 9%
- 7%
- 7%
- 2%
- 2%
- 2%

Chemicals · Machinery and electrical · Food products · Metals · Fuels · Animals · Minerals · Others · Vegetables

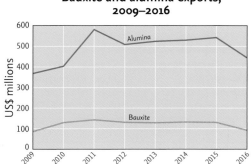

Bauxite and alumina exports, 2009–2016

(US$ millions) — Alumina, Bauxite

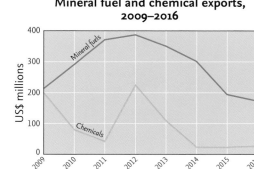

Mineral fuel and chemical exports, 2009–2016

(US$ millions) — Mineral fuels, Chemicals

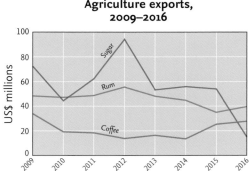

Agriculture exports, 2009–2016

(US$ millions) — Sugar, Rum, Coffee

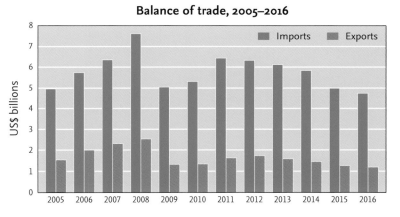

Balance of trade, 2005–2016

(US$ billions) — Imports, Exports

Kingston container terminal is the largest port in Jamaica. Around 15 million pallets of cargo are handled here every year.

Communications

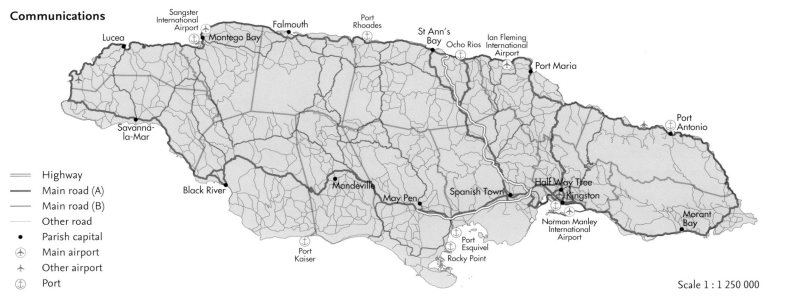

Lucea · Sangster International Airport · Montego Bay · Falmouth · Port Rhoades · St Ann's Bay · Ocho Rios · Ian Fleming International Airport · Port Maria · Savanna-la-Mar · Port Antonio · Black River · Mandeville · May Pen · Spanish Town · Half Way Tree · Kingston · Morant Bay · Port Kaiser · Port Esquivel · Rocky Point · Norman Manley International Airport

Legend:
- Highway
- Main road (A)
- Main road (B)
- Other road
- • Parish capital
- ✈ Main airport
- ✈ Other airport
- ⊕ Port

Scale 1 : 1 250 000

Urban centres

- Important town
- Other town
- Urban area

Scale 1 : 1 500 000

Population density, 2016

Persons per sq km

- over 500
- 250 – 500
- 200 – 250
- 150 – 200
- under 150

- Parish capital

Scale 1 : 2 500 000

Population statistics

Population (2016)	2 730 894
Population density (2016)	248 per sq km
Annual population growth rate (2011)	0.36%
Male life expectancy (2015)	74 years
Female life expectancy (2015)	79 years
Birth rate (2013)	14 per 1000 population
Death rate (2013)	6 per 1000 population
Infant mortality (2015)	13.6 per 1000 live births

Population change, 2001–2016

Percentage population change 2001–2016

- over 7.0
- 5.0 – 6.9
- 4.0 – 4.9
- 3.0 – 3.9
- 2.0 – 2.9

Scale 1 : 2 500 000

Parish	Population (2016, est.)
St Andrew	580 626
St Catherine	522 057
Clarendon	248 087
Manchester	192 178
St James	185 985
St Ann	174 473
St Elizabeth	152 074
Westmoreland	145 854
St Mary	115 045
St Thomas	95 087
Kingston	90 184
Portland	82 771
Trelawny	76 099
Hanover	70 374

Kingston-Spanish Town conurbation

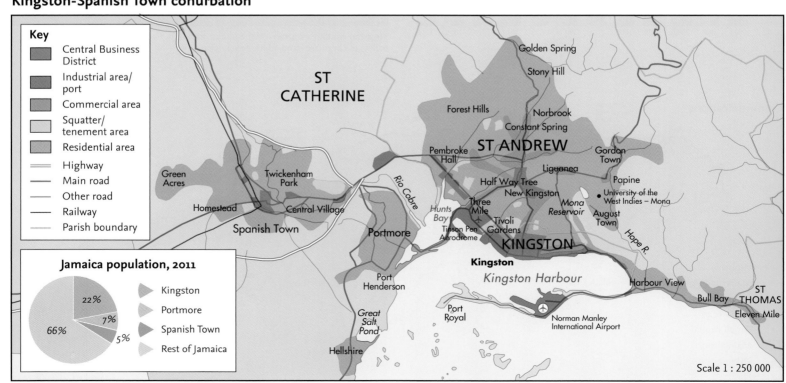

Key

- Central Business District
- Industrial area/ port
- Commercial area
- Squatter/ tenement area
- Residential area
- Highway
- Main road
- Other road
- Railway
- Parish boundary

Jamaica population, 2011

- 22% Kingston
- 7% Portmore
- 5% Spanish Town
- 66% Rest of Jamaica

Scale 1 : 250 000

Population growth, 1960–2016

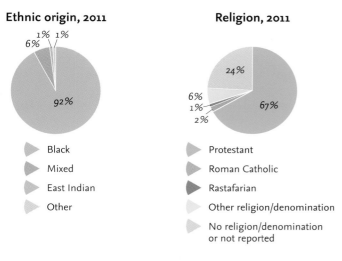

Population structure

1957

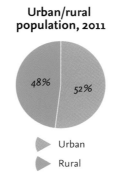

2017

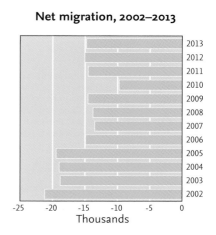

Each full square represents 1% of the total population

Ethnic origin, 2011

- 92% Black
- 6%
- 1%
- 1%

- Black
- Mixed
- East Indian
- Other

Religion, 2011

- 67% Protestant
- 24%
- 6%
- 1%
- 2%

- Protestant
- Roman Catholic
- Rastafarian
- Other religion/denomination
- No religion/denomination or not reported

Urban/rural population, 2011

- 48% Urban
- 52% Rural

- Urban
- Rural

Net migration, 2002–2013

2013
2012
2011
2010
2009
2008
2007
2006
2005
2004
2003
2002

-25 -20 -15 -10 -5 0
Thousands

Hospitals

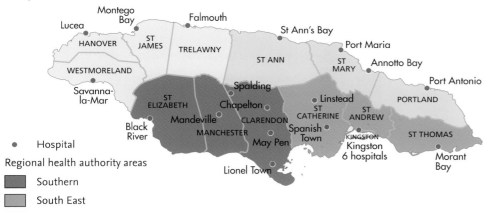

- Hospital

Regional health authority areas
- Southern
- South East
- North East
- Western

Scale 1 : 2 000 000

AIDS/HIV

AIDS means **Acquired Immune Deficiency Syndrome**. It is caused by the **Human Immunodeficiency Virus (HIV)**. The main symptoms of the virus are prolonged fever, chronic diarrhoea and weight loss, and those infected become susceptible to other diseases.
More than 90% of AIDS cases occur in the 15-49 age group. As this is the most productive segment of the population, sickness and death have a huge impact on the economy as well as other sectors of society such as health, education and the labour force.

Prevalence of HIV, 1990–2016

Percentage of population aged 15–49 infected with HIV

1990 1992 1994 1996 1998 2000 2002 2004 2006 2008 2010 2012 2014 2016

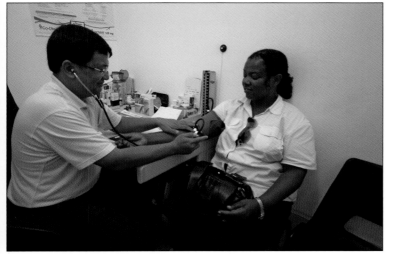

A doctor taking a patient's blood pressure at a clinic at Montego Bay.

Health statistics

Annual number of births *(average 2003–2013)*	42 343
Fertility rate *(2013)*	2.3 per woman
Doctors *(2008)*	41 per 100 000 population
Nurses *(2008)*	108 per 100 000 population
Dentists *(2008)*	9 per 100 000 population
Prevalence of HIV *(2016)*	1.7%
Deaths due to HIV/AIDS *(2012)*	46 per 100 000 population
Incidence of tuberculosis *(2015)*	4.5 per 100 000 population
Use of improved drinking-water *(2015)*	93.8%
Use of improved sanitation *(2015)*	81.8%
Expenditure on health *(2014)*	5.4% of GDP

Tainos

The earliest known inhabitants of Jamaica were the Tainos. They migrated northwards from South America, arriving in Jamaica around AD 500. They settled mainly along the coast, in the plains and near rivers. They hunted, fished and farmed the land, growing crops such as sweet potatoes and cassava. The Tainos used rock carvings (petroglyphs) and rock paintings (pictographs) to illustrate their lives and beliefs. Many have been found in caves which were used for Taino rituals.

- ● Petroglyphs (rock carvings)
- ■ Pictographs (rock paintings)

Scale 1 : 2 500 000

Spanish settlement

Christopher Columbus arrived in Jamaica in 1494 and claimed the island for Spain. In 1509 the first Spanish settlement was established at Sevilla la Nueva and Juan de Esquivel was appointed governor. A number of towns were set up by the settlers across the island. Under Spanish rule the Taino population dramatically declined due to the introduction of European diseases and the harsh treatment they endured through the colonists' implementation of the encomienda labour system.

Scale 1 : 2 500 000

British rule

In 1655 the British captured Jamaica from the Spanish and ruled the island until 1962. In 1656 about 1600 immigrants from Britain settled around Port Morant. Kingston Harbour expanded rapidly and Port Royal became the most important British port in the Western Caribbean. Under British rule, Jamaica became one of the world's main producers and exporters of sugar using a plantation economy and slave labour.

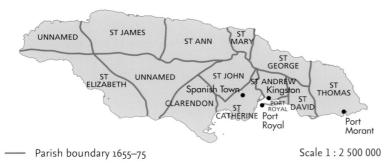

— Parish boundary 1655–75

Scale 1 : 2 500 000

Maroons

When the British took Jamaica from Spain in 1655, the African slaves on the Spanish-owned plantations took the opportunity to escape to the mountainous interior of the island. They formed independent communities and became known as Maroons, their numbers growing as rebel slaves escaped to join them. Fighting between the British and Maroons eventually led to treaties being made whereby the Maroons agreed to peace with the British; part of the agreement was for them to refrain from raiding British settlements which disrupted the plantation economy.

◾ Maroon areas

Scale 1 : 2 500 000

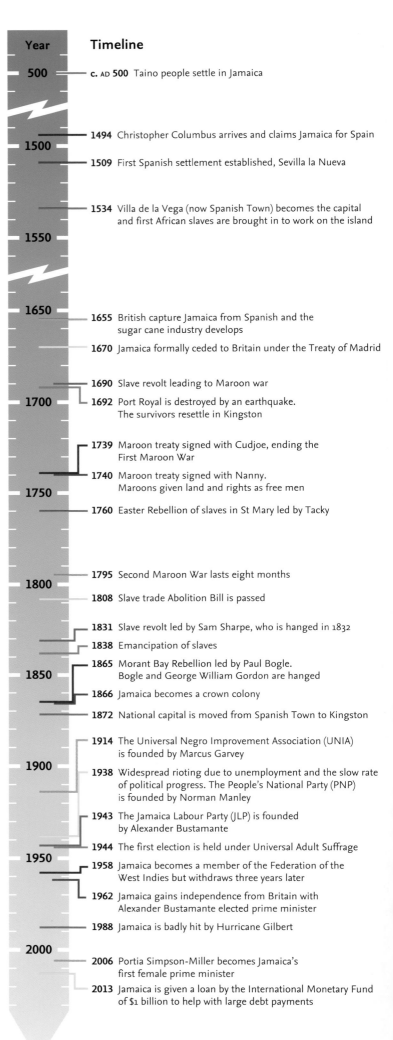

Year **Timeline**

500

c. AD 500 Taino people settle in Jamaica

1500 1494 Christopher Columbus arrives and claims Jamaica for Spain

1509 First Spanish settlement established, Sevilla la Nueva

1534 Villa de la Vega (now Spanish Town) becomes the capital and first African slaves are brought in to work on the island

1550

1650

1655 British capture Jamaica from Spanish and the sugar cane industry develops

1670 Jamaica formally ceded to Britain under the Treaty of Madrid

1690 Slave revolt leading to Maroon war

1700 1692 Port Royal is destroyed by an earthquake. The survivors resettle in Kingston

1739 Maroon treaty signed with Cudjoe, ending the First Maroon War

1740 Maroon treaty signed with Nanny. Maroons given land and rights as free men

1750

1760 Easter Rebellion of slaves in St Mary led by Tacky

1800 1795 Second Maroon War lasts eight months

1808 Slave trade Abolition Bill is passed

1831 Slave revolt led by Sam Sharpe, who is hanged in 1832

1838 Emancipation of slaves

1865 Morant Bay Rebellion led by Paul Bogle. Bogle and George William Gordon are hanged

1850

1866 Jamaica becomes a crown colony

1872 National capital is moved from Spanish Town to Kingston

1914 The Universal Negro Improvement Association (UNIA) is founded by Marcus Garvey

1900 1938 Widespread rioting due to unemployment and the slow rate of political progress. The People's National Party (PNP) is founded by Norman Manley

1943 The Jamaica Labour Party (JLP) is founded by Alexander Bustamante

1944 The first election is held under Universal Adult Suffrage

1950 1958 Jamaica becomes a member of the Federation of the West Indies but withdraws three years later

1962 Jamaica gains independence from Britain with Alexander Bustamante elected prime minister

1988 Jamaica is badly hit by Hurricane Gilbert

2000

2006 Portia Simpson-Miller becomes Jamaica's first female prime minister

2013 Jamaica is given a loan by the International Monetary Fund of $1 billion to help with large debt payments

National Heroes

The honour of the Order of National Hero, established in 1969, is the highest decoration awarded by the government of Jamaica. It may be given only to Jamaican citizens for "services of the most distinguished nature" to the nation.

Heroes are given the title "The Right Excellent" and allowed to wear the insignia of the order. This is a medallion of a fourteen-pointed gold and white star, surrounding the Jamaican coat of arms and the motto of the Order: "He built a city which hath foundations."

Seven people have now been awarded the honour of National Hero.

Paul Bogle
c.1822–1865

A Baptist deacon, Bogle led protests to end poverty and social injustice. After marching on the Morant Bay courthouse on 11 October 1865, he was captured and hanged, but this paved the way for more just treatment of people in the courts. There is some debate about whether the illustration here is actually Bogle himself.

Sir Alexander Bustamante
1884–1977

Bustamante began working to better the pay and working conditions of people when Jamaica was still a British colony. In 1943 he founded the Jamaica Labour Party, and in 1962 he became the first Prime Minister of independent Jamaica.

Marcus Garvey
1887–1940

Marcus Mosiah Garvey did much political work to improve people's lives. He founded the Universal Negro Improvement Association in 1914 and the People's Political Party in 1929.

George William Gordon
c.1820s–1865

George William Gordon was a businessman, politician, and landowner. He sold his land cheaply to freed slaves and ensured they could earn a fair income. A friend of Paul Bogle, he was charged with complicity in the Morant Bay Rebellion of 1865, illegally tried, and executed.

Norman Manley
1893–1969

Norman Washington Manley founded the People's National Party in 1938 and was an advocate of universal suffrage. This was introduced to Jamaica in 1944.

Queen Nanny
c.1686–c.1740s

"Nanny of the Maroons" or "Queen Nanny" was a leader of the Maroons at the beginning of the 18th century. Not much is known about her life, but she is documented as a great military strategist against the British during the First Maroon War from 1720–1739.

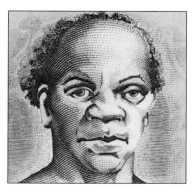

Samuel Sharpe
?–1832

Samuel Sharpe was the leader of the 1831–2 "Christmas Rebellion". He encouraged slaves to refuse to work on Christmas Day unless they were treated better and their pleas for freedom considered. The rebellion was quashed and Sharpe was hanged.

Famous Jamaicans

As well as Bolt and Fraser-Pryce (see right), there have been several other recent Jamaican sprinting stars. Yohan Blake is the second-fastest 100 m and 200 m sprinter of all time (behind Bolt). Veronica Campbell-Brown won the Olympic gold for the 200 m in both 2004 and 2008, becoming the first Caribbean woman to win this event and also to retain the title.

Some of the world's most famous cricketers have come from Jamaica, including Michael Holding, Courtney Walsh and Chris Gayle.

Many famous musicians were born in Jamaica, including Bob Marley (see right), Jimmy Cliff, Grace Jones, Dawn Penn and Lee "Scratch" Perry. Chronixx (born Jamar Rolando McNaughton) is a young, versatile musician who received a Grammy Award nomination in 2017 for his debut album, *Chronology*.

Elsewhere in the Arts, Barrington "Barry" Watson (1931–2016) was an influential artist who painted several major commissions, including official portraits of Marcus Garvey and Martin Luther King. Ralston Milton "Rex" Nettleford (1933–2010) was a famous dancer, choreographer, author and scholar. Marlon James (see right) is probably the most well-known modern Jamaican author. Though not Jamaican-born, James Bond novelist Ian Fleming lived near Oracabessa and set some of his stories on the island. Finally, Louise Bennett-Coverley (1919–2006) is credited for popularizing the Jamaican Patois language through her folk songs and poetry.

Usain Bolt

Said to be the fastest human ever timed, Bolt is the only sprinter to have won the 100 m and 200 m at three consecutive Olympic Games – in 2008, 2012 and 2016. From 2009 to 2015 (apart from the 100 m in 2011) he won consecutive World Championship gold medals in the 100 m, 200 m and 4 x 100 m relay.

Shelly-Ann Fraser-Pryce

Nicknamed the "Pocket Rocket", Fraser-Pryce won medals for the 100 m at three consecutive Olympics – gold in 2008 and 2012, and bronze in 2016 – the first woman ever to do so. She has won a number of awards in her home country and was named IAAF World Athlete of the Year in 2015.

Bob Marley

One of the most influential musicians of all time, Bob Marley popularized reggae music around the world, both with the Wailers and as a solo artist, having hits such as *Jamming* and *No Woman No Cry*. Shortly before his death in 1981, he was awarded the Order of Merit and is now being considered for the Order of National Hero.

Marlon James

James is a Jamaican-born writer who has written three novels, the most recent of which, *A Brief History of Seven Killings*, has won several awards, including the 2015 Man Booker Prize. He teaches literature in St Paul, Minnesota, USA, and is currently working on his next novel, the first of a planned fantasy series.

Jamaica Tourism

Rose Hall Great House
Greenwood Great House
Columbus Park
Green Grotto Caves
Seville Great House and Heritage Park
Montego Bay Marine Park
Bellefield Great House and Gardens
Martha Brae Rafter's Village
Rocklands Bird Sanctuary
Good Hope Estate
Dunns River Falls and Park
Fern Gully
Seven Mile Beach
Mayfield Falls
Croydon Plantation
The Cockpit Country
Bob Marley Mausoleum
Fort George
Negril Cliffs and Lighthouse
Blue Hole Mineral Spring
Y.S. Falls
Appleton Sugar and Rum Estate
Castleton Botanical Gardens
Somerset Falls
Blue Lagoon
Boston Bay Beach
Long Bay Beach
Cinchona Botanical Gardens
Blue and John Crow Mountains National Park
Holywell National Park
Marshall's Pen Great House
Hope Botanical Gardens and Zoo
Fort Augusta
Bath Botanical Gardens and Spa
Hellshire Beach
Portland Point Lighthouse

Kingston:
National Heroes Park
Port Royal and Fort Charles
National Gallery
Sabina Park Cricket Stadium
Bob Marley Museum
Devon House

Features

- ● National park
- ★ Point of interest
- □ Major resort
- ⊕ Main airport
- ⊕ Port
- Cruise ships
- Major marina
- Fishing port

Scale 1 : 1 250 000

Bamboo rafting, seen here on the Martha Brae River, is a popular tourist activity. The rafts were once used by farmers to transport their crops to port.

In the last 50 years, Ocho Rios has grown from a fishing village to a major resort city and cruise port. It benefits from its attractive coastal setting and the nearby Dunns River Falls, Jamaica's most visited tourist site.

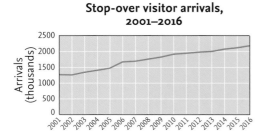

Stop-over visitor arrivals, 2001–2016
Arrivals (thousands)

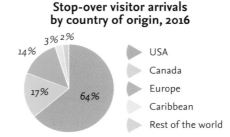

Stop-over visitor arrivals by country of origin, 2016
- 64% USA
- 17% Canada
- 14% Europe
- 3% Caribbean
- 2% Rest of the world

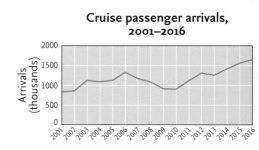

Cruise passenger arrivals, 2001–2016
Arrivals (thousands)

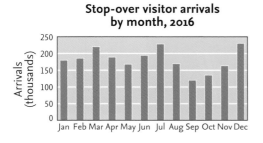

Stop-over visitor arrivals by month, 2016
Arrivals (thousands)
Jan Feb Mar Apr May Jun Jul Aug Sep Oct Nov Dec

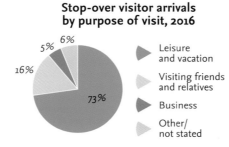

Stop-over visitor arrivals by purpose of visit, 2016
- 73% Leisure and vacation
- 16% Visiting friends and relatives
- 5% Business
- 6% Other/ not stated

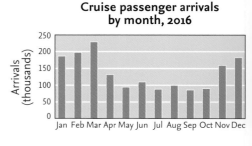

Cruise passenger arrivals by month, 2016
Arrivals (thousands)
Jan Feb Mar Apr May Jun Jul Aug Sep Oct Nov Dec

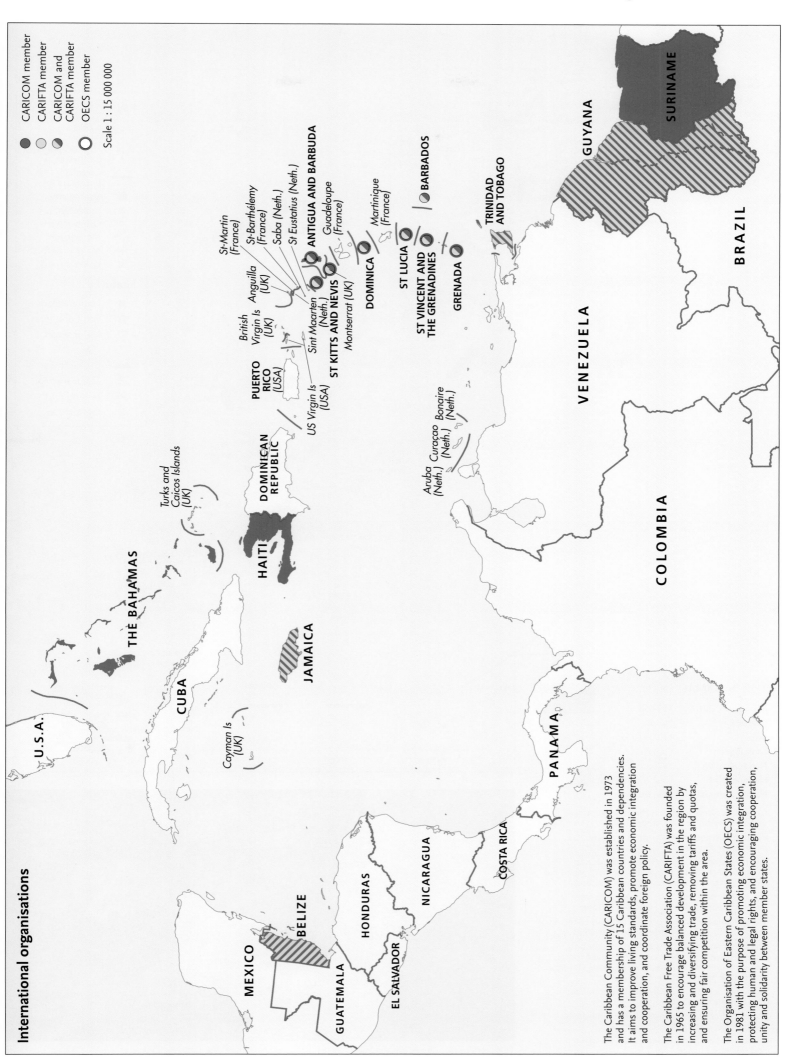

International organisations

CARICOM member
CARIFTA member
CARICOM and CARIFTA member
OECS member

Scale 1 : 15 000 000

The Caribbean Community (CARICOM) was established in 1973 and has a membership of 15 Caribbean countries and dependencies. It aims to improve living standards, promote economic integration and cooperation, and coordinate foreign policy.

The Caribbean Free Trade Association (CARIFTA) was founded in 1965 to encourage balanced development in the region by increasing and diversifying trade, removing tariffs and quotas, and ensuring fair competition within the area.

The Organisation of Eastern Caribbean States (OECS) was created in 1981 with the purpose of promoting economic integration, protecting human and legal rights, and encouraging cooperation, unity and solidarity between member states.

U.S.A.

THE BAHAMAS

CUBA

Cayman Is
(UK)

JAMAICA

Turks and
Caicos Islands
(UK)

DOMINICAN
REPUBLIC

HAITI

PUERTO
RICO
(USA)

US Virgin Is
(USA)

British
Virgin Is
(UK)

Anguilla
(UK)

St-Martin
(France)

St-Barthélemy
(France)

Saba (Neth.)

St Eustatius (Neth.)

Sint Maarten
(Neth.)

ST KITTS AND NEVIS

Montserrat (UK)

ANTIGUA AND BARBUDA

Guadeloupe
(France)

DOMINICA

Martinique
(France)

ST LUCIA

ST VINCENT AND
THE GRENADINES

BARBADOS

GRENADA

TRINIDAD
AND TOBAGO

Aruba
(Neth.)

Curaçao
(Neth.)

Bonaire
(Neth.)

MEXICO

GUATEMALA

BELIZE

EL SALVADOR

HONDURAS

NICARAGUA

COSTA RICA

PANAMA

COLOMBIA

VENEZUELA

GUYANA

SURINAME

BRAZIL

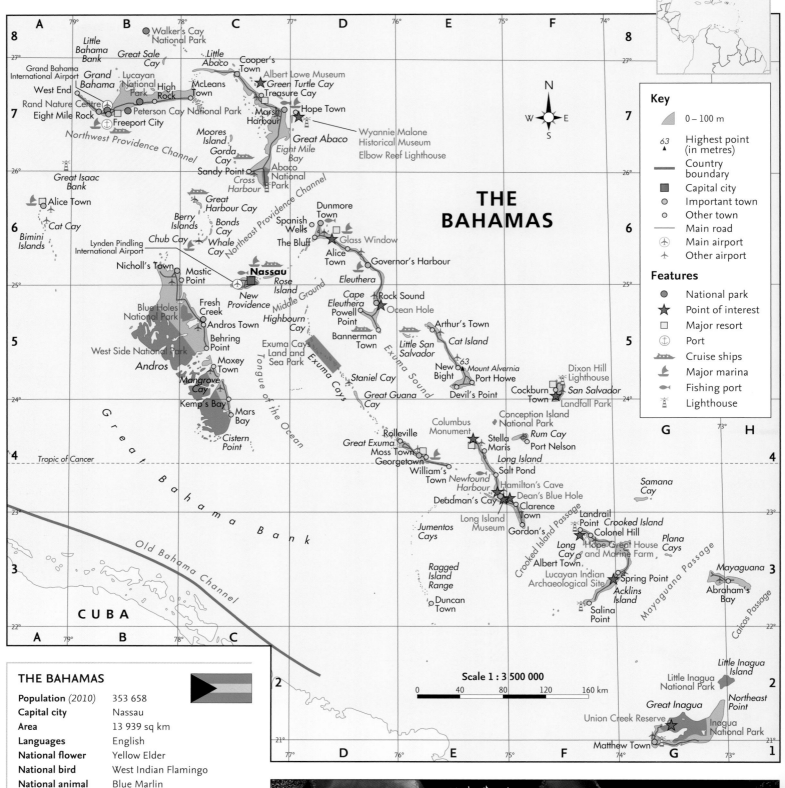

Key

	0 – 100 m
63 ▲	Highest point (in metres)
▬▬▬	Country boundary
■	Capital city
⊙	Important town
○	Other town
▬▬	Main road
✈	Main airport
✈	Other airport

Features

●	National park
★	Point of interest
□	Major resort
⊕	Port
🚢	Cruise ships
⛵	Major marina
🐟	Fishing port
🗼	Lighthouse

Scale 1 : 3 500 000

0   40   80   120   160 km

THE BAHAMAS

Population (2010)	353 658
Capital city	Nassau
Area	13 939 sq km
Languages	English
National flower	Yellow Elder
National bird	West Indian Flamingo
National animal	Blue Marlin

Columbus's first landfall in the New World was on San Salvador on 14 October **1492**

Columbus visited four islands in the Bahamas before travelling on

The prehistoric inhabitants were the Lucayans, a branch of the Taino people, but all were wiped out within 50 years of the country's first sighting

The first settlers were religious refugees from Bermuda who settled on Eleuthera in **1648**

The Bahamas became a British colony in **1718** and remained British until independence in **1973**

The Bahamas never had a plantation economy, but subsisted on shifting cultivation and fishing, and occasionally from wrecking, blockade running and other opportunistic enterprises

New Providence is the most densely populated island in the Caribbean region

The extent of the archipelago is the same as the distance from Antigua to Trinidad

The current economy is dependent on tourism and offshore finance

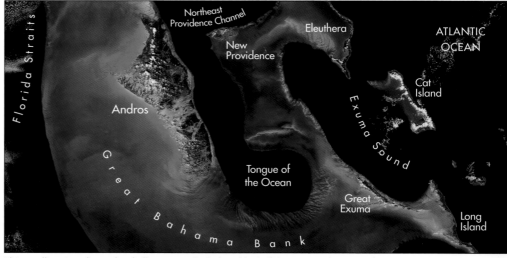

This satellite view shows the shallow waters (in lighter blue) of the Great Bahama Bank.

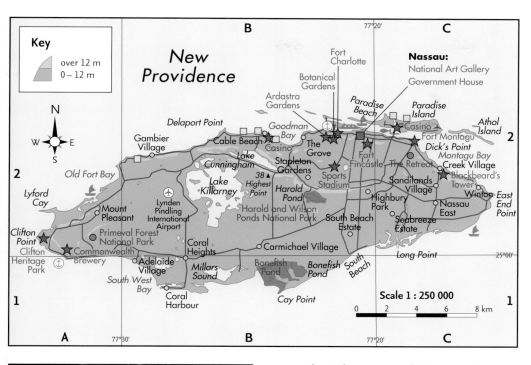

THE BAHAMAS island data	Area (sq km)	Population (2010)	Pop. density (per sq km)
TOTAL	13 939	353 658	25
New Providence	207	248 948	1203
Grand Bahama	1373	51 756	38
Abaco	1681	16 692	10
Acklins	497	560	1
Andros	5957	7386	1
Berry Islands	31	798	26
Bimini Islands	23	2008	87
Cat Island	389	1503	4
Cay Sal Bank	5	0	0
Crooked Island/ Long Cay	241	323	1
Eleuthera	518	11 065	21
Exuma and Cays	290	7314	25
Inagua	1551	911	1
Long Island	596	3024	5
Mayaguana	285	271	1
Ragged Island	36	70	2
Rum Cay	78	99	1
San Salvador	163	930	6

Each Boxing Day and New Year's Day Junkanoo street parades take place across The Bahamas, the largest being in the capital, Nassau. It is believed that these festivals of music, dance and costumes originated in the days of slavery.

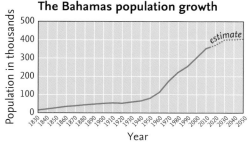

Blue holes

- These are deep solution holes in the flat limestone islands and shallow seas
- Those in the sea are known as ocean holes
- Some exist in The Cockpit Country of Jamaica and many in the Yucatán area of Mexico
- There are hundreds in The Bahamas, many over 100 metres deep
- The deepest blue hole is Dean's Blue Hole on Long Island, 202 metres deep
- This blue hole has been the scene of a number of recent free diving record attempts
- Many artifacts from the original Amerindian inhabitants (known as the Lucayans) have been found in the blue holes which these people used as burial sites

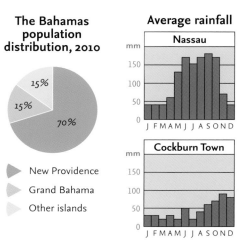

TURKS & CAICOS island data	Area (sq km)	Population (2012)	Pop. density (per sq km)
TOTAL	616	31 458	51
Grand Turk	17	4831	284
Middle Caicos	144	168	1
North Caicos	116	1312	11
Parrot Cay	6	131	22
Providenciales	122	23 769	195
Salt Cay	7	108	15
South Caicos	21	1139	54

TURKS AND CAICOS ISLANDS

British Overseas Territory

Population (2012)   31 458
Capital town   Cockburn Town
Area   616 sq km
Languages   English
National flower   Turk's Head Cactus
National bird   Brown Pelican
National animal   Rock Iguana

The prehistoric inhabitants were the Taino
First sighted by Ponce de León in **1512**
Settled by Bermudans collecting salt after **1680**
Occupied by the French **1765–1799**
Became part of the British Bahamas in **1799**
Governed variously by Jamaica and The Bahamas until **1973** when it became a British Overseas Territory

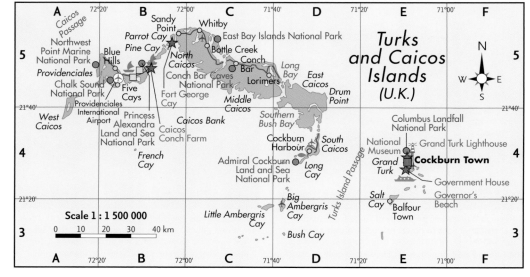

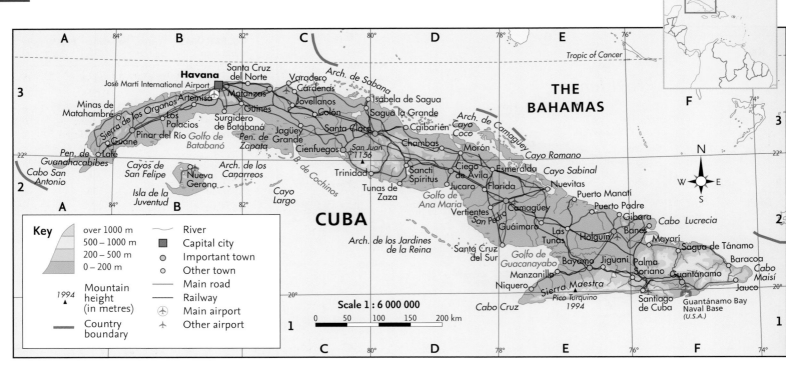

Key

over 1000 m	River
500 – 1000 m	Capital city
200 – 500 m	Important town
0 – 200 m	Other town
	Main road
1994 Mountain height (in metres)	Railway
	Main airport
Country boundary	Other airport

Scale 1 : 6 000 000

0 50 100 150 200 km

Features

Havana:
Old Havana: Plaza de la Catedral,
Catedral de San Cristóbal, Bodeguita del Medio,
Castillo de la Real Fuerza, Casa del Conde Jaruco,
Museo Nacional de Bellas Artes
Malecón
Parque Histórico Militar
El Capitolio
Acuario Nacional
Jardín Botánico
Nacional

Parque Nacional
Peninsula de
Guanahacabibes

Cienfuegos:
Palacio de Valle
Castillo de Jagua
Museo Naval
Oil Refinery

Varadero:
Parque Natural Punta Hicacos
Cueva de Musulmanes
Parque Josone

Santa Clara:
Museo Histórico de la Revolución
Memorial Comandante Ernesto 'Che' Guevara
Monumento a la Toma del Tren Blindado
Teatro de La Caridad

Trinidad:
Iglesia Parroquial de la
Santisima Trinidad
Iglesia y Convento de San Francisco
Museo de Arquitectura Colonial
Casa de Aldeman Ortiz
Palacio Brunet

Camagüey:
Plaza San Juan de Díos
Iglesia de Nuestra Señora de la Merced

Baracoa:
Fortaleza Matachín
El Castillo de
Seboruco
El Yunque

Santiago de Cuba:
Casa de Diego Velazquez
Castillo del Morro

Scale 1 : 8 000 000

●	National park
★	Point of interest
□	Major resort
⊕	Main airport
⚓	Port
🚢	Cruise ships
⚓	Major marina
🐟	Fishing port

Economic activity

11%
19%
70%

▸ Services
▸ Agriculture, fishing and forestry
▸ Manufacturing

Average rainfall

Havana

mm
150
100
50
0
J F M A M J J A S O N D

Fulgencio Batista was president of Cuba from 1940 to 1944. He came back to power in 1952 through a military coup and remained dictator of Cuba until deposed by the Cuban Revolution in 1959. He died in exile in Spain in 1973.

Fidel Castro was the ruler of Cuba from 1959 until 2008. He gained power through the Cuban Revolution, which he led with Che Guevara and his brother Raúl Castro. Due to failing health he passed the presidency to his brother in 2008, and died in 2016.

CUBA

Population (2012)	11 167 325
Capital city	Havana
Area	110 860 sq km
Languages	Spanish
National flower	White Mariposa
National bird	Tocororo
National animal	Cuban Trogon

First sighted by Columbus on his first voyage in **1492**. Columbus thought he had reached Japan (Cipangu)

Original inhabitants were the Taino and Ciboney. Both groups had died out, mainly from disease, by **1600**

Cuba was a Spanish colony from its sighting by Columbus until **1898**

The Spanish-American war of **1898** led to the independence of Cuba, but until **1902** it was governed by the USA

In **1959** the Cuban Revolution took over the government and founded a socialist state, and by **1965** a communist state

In **1961** a US supported invasion at the Bay of Pigs was repelled by the Cubans

A US embargo on trade and travel to Cuba was begun in **1960**, but was partly reduced in **2015**

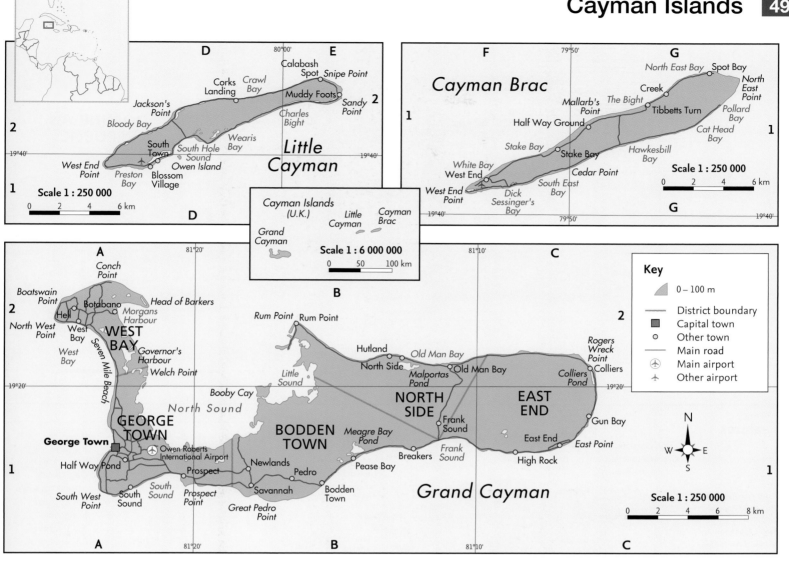

Little Cayman

Scale 1 : 250 000

Calabash Spot · Snipe Point
Corks Landing · Crawl Bay
Jackson's Point · Muddy Foots
Bloody Bay · Charles Bight · Sandy Point
South Town · Wearis Bay
West End Point · South Hole Sound · Owen Island
Preston Bay · Blossom Village

Cayman Brac

Scale 1 : 250 000

North East Bay · Spot Bay
Creek · North East Point
Mallarb's Point · The Bight · Tibbetts Turn · Pollard Bay
Half Way Ground · Cat Head Bay
Stake Bay · Hawkesbill Bay
White Bay · Stake Bay · Cedar Point
West End · Dick Sessinger's Bay · South East Bay
West End Point

Cayman Islands (U.K.)
Scale 1 : 6 000 000
Grand Cayman · Little Cayman · Cayman Brac

Grand Cayman

Scale 1 : 250 000

Conch Point · Boatswain Point · Head of Barkers
North West Point · Botabano · Morgans Harbour
Hell · West Bay · WEST BAY
West Bay · Governor's Harbour · Welch Point
Seven Mile Beach · Rum Point · Rum Point
GEORGE TOWN · **George Town** · North Sound
Little Sound · Hutland · North Side · Old Man Bay · Old Man Bay
Booby Cay · Malportas Pond · Colliers Pond · Colliers
Rogers Wreck Point
Owen Roberts International Airport · BODDEN TOWN · NORTH SIDE · EAST END
Half Way Pond · Prospect · Newlands · Pedro · Meagre Bay Pond · Frank Sound · Frank Sound · Gun Bay
Savannah · Pease Bay · Breakers · East End · East Point
South West Point · South Sound · Prospect Point · Bodden Town · High Rock
Great Pedro Point

Key
	0 – 100 m
—	District boundary
◼	Capital town
○	Other town
—	Main road
✈	Main airport
✈	Other airport

CAYMAN ISLANDS

British Overseas Territory

Population (2010)	55 036
Capital town	George Town
Area	264 sq km
Languages	English
National flower	Wild Banana Orchid
National bird	Cayman Parrot

No prehistoric settlement is known

Little Cayman and Cayman Brac were first sighted by Columbus in **1503**

Occasional European settlements were attempted on Grand Cayman in the **17th** century

The Cayman Islands formally became British in **1670**, and permanent settlement was established after **1730**

The Caymans were governed as a British colony with Jamaica until **1962**, when it became a separate crown colony, and subsequently a British Overseas Territory

It has since become a tax haven and a major tourist destination in the modern era

The Blue Iguana is found only on Grand Cayman. It can reach 1.5 metres in length and live for over 60 years. It is an endangered species and only 750 are believed to exist.

Features

●	National park	✈	Main airport
★	Point of interest	⌖	Port
☐	Major resort	⛴	Cruise ships
		⚓	Major marina
		🐟	Fishing port

Hell Rock Formations · Barker's National Park
Cayman Turtle Farm · Stingray City
Cemetery Beach and Reef · Davinoff's Concrete Sculpture Garden
Kittiwake Shipwreck and Artificial Reef · Blue Iguana Nature Reserve
Seven Mile Beach · Mastic Trail
Government House · Queen Elizabeth II Botanic Park · East End Lighthouse Park
Devil's Grotto
Pedro St James National Historic Site

George Town:
Fort George
Government Buildings
National Museum
National Gallery

Scale 1 : 400 000

	Area (sq km)	Population (2010)	Population density (per sq km)
Grand Cayman	197	52 740	268
Cayman Brac	39	2098	54
Little Cayman	28	198	7

Tourist arrivals, 2000–2014

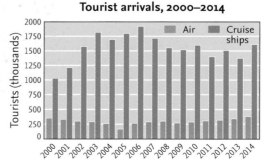

Tourists (thousands) · Air · Cruise ships
2000 2001 2002 2003 2004 2005 2006 2007 2008 2009 2010 2011 2012 2013 2014

Average rainfall

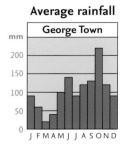

George Town

mm · 200 · 150 · 100 · 50
J F M A M J J A S O N D

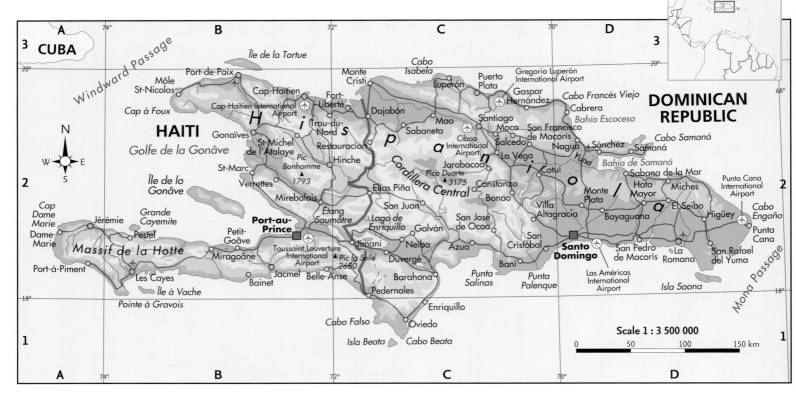

Features

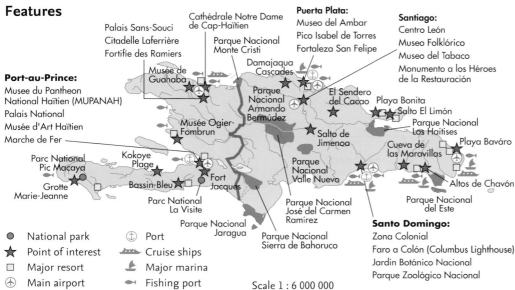

Port-au-Prince:
- Palais Sans-Souci
- Citadelle Laferrière
- Fortifié des Ramiers
- Musée de Guahaba

Cathédrale Notre Dame de Cap-Haïtien
Parque Nacional Monte Cristi
Damajagua Cascades

Puerta Plata:
- Museo del Ambar
- Pico Isabel de Torres
- Fortaleza San Felipe

Santiago:
- Centro León
- Museo Folklórico
- Museo del Tabaco
- Monumento a los Héroes de la Restauración

Port-au-Prince:
- Musee du Pantheon National Haïtien (MUPANAH)
- Palais National
- Musée d'Art Haïtien
- Marche de Fer

Parque Nacional Armando Bermúdez
Musée Ogier-Fombrun

El Sendero del Cacao
Playa Bonita
Salto El Limón
Parque Nacional Los Haitises

Parc National Pic Macaya
Kokoye Plage
Grotte Marie-Jeanne
Bassin-Bleu
Fort Jacques
Salto de Jimenoa

Cueva de las Maravillas
Playa Baváro
Altos de Chavón

Parc National La Visite
Parque Nacional Valle Nuevo

Parque Nacional del Este

Santo Domingo:
- Zona Colonial
- Faro a Colón (Columbus Lighthouse)
- Jardin Botánico Nacional
- Parque Zoológico Nacional

Parque Nacional Jaragua
Parque Nacional Sierra de Bahoruco
Parque Nacional José del Carmen Ramírez

- ● National park
- ★ Point of interest
- ▢ Major resort
- ⊕ Main airport
- ⊕ Port
- ⛴ Cruise ships
- ⚓ Major marina
- 🐟 Fishing port

Scale 1 : 6 000 000

Key
- over 3000 m
- 2000 – 3000 m
- 1000 – 2000 m
- 500 – 1000 m
- 200 – 500 m
- 0 – 200 m
- 3175 ▲ Mountain height (in metres)
- ⌢ River
- ▬ Country boundary
- ▢ Capital city
- ◉ Important town
- ○ Other town
- ▬ Main road
- ⊕ Main airport
- ✈ Other airport

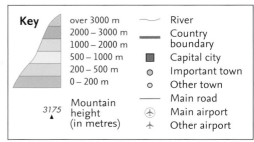

Average rainfall
Port-au-Prince
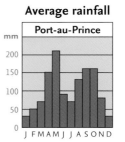

Average rainfall
Santo Domingo
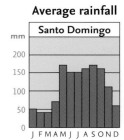

HAITI

Population (2013 est.)	10 320 000
Capital city	Port-au-Prince
Area	27 750 sq km
Languages	French, creole
National flower	Hibiscus
National bird	Hispaniolan Trogon

First sighted by Columbus, who thought he had reached India, on his first voyage in **1492**

The original inhabitants were the Taino who died out mainly from disease in the next 100 years

Initially part of the larger Spanish colony of Hispaniola, the whole island was ceded to France in **1625**. In **1697** Hispaniola became a French colony called Saint-Domingue

The French created a sugar plantation economy for their new colony

In **1804** the Haitian Revolution (began **1791**) created the Republic of Haiti, the first independent country in the Caribbean

From **1915** until **1934** the country was occupied by the United States

On 12 January **2010** a major earthquake destroyed much of the capital Port-au-Prince and killed an estimated 100 000 people

DOMINICAN REPUBLIC

Population (2010)	9 445 281
Capital city	Santo Domingo
Area	48 442 sq km
Languages	Spanish, creole
National flower	Bayahibe Rose
National bird	Palm Chat

First sighted by Columbus on his first voyage in **1492**

The original inhabitants were the Taino who died out mainly from disease in the next 100 years

The colony of Hispaniola remained Spanish until the French took over in **1625**

French rule continued after the Haitian revolution until **1809** when the present Dominican Republic's boundaries were established

The Dominican Republic, part of Saint-Domingue, again became Spanish, until **1821**, when it was occupied by Haiti, and the whole island became Haitian until **1844**

The modern Dominican Republic was created as an independent country on 27 February **1844** (independence from Haiti), but was commonly called Santo Domingo

From **1861** until 16 August **1865** the Dominican Republic was again a Spanish colony, so there are two independence days (independence from Spain)

Street sellers are often the main sellers of food in Haiti.

Spanish historic remains in Santo Domingo.

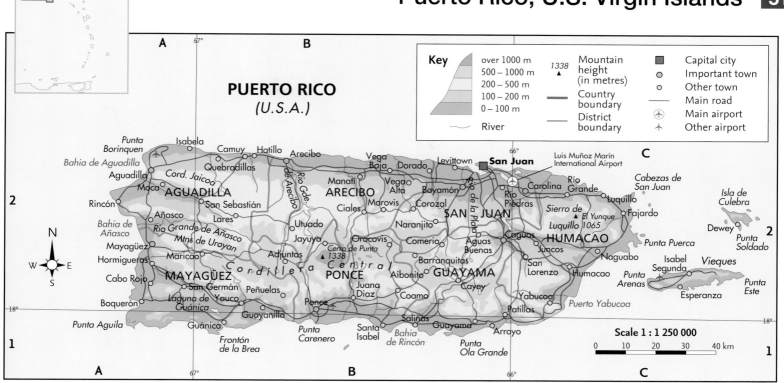

Key

over 1000 m	
500 – 1000 m	
200 – 500 m	
100 – 200 m	
0 – 100 m	
River	

1338 ▲ Mountain height (in metres)

━━ Country boundary

━━ District boundary

■ Capital city
◉ Important town
○ Other town
── Main road
✈ Main airport
✈ Other airport

PUERTO RICO
(U.S.A.)

Scale 1 : 1 250 000

0 10 20 30 40 km

Features

◉ National park
★ Point of interest
□ Major resort
✈ Main airport
⚓ Port
🚢 Cruise ships
⚓ Major marina

Faro de Punta Higuero
Bosque Estatal de Guajataca
Arecibo Radio Telescope Observatory
Arecibo Lighthouse and Historical Park
Cueva del Indio
Museo del Café
Jardín Botánico y Cultural de Caguas
Reserva Natural de las Cabezas de San Juan
Culebra National Wildlife Refuge
Parque de las Cavernas del Río Camuy
Zoologico
Reserve Natural Laguna de Joyuda
Hacienda Buena Vista
Centro Ceremonial Indígena de Tibes
Reserve Natural de Humacao
El Yunque National Forest
Vieques National Wildlife Refuge
Fortín Conde de Mirasol
Bosque Estatal de Guánica

Ponce: Museo de Arte de Ponce; Parque de Bombas; Museo de la Historia de Ponce; Museo de la Música Puertorriqueña

San Juan:
San Juan National Historic Site: La Fortaleza; Castillo San Cristóbal; Castillo San Felipe del Morro
Catedral San Juan Bautista
Museo de Arte de Puerto Rico
Museo de Las Americas

Scale 1 : 2 500 000

St Thomas
British Virgin Islands (U.K.)
Cruz Bay
Charlotte Amalie
St John
U.S. Virgin Islands (U.S.A.)
St Croix
356 ▲
Christiansted
Henry E. Rohlsen International Airport

Scale 1 : 3 000 000

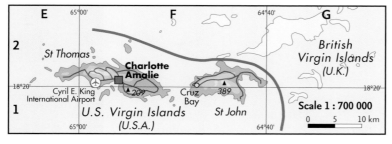

St Thomas
Charlotte Amalie
Cyril E. King International Airport
209 ▲
Cruz Bay
389 ▲
British Virgin Islands (U.K.)
U.S. Virgin Islands (U.S.A.)
St John

Scale 1 : 700 000

0 5 10 km

Features

Coral World Ocean Park
St Peter Greathouse and Botanical Gardens
Trunk Bay Beach
Virgin Islands National Park
Buck Island National Wildlife Refuge

Charlotte Amalie:
Blackbeard's Castle
Fort Christian
St Thomas Synagogue
Frederick Lutheran Church

Salt River Bay National Historic Park and Ecological Preserve
Frederiksted Historic District: Fort Frederik
Sandy Point National Wildlife Refuge
Cruzan Rum Distillery
Buck Island Reef National Monument
Christiansted National Historic Site: Fort Christiansværn; Steeple Building; Danish Custom House

Scale 1 : 2 000 000

PUERTO RICO

United States Commonwealth

Population *(2010)*	3 725 789
Capital city	San Juan
Area	9104 sq km
Languages	Spanish, English
National flower	Flor de Maga
National bird	Stripe-headed Tanager
National animal	Coqui Frog

First sighted by Columbus on his second voyage in **1493**

The original inhabitants were the Taino who died out mainly from disease in the next 100 years

Puerto Rico remained a Spanish colony until **1898**

In **1898** Puerto Rico was invaded by the USA and became a US possession

In **1952** the island became self-governing under its own constitution, but remains an unincorporated US territory

U.S. VIRGIN ISLANDS

United States Unincorporated Territory

Population *(2010)*	106 405
Capital city	Charlotte Amalie
Area	347 sq km
Languages	English, Spanish
National flower	Yellow Cedar
National bird	Bananaquit

First sighted and named by Columbus on his second voyage in **1493**

The Taino (Arawaks and Caribs) were the original inhabitants

Spain and France at times colonized the islands, but permanent settlement only came when the Danish settled in St Thomas in **1672**, followed by St John in **1694**. Denmark also bought St Croix from the French in **1733**. From **1754** the islands were officially Royal Danish colonies with sugar plantations

Denmark sold the islands to the United States which took possession on 31 March **1917**, now known as Transfer Day, a public holiday

Average rainfall

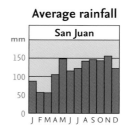

San Juan

Average rainfall

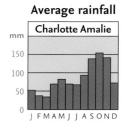

Charlotte Amalie

The busy harbour of San Juan with the skyline of the city across the bay.

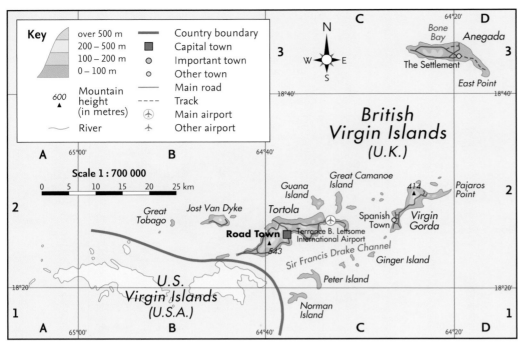

Key

- over 500 m
- 200 – 500 m
- 100 – 200 m
- 0 – 100 m

600 ▲ Mountain height (in metres)

~ River

━ Country boundary
■ Capital town
⊚ Important town
○ Other town
── Main road
--- Track
⊕ Main airport
✈ Other airport

Scale 1 : 700 000

0 5 10 15 20 25 km

British Virgin Islands (U.K.)

Bone Bay
Anegada
The Settlement
East Point

Great Camanoe Island
Pajaros Point
Guana Island
414 ▲
Spanish Town
Virgin Gorda
Tortola
Jost Van Dyke
Great Tobago
Road Town
Terrance B. Lettsome International Airport
543 ▲
Sir Francis Drake Channel
Ginger Island
Peter Island

U.S. Virgin Islands (U.S.A.)

Norman Island

Features

- ● National park
- ★ Point of interest
- □ Major resort
- ⊕ Main airport
- ⚓ Port
- 🚢 Cruise ships
- ⚓ Major marina

Scale 1 : 500 000

Diamond Cay
Shark Bay National Park
Mount Healthy National Park
Road Town
Callwood Distillery
J.R. O'Neal Botanic Gardens
Smuggler's Cove
Fort Burt
Folk Museum
Sage Mountain National Park
Tortola
Sugar Works Museum

Shoal Bay East
Shoal Bay-Island Harbour Marine Park
Little Bay Marine Park
The Valley
Heritage Collection Museum
Wallblake Historic House
Meads Bay
Rendezvous Bay
Anguilla

St-Martin
National Nature Reserve
Marigot
Baie Orientale
Fort Louis
Loterie Farm
St-Martin's Museum
St Maarten Zoo and Botanical Park
Mullet Beach
Fort Amsterdam
Philipsburg
St Maarten Museum
Sint Maarten
The Courthouse

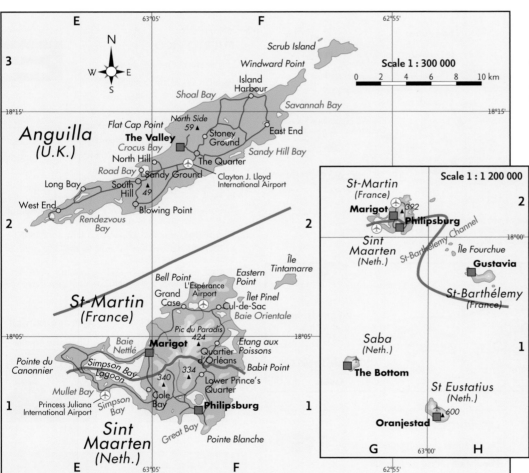

Scale 1 : 300 000

0 2 4 6 8 10 km

Anguilla (U.K.)

Scrub Island
Windward Point
Island Harbour
Shoal Bay
Savannah Bay
Flat Cap Point
North Side 59 ▲
Stoney Ground
East End
The Valley
Crocus Bay
North Hill
The Quarter
Sandy Hill Bay
Road Bay
Sandy Ground
Clayton J. Lloyd International Airport
Long Bay
South Hill 49 ▲
West End
Blowing Point
Rendezvous Bay

St-Martin (France)

Île Tintamarre
Bell Point
Eastern Point
Grand Case
L'Espérance Airport
Île Pinel
Cul-de-Sac
Baie Orientale
Pic du Paradis 424 ▲
Baie Nettlé
Marigot
Quartier d'Orléans
Etang aux Poissons
Babit Point
Pointe du Canonnier
Simpson Bay Lagoon
340 ▲ 334 ▲
Lower Prince's Quarter
Mullet Bay
Cole Bay
Philipsburg
Princess Juliana International Airport
Simpson Bay
Sint Maarten (Neth.)
Great Bay
Pointe Blanche

Scale 1 : 1 200 000

St-Martin (France)
Marigot 392 ▲
Philipsburg
St-Barthélemy Channel
Sint Maarten (Neth.)
Île Fourchue
Gustavia
St-Barthélemy (France)

Saba (Neth.)
The Bottom

St Eustatius (Neth.)
600 ▲
Oranjestad

Saba can be seen from Fort Oranje on St Eustatius. Both islands have a volcanic origin.

BRITISH VIRGIN ISLANDS

ANGUILLA

ST-MARTIN

SINT MAARTEN

SABA

ST EUSTATIUS

ST-BARTHÉLEM

	BRITISH VIRGIN ISLANDS	ANGUILLA	ST-MARTIN	SINT MAARTEN	SABA	ST EUSTATIUS	ST-BARTHÉLEM
	British Overseas Territory	*British Overseas Territory*	*French Overseas Collectivity*	*Self-governing Netherlands Territory*	*Netherlands Special Municipality*	*Netherlands Special Municipality*	*French Overseas Collectivity*
Population	28 054 (2010)	13 037 (2011)	36 286 (2011)	33 609 (2011)	1971 (2014 est.)	3791 (2014 est.)	9072 (2010)
Capital town	Road Town	The Valley	Marigot	Philipsburg	The Bottom	Oranjestad	Gustavia
Area	153 sq km	91 sq km	54 sq km	34 sq km	13 sq km	21 sq km	21 sq km
Languages	English	English	French	Dutch, English	Dutch, English	Dutch, English	French
National flower	White Cedar Flower	White Cedar	Hibiscus	Orange-yellow Sage	Black-eyed Susan	Morning Glory	Lily
National bird	Zenaida Dove	Zenaida Dove	Brown Pelican	Brown Pelican	Audubon's Shearwater	Nahamaya	-

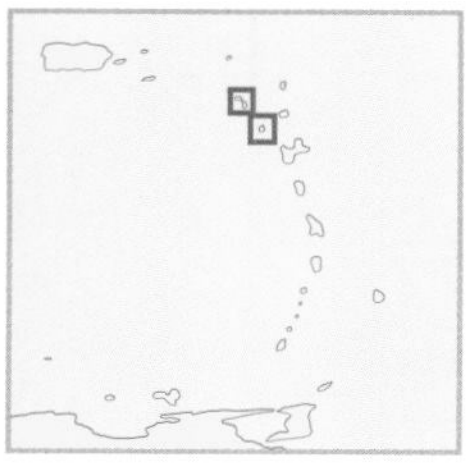

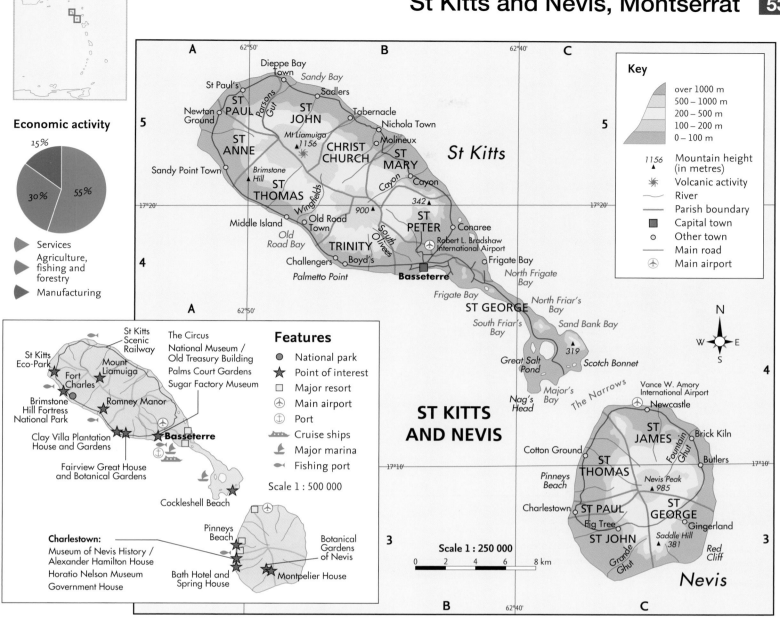

Economic activity

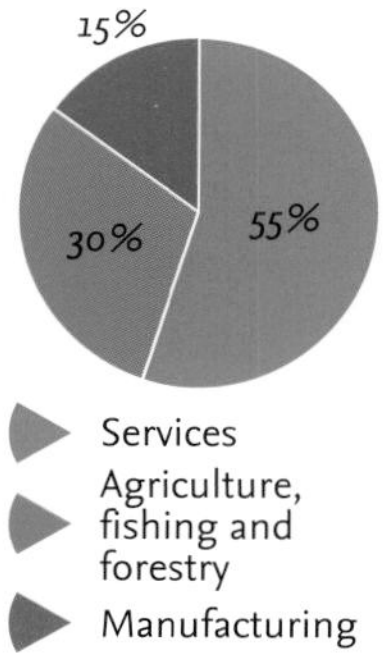
15%
30%
55%
Services
Agriculture, fishing and forestry
Manufacturing

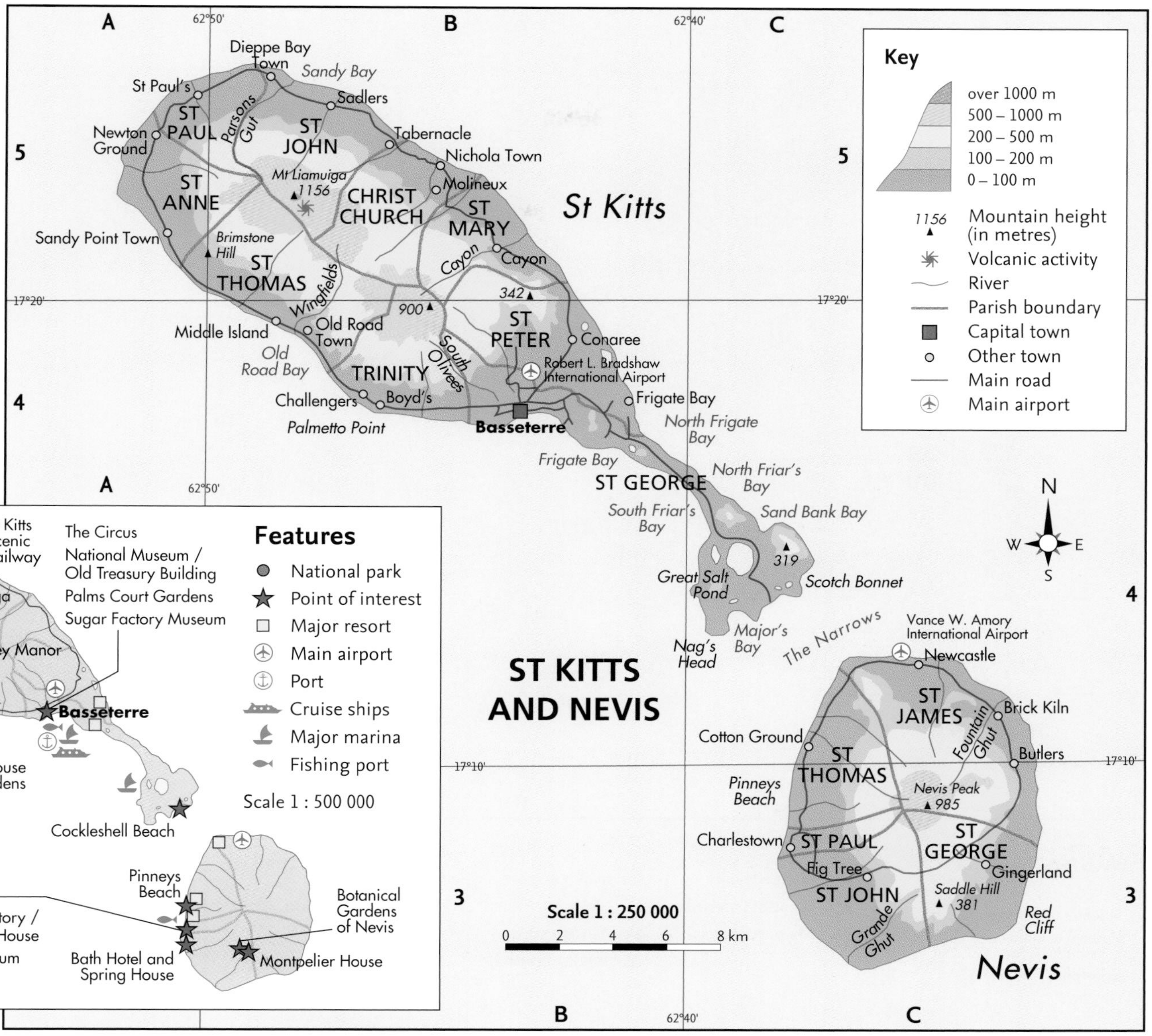
St Kitts
ST KITTS AND NEVIS
Nevis
Key
over 1000 m
500 – 1000 m
200 – 500 m
100 – 200 m
0 – 100 m
1156 Mountain height (in metres)
Volcanic activity
River
Parish boundary
Capital town
Other town
Main road
Main airport
Dieppe Bay Town
Sandy Bay
St Paul's
Sadlers
ST PAUL
Parsons Gut
ST JOHN
Newton Ground
Tabernacle
Nichola Town
Mt Liamuiga 1156
Molineux
ST ANNE
CHRIST CHURCH
ST MARY
Sandy Point Town
Brimstone Hill
ST THOMAS
Cayon
Wingfields
342
900
ST PETER
Middle Island
Old Road Town
Conaree
Old Road Bay
TRINITY
South Olivees
Robert L. Bradshaw International Airport
Challengers
Boyd's
Frigate Bay
Palmetto Point
Basseterre
North Frigate Bay
Frigate Bay
ST GEORGE
North Friar's Bay
South Friar's Bay
Sand Bank Bay
319
Great Salt Pond
Scotch Bonnet
Nag's Head
Major's Bay
The Narrows
Vance W. Amory International Airport
Newcastle
ST JAMES
Brick Kiln
Fountain Ghut
Cotton Ground
ST THOMAS
Butlers
Pinneys Beach
Nevis Peak 985
Charlestown
ST PAUL
ST GEORGE
Fig Tree
Gingerland
ST JOHN
Saddle Hill 381
Red Cliff
Grande Ghut
Scale 1 : 250 000
0 2 4 6 8 km
62°50'
62°40'
17°20'
17°10'
N
W
E
S
Features
National park
Point of interest
Major resort
Main airport
Port
Cruise ships
Major marina
Fishing port
Scale 1 : 500 000
St Kitts Eco-Park
St Kitts Scenic Railway
The Circus
National Museum / Old Treasury Building
Palms Court Gardens
Sugar Factory Museum
Mount Liamuiga
Fort Charles
Brimstone Hill Fortress National Park
Romney Manor
Clay Villa Plantation House and Gardens
Basseterre
Fairview Great House and Botanical Gardens
Cockleshell Beach
Pinneys Beach
Charlestown:
Museum of Nevis History / Alexander Hamilton House
Horatio Nelson Museum
Government House
Bath Hotel and Spring House
Botanical Gardens of Nevis
Montpelier House

ST KITTS AND NEVIS

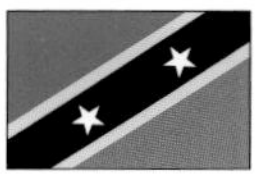

Population *(2014 est.)*	54 940
Capital town	Basseterre
Area *(St Kitts)*	168 sq km
Area *(Nevis)*	93 sq km
Languages	English, creole
National flower	Flamboyant
National bird	Brown Pelican

First sighted by Columbus **1493**

Occupied by Arawaks and later Caribs

Jointly settled by English in **1623** and French in **1625**

Alternately occupied by English and French until became British in **1783**

A sugar colony into the **20th** century. Sugar cultivation ended in **2005**

Average rainfall

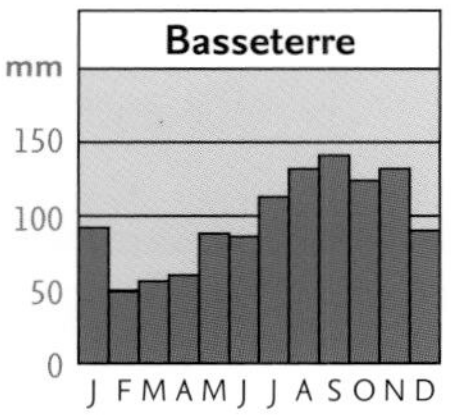
Basseterre
mm
150
100
50
0
J F M A M J J A S O N D

MONTSERRAT

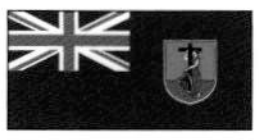

British Overseas Territory

Population *(2011)*	4922
Capital town	Brades
Area	102 sq km
Languages	English
National flower	Heliconia
National bird	Montserrat Oriole

First sighted by Columbus **1493**

Occupied by Irish settlers **1632**

Sugar, and later lime, plantations were established, but none exist today

In **1995** the Soufrière Hills volcano erupted. Ultimately the town of Plymouth was buried and two thirds of the island was abandoned

The island remains a British Overseas Territory

Features

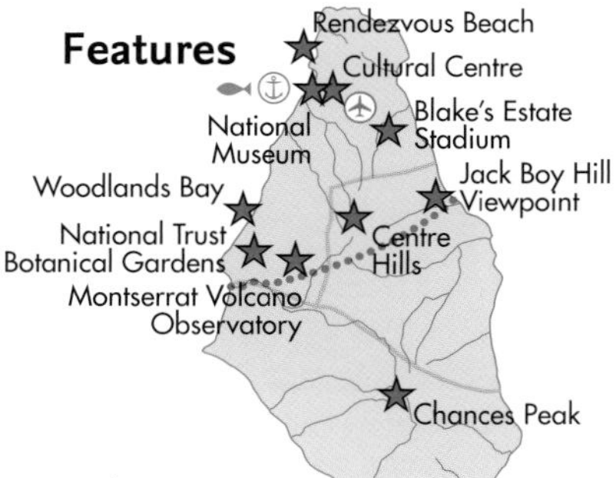
Rendezvous Beach
Cultural Centre
National Museum
Blake's Estate Stadium
Woodlands Bay
Jack Boy Hill Viewpoint
National Trust Botanical Gardens
Centre Hills
Montserrat Volcano Observatory
Chances Peak
Scale 1 : 350 000

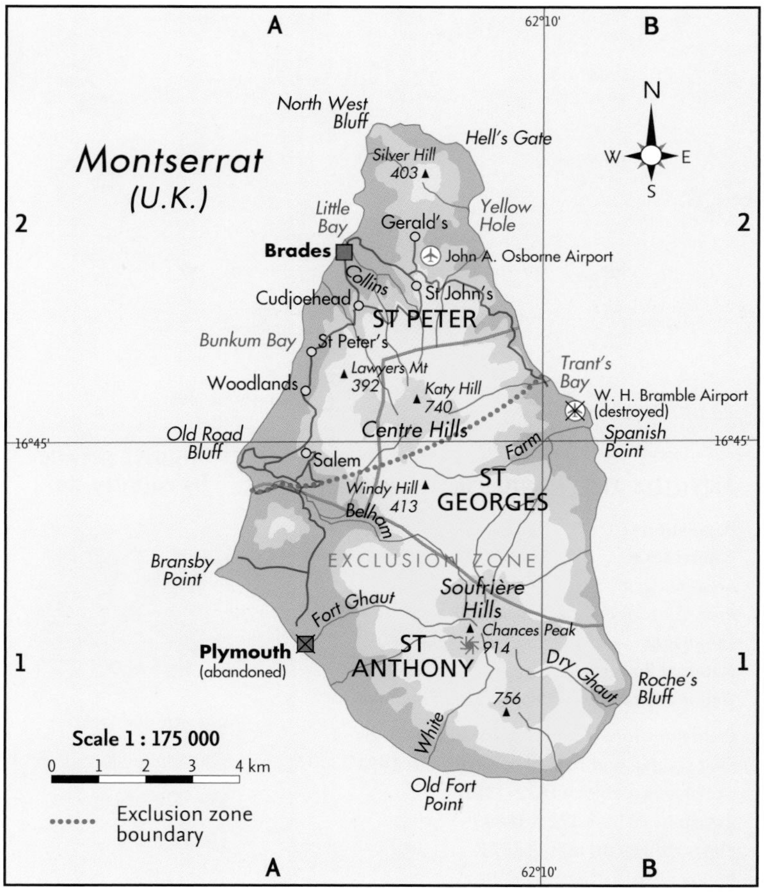
Montserrat (U.K.)
North West Bluff
Hell's Gate
Silver Hill 403
Little Bay
Yellow Hole
Gerald's
Brades
John A. Osborne Airport
Collins
St John's
Cudjoehead
ST PETER
Bunkum Bay
St Peter's
Lawyers Mt 392
Katy Hill 740
Trant's Bay
Woodlands
W. H. Bramble Airport (destroyed)
Centre Hills
Spanish Point
Old Road Bluff
Farm
Salem
Windy Hill 413
ST GEORGES
Belham
EXCLUSION ZONE
Bransby Point
Soufrière Hills
Fort Ghaut
Chances Peak 914
Plymouth (abandoned)
ST ANTHONY
Dry Ghaut
Roche's Bluff
756
White
Old Fort Point
Scale 1 : 175 000
0 1 2 3 4 km
Exclusion zone boundary
62°10'
16°45'
N
W
E
S

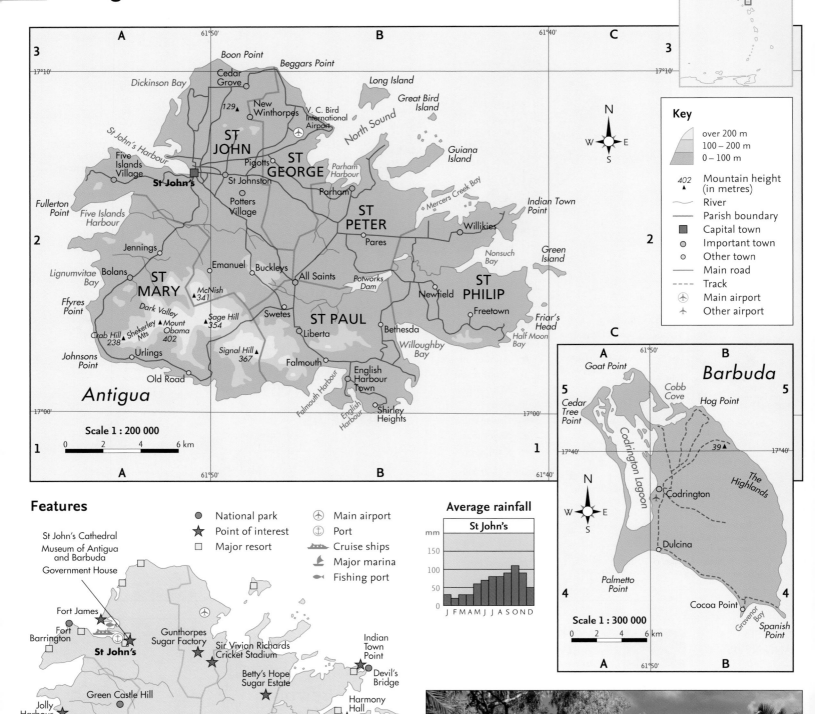

Antigua

Scale 1 : 200 000

0 2 4 6 km

Barbuda

Scale 1 : 300 000

0 2 4 6 km

Key

over 200 m
100 – 200 m
0 – 100 m

402 ▲ Mountain height (in metres)
— River
— Parish boundary
■ Capital town
◉ Important town
○ Other town
— Main road
--- Track
✈ Main airport
✈ Other airport

Features

◉ National park
★ Point of interest
□ Major resort
✈ Main airport
⚓ Port
🚢 Cruise ships
⚓ Major marina
🐟 Fishing port

Scale 1 : 275 000

St John's Cathedral
Museum of Antigua and Barbuda
Government House

Average rainfall

St John's

mm
150
100
50
0
J F M A M J J A S O N D

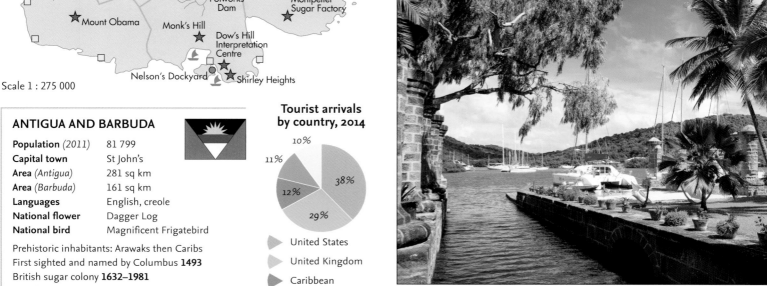

ANTIGUA AND BARBUDA

Population (2011)	81 799
Capital town	St John's
Area (Antigua)	281 sq km
Area (Barbuda)	161 sq km
Languages	English, creole
National flower	Dagger Log
National bird	Magnificent Frigatebird

Prehistoric inhabitants: Arawaks then Caribs
First sighted and named by Columbus **1493**
British sugar colony **1632–1981**
British naval base **1725–1889**
Sugar cultivation ceased **1971**
Independent 1 November **1981**

Tourist arrivals by country, 2014

- 38% United States
- 29% United Kingdom
- 12% Caribbean
- 11% Canada
- 10% Other

Nelson's Dockyard was the Royal Navy's naval base in the Caribbean for over 100 years. It is now a national park and includes a dockyard museum and an active yacht club and marina.

Map

Pointe de la Grande Vigie

Anse-Bertrand
Massioux
Campêche

Pointe d'Antigues
Gros-Cap
Port-Louis
Beauport
Les Mangles
Petit-Canal
Vieux-Bourg
Grande-
Morne-à-l'Eau
Le Moule
Bosrédon
Château-Gaillard
Terre
Les Abymes
Douville
Pointe-à-Pitre
Besson
St-François
Ste-Anne
Le Gosier
Pointe des Châteaux

Gachet
Salée

Pointe Allègre
Ste-Rose
Ilet à Fajou
Grand Cul-de-Sac Marin
Monplaisir
Goyaves
Lamentin
Baie-Mahault
Petit Cul-de-Sac Marin

Deshaies
Basse-
Morne Jeanneton 744 ▲
Terre
Pointe-Noire
Mahaut
Petit-Bourg
Vernou
Pigeon
Pitons de Bouillante 1088 ▲
La Lézarde
Bouillante
Montebello
▲ 1354 Sans Toucher
Goyave
Marigot
Vieux-Habitants
Capesterre
Ste-Marie
Vieux-Habitants
La Soufrière ✳ 1467 ▲
Carangaise
Baillif
St-Claude
Capesterre-Belle-Eau
Gourbeyre
Basse-Terre
Bananier
Vieux-Fort
Trois-Rivières
Pointe de Vieux-Fort

Pointe-à-Pitre (Le Raizet) International Airport

Guadeloupe (France)

Scale 1 : 500 000
0   5   10   15 km

Îles des Saintes
Terre-de-Bas
Petites-Anses
Terre-de-Haut

Grosse Pointe
St-Louis
Marie-
St Louis
Galante
Grand-Bourg
Capesterre
Pointe des Basses

61°30'   16°30'   16°00'

GUADELOUPE

Department of France

Population (2014 est.)   403 750
Capital town   Basse-Terre
Area   1780 sq km
Languages   French, creole
National flower   Lily
National bird   Gallic Rooster

Original inhabitants: Caribs

First sighted and named by Columbus **1493**

Occupied by the French **1635**

Annexed by France **1674**

Became a major French sugar colony, but occupied by the British at times in the **17th** century

In **1946** became a department (an integral part) of France, and therefore is part of the European Union

Sugar is still exported, along with bananas

Key

over 1000 m
500 – 1000 m
200 – 500 m
100 – 200 m
0 – 100 m

1467 ▲   Mountain height (in metres)
✳   Volcanic activity
～   River
■   Capital town
◉   Important town
○   Other town
—   Main road
✈   Main airport
✈   Other airport

Features

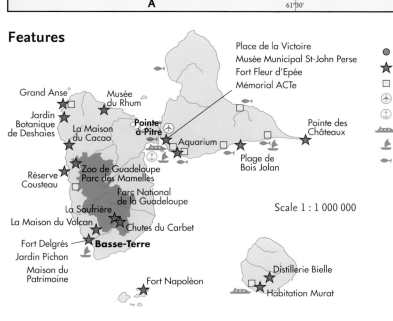

Grand Anse
Musée du Rhum
Jardin Botanique de Deshaies
La Maison du Cacao
Réserve Cousteau
Zoo de Guadeloupe Parc des Mamelles
La Soufrière
La Maison du Volcan
Fort Delgrés
Basse-Terre
Jardin Pichon
Maison du Patrimoine
Chutes du Carbet
Parc National de la Guadeloupe

Place de la Victoire
Musée Municipal St-John Perse
Fort Fleur d'Epée
Mémorial ACTe
Pointe-à-Pitre
Aquarium
Plage de Bois Jolan
Pointe des Châteaux

Fort Napoléon
Distillerie Bielle
Habitation Murat

Scale 1 : 1 000 000

◉   National park
★   Point of interest
□   Major resort
✈   Main airport
⏱   Port
🚢   Cruise ships
⚓   Major marina
🐟   Fishing port

Economic activity

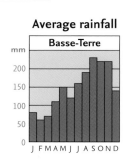

13%
27%
60%

■ Services
■ Agriculture, fishing and forestry
■ Manufacturing

Average rainfall

Basse-Terre

mm
200
150
100
50
0
J F M A M J J A S O N D

Traditional dishes

- *Matete* – a hot crab curry
- *Colombo* – a curry made with chicken or cabri (goat)
- *Callaloo* – a soup made with bacon and leafy greens
- *Bébélé* – a tripe soup with dumplings and green bananas
- *Blaff* – seafood cooked in a seasoned soup
- *Accras* – cod or vegetable fritters
- *Ouassou* – large freshwater shrimp

Although Basse-Terre is the capital of Guadeloupe, Pointe-à-Pitre is the largest city, commercial capital, and the main port. Its population is over 132 000, compared with less than 40 000 for Basse-Terre.

Chicken Colombo, one of the traditional dishes of Guadeloupe.

DOMINICA

Population (2011)	71 293
Capital town	Roseau
Area	750 sq km
Languages	English, creole
National flower	Carib Wood
National bird	Imperial Parrot (Sisserou)

Prehistoric inhabitants: Arawaks followed by Caribs

First sighted and named by Columbus **1493**

Some minor Spanish attempts at settlement resisted by the Caribs in **16th** and **17th** centuries

Colonised by the French as a sugar colony **1690–1763**

British colony **1763–1978**

Occupied by the French **1778–1783**

The sugar plantations were replaced by bananas in the **1960s**

Became independent 3 November **1978** and declared itself a Republic with a President

Banana production

Thousand tonnes (y-axis 0–80)
x-axis: 1961 1971 1981 1991 2001 2013

Average rainfall

Roseau
mm (y-axis 0–200+)
x-axis: J F M A M J J A S O N D

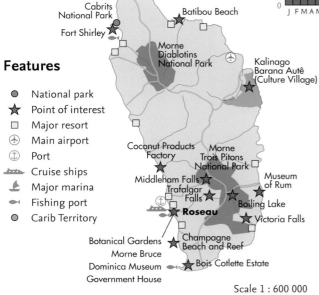

Features

- National park
- ★ Point of interest
- □ Major resort
- ✈ Main airport
- ⚓ Port
- Cruise ships
- Major marina
- Fishing port
- Carib Territory

Cabrits National Park
Fort Shirley
Batibou Beach
Morne Diablotins National Park
Kalinago Barana Autê (Culture Village)
Coconut Products Factory
Morne Trois Pitons National Park
Middleham Falls
Trafalgar Falls
Museum of Rum
Boiling Lake
Roseau
Victoria Falls
Botanical Gardens
Morne Bruce
Champagne Beach and Reef
Dominica Museum
Government House
Bois Cotlette Estate

Scale 1 : 600 000

Key

	over 1000 m
	500 – 1000 m
	200 – 500 m
	100 – 200 m
	0 – 100 m
1447 ▲	Mountain height (in metres)
✳	Volcanic activity
〜	River
⤳	Waterfall
—	Parish boundary
■	Capital town
⦿	Important town
○	Other town
—	Main road
✈	Main airport

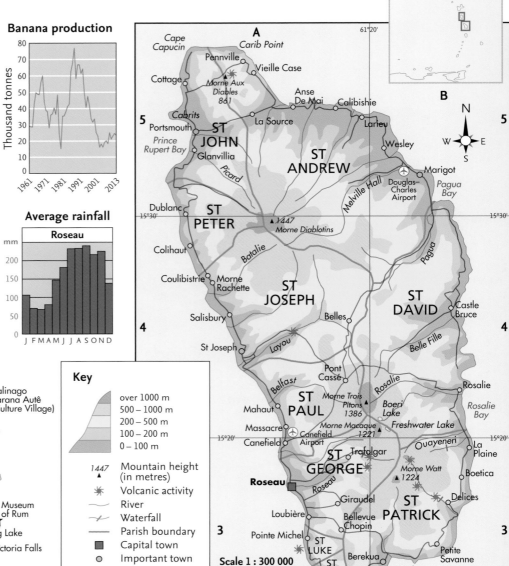

DOMINICA

Scale 1 : 300 000
0 2 4 6 km

MARTINIQUE

Department of France

Population (2014 est.)	381 326
Capital town	Fort-de-France
Area	1079 sq km
Languages	French, creole
National flower	Lily
National bird	Gallic Rooster

Prehistoric inhabitants: Arawaks followed by Caribs

First sighted and named by Columbus **1493**, visited and named by him in **1502** ('Martinica')

Settled by the French from St Kitts **1635**

The French conquered the Caribs and the survivors fled to Dominica

Mainly occupied by the British **1794–1815**

In **1946** became a department of France

Distillerie J M
Montagne Pelée
Les Gorges de la Falaise
La Maison Regionale des Volcans
Le Figuier
Musée Volcanologique
Musée Gauguin
Presqu'île de la Caravelle
Jardin de Balata
Fort-de-France
Fort St-Louis
Habitation Clement
La Savane
Cathédrale St-Louis
Musée de la Pagerie
Bibliothèque Schoelcher
Musée Regional d'Histoire et d'Ethnographie
Le Diamant
Les Salines

Scale 1 : 1 000 000

Montagne Pelée

- This active volcano exploded on 2 May 1902
- About 30 000 persons were killed
- The town of St-Pierre, capital of Martinique, was destroyed
- The capital was later moved to Fort-de-France, far from the volcano
- The nature of the explosion was an incandescent gas cloud known as a Nuée Ardente, which incinerated everything in its path
- Only two persons survived, one in a dungeon and one on a ship

St-Pierre, at the foot of Montagne Pelée.

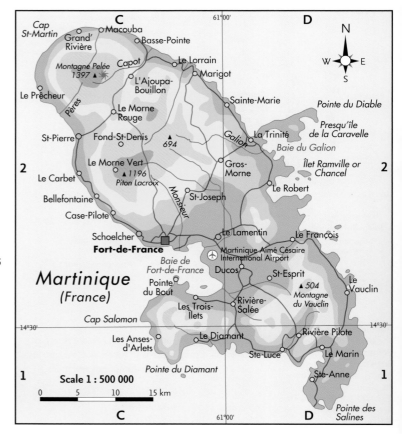

Martinique (France)

Scale 1 : 500 000
0 5 10 15 km

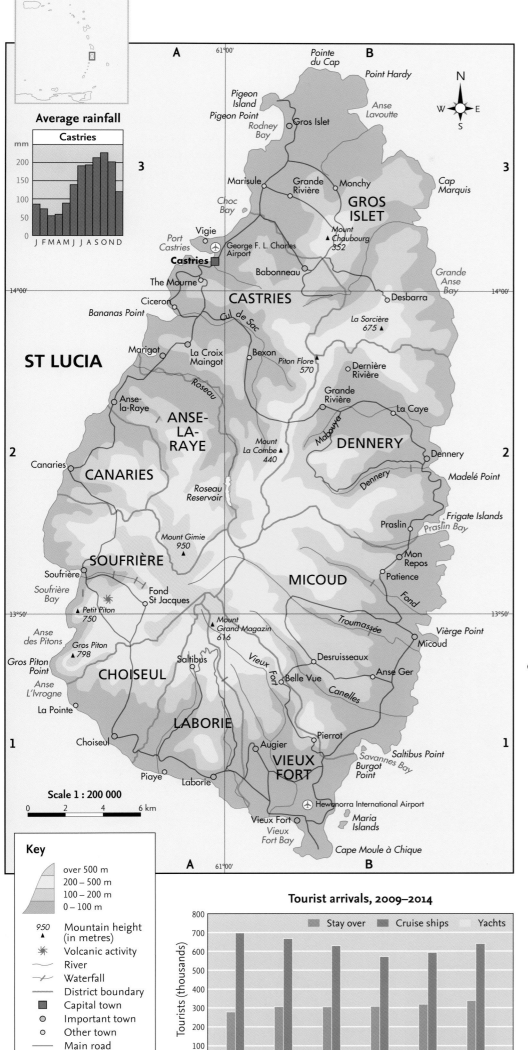

Average rainfall

Castries

mm
200
150
100
50

J F M A M J J A S O N D

Scale 1 : 200 000

0   2   4   6 km

Key

- over 500 m
- 200 – 500 m
- 100 – 200 m
- 0 – 100 m
- 950 ▲ Mountain height (in metres)
- ✳ Volcanic activity
- River
- Waterfall
- District boundary
- ■ Capital town
- ◉ Important town
- ○ Other town
- Main road
- ✈ Main airport

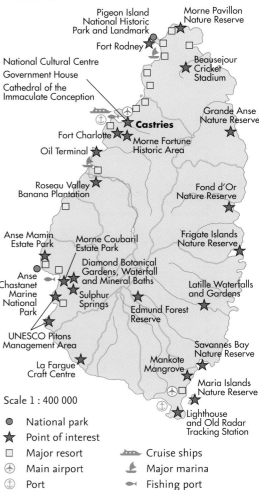

ST LUCIA

Population (2009)   173 765
Capital town   Castries
Area   617 sq km
Languages   English, creole
National flower   Rose
National bird   St Lucian Parrot

Prehistoric inhabitants: Arawaks followed by Caribs

First sighted and named by Columbus **1493**

Many failed attempts at settling the island were made by French, Dutch and British colonists from **1550** until **1640**

Colonised by the French as a sugar colony **1643–1803**. This period included several British occupations

British colony **1803–1979**

The sugar plantations were replaced by bananas in the **1960s**

Independent 22 February **1979**

Two St Lucians have won Nobel Prizes. The Nobel Prize for Economics was won by Sir Arthur Lewis in **1979**, and the Nobel Prize for Literature by Derek Walcott in **1992**

Features

Scale 1 : 400 000

- ◉ National park
- ★ Point of interest
- □ Major resort
- ✈ Main airport
- ⚓ Port
- 🚢 Cruise ships
- ⚓ Major marina
- 🐟 Fishing port

Tourist arrivals, 2009–2014

Tourists (thousands)

800
700
600
500
400
300
200
100

■ Stay over   ■ Cruise ships   □ Yachts

2009 2010 2011 2012 2013 2014

The *Carnival Valor* in Castries. This cruise ship can carry 3000 passengers and has a crew of over 1100.

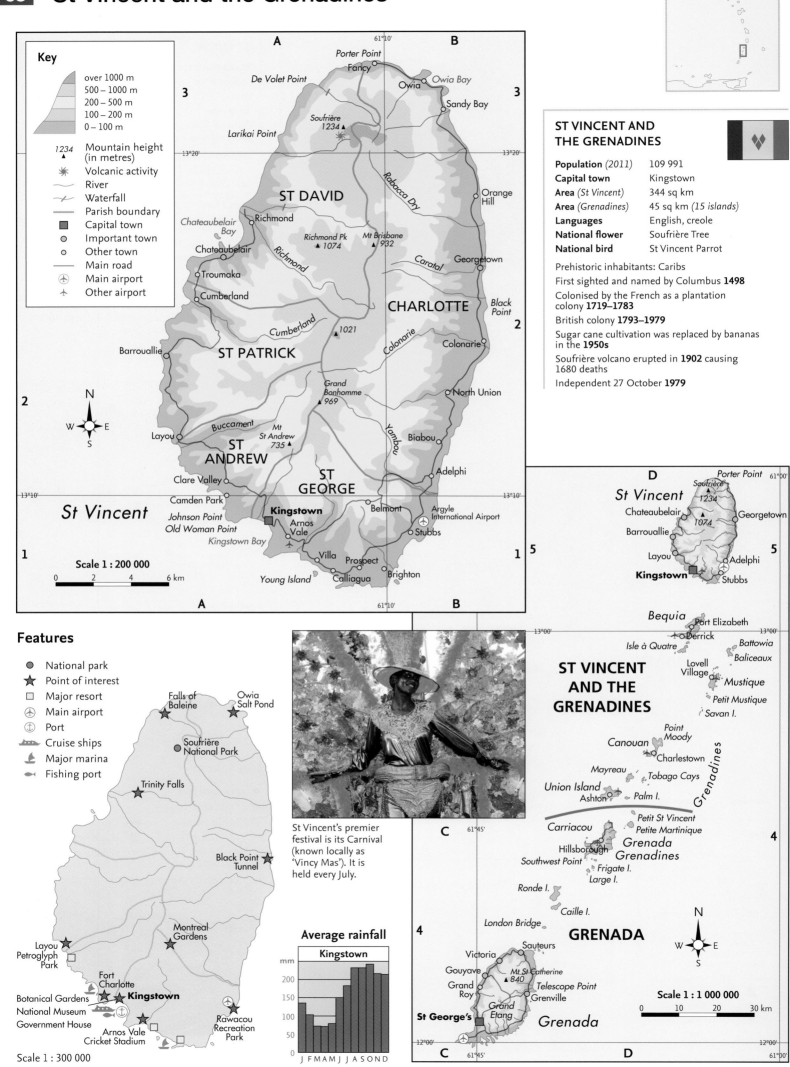

Key

- over 1000 m
- 500 – 1000 m
- 200 – 500 m
- 100 – 200 m
- 0 – 100 m

- 1234 ▲ Mountain height (in metres)
- ✳ Volcanic activity
- River
- Waterfall
- Parish boundary
- ■ Capital town
- ● Important town
- ○ Other town
- Main road
- ✈ Main airport
- ✈ Other airport

Scale 1 : 200 000

0   2   4   6 km

St Vincent

Porter Point
Fancy
De Volet Point
Owia   *Owia Bay*
Sandy Bay
Soufrière 1234 ▲
Larikai Point
Orange Hill

ST DAVID

Chateaubelair Bay
Richmond
Richmond Pk ▲ 1074
Mt Brisbane ▲ 932
Chateaubelair
Georgetown
Troumaka
Black Point
Cumberland
CHARLOTTE
Cumberland
▲ 1021
Colonarie
Colonarie
ST PATRICK
Barrouallie
Caratal
Grand Bonhomme ▲ 969
North Union
Buccament
Layou
Mt St Andrew 735 ▲
Yambou
ST ANDREW
Biabou
Clare Valley
ST GEORGE
Adelphi
Camden Park
Kingstown
Belmont
Johnson Point
Arnos Vale
Argyle International Airport
Old Woman Point
Stubbs
Kingstown Bay
Villa
Prospect
Brighton
Young Island
Calliagua

ST VINCENT AND THE GRENADINES

Population (2011)	109 991
Capital town	Kingstown
Area (St Vincent)	344 sq km
Area (Grenadines)	45 sq km (15 islands)
Languages	English, creole
National flower	Soufrière Tree
National bird	St Vincent Parrot

Prehistoric inhabitants: Caribs

First sighted and named by Columbus **1498**

Colonised by the French as a plantation colony **1719–1783**

British colony **1793–1979**

Sugar cane cultivation was replaced by bananas in the **1950s**

Soufrière volcano erupted in **1902** causing 1680 deaths

Independent 27 October **1979**

St Vincent

Porter Point
Soufrière 1234 ▲
Chateaubelair
▲ 1074
Georgetown
Barrouallie
Layou
Adelphi
Kingstown
Stubbs

Bequia
Port Elizabeth
Derrick
Isle à Quatre
Battowia
Baliceaux
Lovell Village
Mustique
Petit Mustique
Savan I.

ST VINCENT AND THE GRENADINES

Point Moody
Canouan
Charlestown
Mayreau
Tobago Cays
Union Island
Ashton
Palm I.
Petit St Vincent
Petite Martinique
Carriacou
Grenada Grenadines
Hillsborough
Southwest Point
Frigate I.
Large I.
Ronde I.
Caille I.
London Bridge

GRENADA

Victoria
Sauteurs
Gouyave
Mt St Catherine ▲ 840
Grand Roy
Telescope Point
St George's
Grand Etang
Grenville
Grenada

Scale 1 : 1 000 000

0   10   20   30 km

Features

- ● National park
- ★ Point of interest
- □ Major resort
- ✈ Main airport
- ⚓ Port
- 🚢 Cruise ships
- ⚓ Major marina
- 🐟 Fishing port

★ Falls of Baleine
★ Owia Salt Pond
● Soufrière National Park
★ Trinity Falls
★ Black Point Tunnel
★ Montreal Gardens
★ Layou Petroglyph Park
Fort Charlotte
Botanical Gardens ★ **Kingstown**
National Museum
Government House
Arnos Vale Cricket Stadium
★ Rawacou Recreation Park

Scale 1 : 300 000

St Vincent's premier festival is its Carnival (known locally as 'Vincy Mas'). It is held every July.

Average rainfall

Kingstown

mm
200
150
100
50
0

J F M A M J J A S O N D

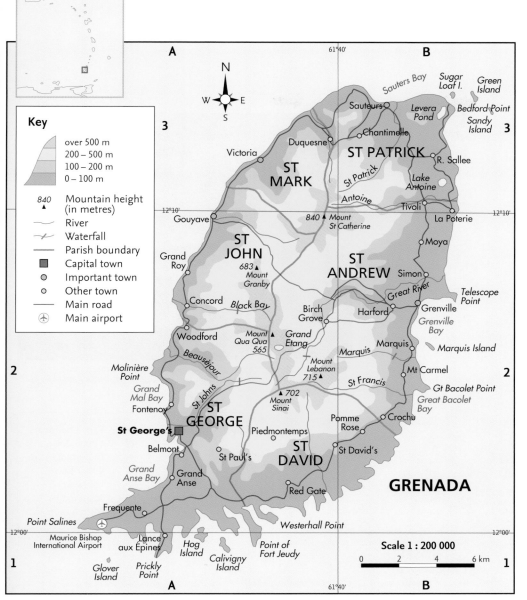

Key

	over 500 m
	200 – 500 m
	100 – 200 m
	0 – 100 m
840 ▲	Mountain height (in metres)
	River
	Waterfall
	Parish boundary
■	Capital town
◉	Important town
○	Other town
	Main road
✈	Main airport

GRENADA

Population (2011) 103 328
Capital town St George's
Total area 348 sq km
Area (Grenada) 313 sq km
Area (Carriacou) 33 sq km
Area (Petite Martinique) 2 sq km
Languages English, creole
National flower Bougainvillea
National bird Grenada Dove

Prehistoric inhabitants: Caribs
First sighted and named by Columbus **1498**
Colonised by the French as a sugar colony **1649–1763**
British colony **1793–1974**
Sugar soon gave way to cocoa production and later bananas
Independent 7 February **1974**
Invaded by USA in **1983**

World renowned producer of nutmeg and other spices. Sugar cane cultivation has largely ceased and bananas are a minor crop

Economic activity

7%
14%
79%

▶ Services
▶ Agriculture, fishing and forestry
▶ Manufacturing

Average rainfall

St George's

Scale 1 : 200 000

0   2   4   6 km

Features

●	National park
★	Point of interest
□	Major resort
✈	Main airport
⊕	Port
	Cruise ships
	Major marina
	Fishing port

Grenada is known as the Spice Island

- *Nutmeg and Mace* – second largest producer after Indonesia (also called 'Spice Islands'). Mace is a coating on the outside of the nutmeg
- *Cinnamon* – production has increased in recent years
- *Cloves* – production has increased in recent years
- *Ginger* – versatile root widely grown
- *Cocoa* – used locally to make cocoa tea and exported as organic dark chocolate
- *Pimento* – also known as allspice, an easily grown tree
- *Turmeric* – produced from a root, also known as saffron. Used in curries and popular for its medicinal value

Tramping through cocoa beans at the Belmont Estate to ensure they dry evenly.

Scale 1 : 300 000

A   59°35'   B   59°30'   C

5

N
W   E
S

Archers Bay   North Point
                    The Spout
                              Seaview
Archers   Greenidge
              Spring Hall   Pie
*Harrison   Corner   *Cockold Point*
Point*   ST LUCY   *Paul's Point*
Bromefield   Nesfield
                                        Boscobelle
Babbs
Fustic   *Mount Stepney*
                              245 ▲
Six Men's   Mile and
Bay   a Quarter
                    ▲ 147
              ST PETER   Greenland

4

13°20'   13°20'
                                        Long Pond

Satellite view of Bridgetown, showing the deep-water harbour and
Constitution River ('The Careenage'), which flows into Carlisle Bay.

13°15'   13°15'
Speightstown   Belleplaine
                    ST
                    ANDREW
Mullins   169   *Chalky
                              Mount
              277 ▲   167*
Lower Carlton   Upper Carlton   Bruce Vale
Westmoreland   *Mount Hillaby*   Cattlewash
          ST   340 ▲   Bathsheba
Alleynes Bay   JAMES   Orange Hillaby Mose   Hillcrest
The Garden   Hill   Bottom   *Joe's River*
                    Mount Misery   ST JOSEPH   306 ▲
                    326 ▲   Chimborazo
Holetown   Welchman   Castle Grant   Hothersal
                         Hall   338 ▲   Newcastle
Sunset Crest   Rock Hall   Coffee Gully   Venture   Glebe
              Arch Hall   ST   Clifton   Clifton Hall
                    THOMAS   Hill
3
13°10'   Coach   St Marks
Paynes   Sandy Lane   228 ▲   Ashbury   Hill   13°10'
Bay   Bagatelle   Redman's   Bridgefield   Four
              Thorpes   Cross Roads   Massiah
Fitts Village   Belair   Street
Prospect   Warrens   Jackson   Hilbury   Cottage
              123   Ellerton   Vale   Church
                                   Rowans   Melverton   Village
          Black   ST   Hothersal   ST GEORGE
          Rock   MICHAEL   Turning
2
Brighton   Dash   Boarded   Marchfield
          Bush Hall   Howells   Valley   Hall   Brereton   Six Cross
                                                                      Roads
                    Mapp   Mount   St Patricks   Four
          Constitution   Hill   Friendship   St Davids   Roads
Bridgetown ■   ▲ 83   CHRISTCHURCH
Carlisle   Sargeants   Charnocks
Bay   Garrison   Village   Newton
Needham's   Rockley   Vauxhall   Lodge   Terrace   Providence
Point   Hastings   St Lawrence   Road   Pegwell
1   Worthing   Welches   Oistins   Scarborough
                         Oistins   Enterprise
                         Bay   Inch
                                   South Point   Marlowe

Scale 1 : 145 000

0 1 2 3 4 5 km

59°40'   A   59°35'   B   59°30'   C

Key

over 200 m
100 – 200 m
0 – 100 m

340 ▲ Mountain height (in metres)

~~~ River

——— Parish boundary
■ Capital town
◉ Important town
○ Other town
═══ Highway
——— Main road
✈ Main airport

---

*Conset
Bay*   *Conset Point*
              Bell Point
ST JOHN
                    Bayfield   *Ragged Point*
                              Marley Vale
              164 ▲   Thicket   *Kitridge
                                        Point*
                         Wellhouse
          ST PHILIP
                                   Robinsons
                              The Crane
          62 ▲   *Cobbler's Rock*
              St Martins   *Foul Bay*
Salt Cave Point
✈ Grantley Adams
International Airport
Chancery   *Long
Lane   Bay*

BARBADOS

BARBADOS

Population (2010)	277 821
Capital town	Bridgetown
Area	430 sq km
Languages	English, creole
National flower	Pride of Barbados
National animal	Dolphin (the fish, also known as Mahi-mahi)

The original inhabitants were various Amerindians (Arawaks and Caribs), the last tribe being the Kalingo (Caribs). Barbados was uninhabited when it was settled

Unlike most Caribbean islands Barbados was not first sighted by Columbus – rather, it was by unknown Spanish mariners. The first recorded visit was by the Portuguese in **1536**

From **1625** English settlers arrived and the country became, and remained, a British colony until **1966**

Initially the colony grew tobacco and cotton and other non-plantation crops

In **1640** the economy changed to one of sugar plantations

Internal self-government was granted from **1961** until independence on 30 November **1966**

The economy diversified by the **1980s** to include tourism, and sugar is no longer the main source of income

Became a republic on 30 November **2021**

Economic activity

6% 3%

91%

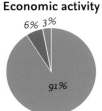

- ▶ Services
- ▶ Manufacturing
- ▶ Agriculture, fishing and forestry

Average rainfall

Bridgetown

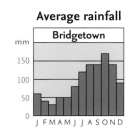

mm
150
100
50
0
J F M A M J J A S O N D

Fishing industry

- Flying fish account for over half the total catch
- Flying fish and dolphin (the fish) are major restaurant dishes for the tourist industry
- Kingfish (wahoo) and shark are also popular
- Oistins and Bridgetown have the two largest fish markets
- About 6000 people are employed in the fisheries industry
- The white sea egg is a local delicacy with a fishing season limited to September through December

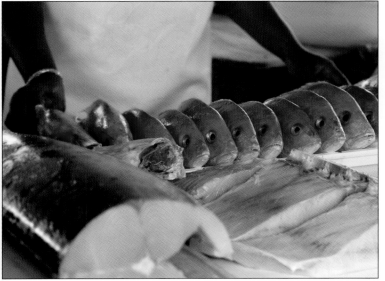

Berinda Cox Fish Market, Oistins.

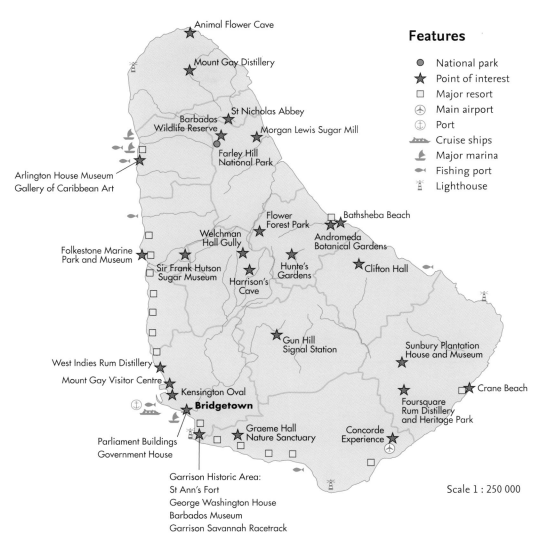

Animal Flower Cave
Mount Gay Distillery
St Nicholas Abbey
Barbados Wildlife Reserve
Morgan Lewis Sugar Mill
Farley Hill National Park
Arlington House Museum Gallery of Caribbean Art
Bathsheba Beach
Flower Forest Park
Welchman Hall Gully
Andromeda Botanical Gardens
Folkestone Marine Park and Museum
Sir Frank Hutson Sugar Museum
Hunte's Gardens
Clifton Hall
Harrison's Cave
Gun Hill Signal Station
Sunbury Plantation House and Museum
West Indies Rum Distillery
Mount Gay Visitor Centre
Kensington Oval
Crane Beach
Bridgetown
Foursquare Rum Distillery and Heritage Park
Parliament Buildings Government House
Graeme Hall Nature Sanctuary
Concorde Experience
Garrison Historic Area:
St Ann's Fort
George Washington House
Barbados Museum
Garrison Savannah Racetrack
Scale 1 : 250 000

Features

- ● National park
- ★ Point of interest
- ☐ Major resort
- ⊕ Main airport
- ⊕ Port
- ⚓ Cruise ships
- ⚓ Major marina
- ⚓ Fishing port
- ☼ Lighthouse

Sugar and rum

- Barbados is noted for its sugar and rum. Over the years the sugar industry has declined, but rum has been very successful
- In the 19th century there were 12 **sugar** factories that crushed the cane, but as sugar sales declined these were closed one by one
- By 2000 there were only two factories still working, Andrew's and Portvale
- In 2014 the Andrew's Factory closed and is being dismantled. A new factory to produce multiple sugar products will eventually be built
- The Portvale Factory is now the only working factory in Barbados. There is a Sugar Museum in the grounds of the factory and both are open to visitors
- Foursquare Factory closed in the 1980s and is now a museum and park, with a modern rum distillery built on the site
- There are 3 **rum** distilleries in Barbados
- Mount Gay in the north in St Lucy has had great success in exporting its rum worldwide. It is now owned by the French Rémy Cointreau liquor company
- The West Indies Distillery is located in Brighton and is used by several rum companies to produce Cockspur and other rums

Crop Over in Barbados is a harvest festival which first began in the 17th century, celebrating the end of the sugar cane season. It is now the island's biggest event running from June until the first Monday in August, ending with the Grand Kadooment Day Parade.

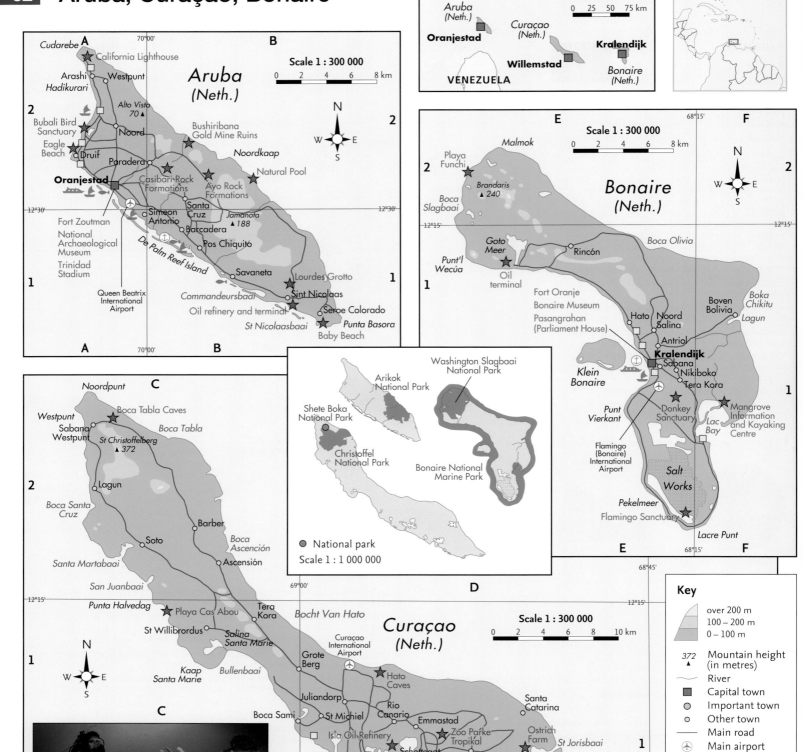

Scale 1 : 5 000 000

Aruba (Neth.)
Oranjestad
Curaçao (Neth.)
Willemstad
Kralendijk
Bonaire (Neth.)
VENEZUELA

Aruba (Neth.)
Scale 1 : 300 000
0 2 4 6 8 km

Cudarebe
California Lighthouse
Arashi
Westpunt
Hadikurari
Alto Vista 70 ▲
Bubali Bird Sanctuary
Noord
Bushiribana Gold Mine Ruins
Noordkaap
Eagle Beach
Druif
Paradera
Natural Pool
Oranjestad
Casibari Rock Formations
Ayo Rock Formations
Fort Zoutman
Santa Cruz
National Archaeological Museum
Simeon Antonio
Jamanota ▲ 188
Trinidad Stadium
Barcadera
Pos Chiquito
De Palm Reef Island
Queen Beatrix International Airport
Savaneta
Lourdes Grotto
Commandeursbaai
Sint Nicolaas
Oil refinery and terminal
Seroe Colorado
St Nicolaasbaai
Punta Basora
Baby Beach

Bonaire (Neth.)
Scale 1 : 300 000
0 2 4 6 8 km

Malmok
Playa Funchi
Brandaris ▲ 240
Boca Slagbaai
Boca Olivia
Goto Meer
Rincón
Punt'l Wecúa
Oil terminal
Fort Oranje
Bonaire Museum
Pasangrahan (Parliament House)
Hato
Noord Salina
Boven Bolivia
Boka Chikitu
Lagun
Antriol
Kralendijk
Sabana
Klein Bonaire
Nikiboko
Tera Kora
Punt Vierkant
Donkey Sanctuary
Mangrove Information and Kayaking Centre
Flamingo (Bonaire) International Airport
Lac Bay
Salt Works
Pekelmeer
Flamingo Sanctuary
Lacre Punt

Curaçao (Neth.)
Scale 1 : 300 000
0 2 4 6 8 10 km

Noordpunt
Boca Tabla Caves
Westpunt
Sabana Westpunt
St Christoffelberg ▲ 372
Boca Tabla
Lagun
Boca Santa Cruz
Barber
Boca Ascención
Soto
Ascención
Santa Martabaai
San Juanbaai
Punta Halvedag
Playa Cas Abou
Tera Kora
Bocht Van Hato
St Willibrordus
Solina Santa Marie
Kaap Santa Marie
Bullenbaai
Grote Berg
Curaçao International Airport
Hato Caves
Santa Catarina
Juliandorp
Rio Canario
Emmastad
Boca Sami
St Michiel
Zoo Parke Tropikal
Ostrich Farm
St Jorisbaai
Isla Oil Refinery
Schottegat
Santa Rosa
Piscaderabaai
Otrobanda
Bottelier
Punda
Maritime Museum
Curaçao Underwater Marine Park
Willemstad:
Fort Amsterdam
Rif Fort
Handelskade
Kura Hulanda Museum
Jewish Cultural Historical Museum
Dolphin Academy
Sea Aquarium
Lagun Jan Thiel
Jan Thiel
Spaanse Water
Santa Barbara
New Port
Oostpunt

Arikok National Park
Washington Slagbaai National Park
Shete Boka National Park
Christoffel National Park
Bonaire National Marine Park
● National park
Scale 1 : 1 000 000

A diver examines a wreck on the Front Porch dive site, Bonaire.

Key
over 200 m
100 – 200 m
0 – 100 m
372 ▲ Mountain height (in metres)
River
Capital town
Important town
Other town
Main road
Main airport

Features
★ Point of interest
□ Major resort
⚓ Port
Cruise ships
Major marina
Fishing port

Oil refineries

- The large Isla refinery was built on Curaçao in 1918
- It was the largest refinery in the world for many years
- It is still operating and contributes 90% of the export earnings to the economy
- Copying Curaçao, two large refineries were built on Aruba in 1929 and 1930
- They refined oil from Venezuela, and later Brazil
- The Eagle refinery closed in 1950
- The Lago refinery was attacked by a U-Boat in 1942
- The Lago refinery, once one of the world's largest, closed in 2009
- Due to the loss of jobs from the closed refineries, Aruba started its modern tourist industry

Aruba and Curaçao are Self-governing Netherlands Territories. Bonaire is a Netherlands Special Municipality

	ARUBA	**CURAÇAO**	**BONAIRE**
Population	101 484 (2010)	150 563 (2011)	16 541 (2014 est.)
Capital town	Oranjestad	Willemstad	Kralendijk
Area	193 sq km	444 sq km	288 sq km
National flower	Wanglo Flower	Kibrahacha	Divi-divi
National bird	Burrowing Owl	Majestic Oriole	Greater Flamingo
Languages	Dutch, Papiamento, English		

TRINIDAD AND TOBAGO

Population (2011)	1 328 019
Capital city	Port of Spain
Area	5128 sq km
Languages	English, creole, Hindi
National flower	Wild Poinsettia (Chaconia)
National bird (Trinidad)	Scarlet Ibis
National bird (Tobago)	Chachalaca (Cocrico)

Island	Area (sq km)	Population (2011)	Pop. density (per sq km)
Trinidad	4828	1 267 145	262
Tobago	300	60 874	203

Scale 1 : 8 000 000

Tobago

Trinidad

Port of Spain

VENEZUELA

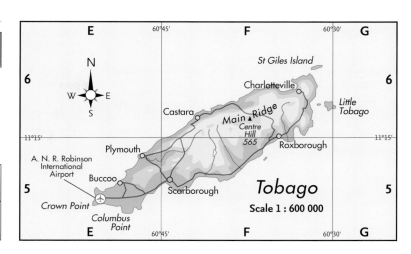

Tobago
Scale 1 : 600 000

St Giles Island
Charlotteville
Castara
Main Ridge
Centre Hill 565
Little Tobago
Plymouth
A. N. R. Robinson International Airport
Buccoo
Roxborough
Scarborough
Crown Point
Columbus Point

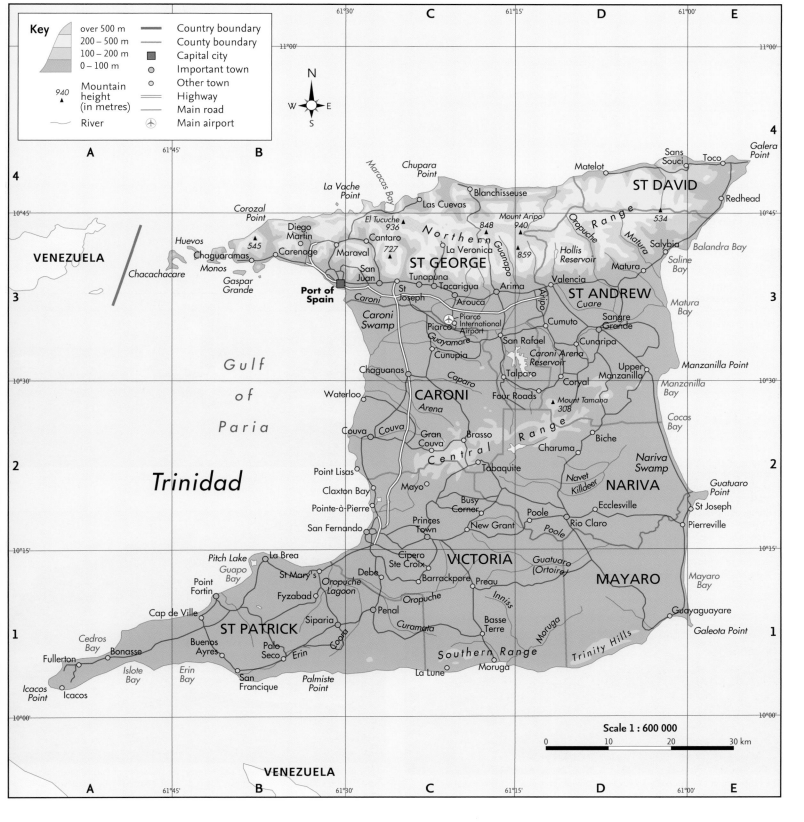

Key

over 500 m	
200 – 500 m	
100 – 200 m	
0 – 100 m	
940 ▲	Mountain height (in metres)
	River

▬▬▬	Country boundary
▬▬	County boundary
◼	Capital city
⊙	Important town
○	Other town
═══	Highway
───	Main road
✈	Main airport

Trinidad
Scale 1 : 600 000

0   10   20   30 km

VENEZUELA

Gulf of Paria

Maracas Bay
Chupara Point
La Vache Point
Corozal Point
Huevos
Chaguaramas
Monos
Gaspar Grande
Chacachacare
Diego Martin
Carenage
545
Maraval
San Juan
Port of Spain
Caroni
Caroni Swamp
St Joseph
Cantaro
El Tucuche 936
727
La Veronica
ST GEORGE
Tunapuna
Tacarigua
Arouca
Piarco International Airport
Piarco
Guayamare
Cunupia
Las Cuevas
Blanchisseuse
Northern Range
Mount Aripo 940
848
859
Hollis Reservoir
Arima
Valencia
San Rafael
Cumuto
Cuare
ST ANDREW
Sangre Grande
Cunaripa
Matelot
Sans Souci
Toco
Galera Point
ST DAVID
Redhead
534
Oropuche Range
Matura
Salybia
Balandra Bay
Saline Bay
Matura Bay
Manzanilla Point
Upper Manzanilla
Manzanilla Bay
Cocos Bay
Chaguanas
Waterloo
Couva
Couva
Gran Couva
Arena
Caparo
Brasso
Four Roads
Talparo
Coryal
Caroni Arena Reservoir
Central Range
Tabaquite
Mount Tamana 308
Charuma
Biche
Nariva Swamp
NARIVA
Guatuaro Point
Point Lisas
Claxton Bay
Pointe-à-Pierre
San Fernando
Mayo
Busy Corner
Princes Town
New Grant
Poole
Poole
Rio Claro
Ecclesville
St Joseph
Pierreville
Navet Killdeer
Mayaro Bay
MAYARO
Guayaguayare
Galeota Point
Pitch Lake
La Brea
Guapo Bay
St Mary's
Debe
Cipero
Ste Croix
VICTORIA
Barrackpore
Preau
Guatuaro (Ortoire)
Point Fortin
Fyzabad
Oropuche Lagoon
Oropuche
Penal
Inniss
Basse Terre
Cap de Ville
Siparia
ST PATRICK
Cedros Bay
Fullerton
Bonasse
Buenos Ayres
Palo Seco
Erin
Guapo
Curamata
Moruga
La Lune
Southern Range
Trinity Hills
Icacos Point
Icacos
Islote Bay
Erin Bay
San Francique
Palmiste Point

VENEZUELA

Trinidad

CARONI

Features

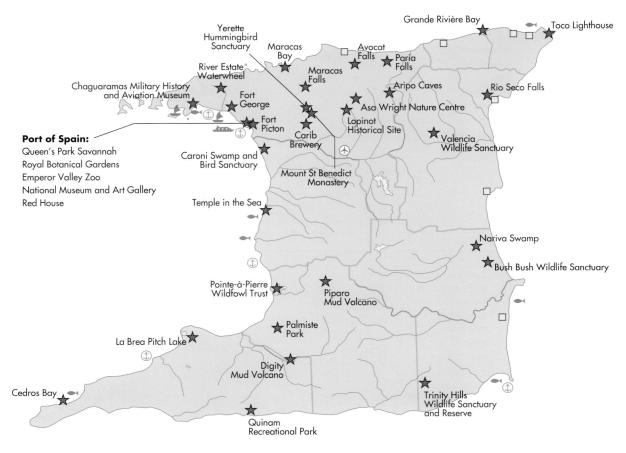

★ Point of interest
☐ Major resort
✈ Main airport
⊕ Port
⛴ Cruise ships
⚓ Major marina
🐟 Fishing port

Scale 1 : 800 000

Grande Rivière Bay
Toco Lighthouse
Yerette Hummingbird Sanctuary
Maracas Bay
Avocat Falls
Paria Falls
River Estate Waterwheel
Maracas Falls
Aripo Caves
Rio Seco Falls
Chaguaramas Military History and Aviation Museum
Fort George
Asa Wright Nature Centre
Fort Picton
Lopinot Historical Site
Valencia Wildlife Sanctuary
Carib Brewery
Mount St Benedict Monastery
Caroni Swamp and Bird Sanctuary

Port of Spain:
Queen's Park Savannah
Royal Botanical Gardens
Emperor Valley Zoo
National Museum and Art Gallery
Red House

Temple in the Sea
Nariva Swamp
Bush Bush Wildlife Sanctuary
Pointe-à-Pierre Wildfowl Trust
Piparo Mud Volcano
Palmiste Park
La Brea Pitch Lake
Digity Mud Volcano
Trinity Hills Wildlife Sanctuary and Reserve
Cedros Bay
Quinam Recreational Park

Local Government

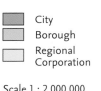

☐ City
☐ Borough
☐ Regional Corporation

Scale 1 : 2 000 000

SAN JUAN-LAVENTILLE
DIEGO MARTIN
TUNAPUNA-PIARCO
SANGRE GRANDE
PORT OF SPAIN
ARIMA
CHAGUANAS
COUVA-TABAQUITE-TALPARO
MAYARO-RIO CLARO
SAN FERNANDO
POINT FORTIN
PRINCES TOWN
PENAL-DEBE
SIPARIA

As its name suggests, Port of Spain became the entry point into the country under Spanish rule, and is still the main port for general cargo today.

Pitch Lake at La Brea (aka *Trinidad Lake Asphalt*)

- The Pitch Lake is the world's largest natural deposit of asphalt covering about 410 000 sq m with an estimated depth of 76 m at the centre
- Mining of asphalt started in 1867 and an estimated 10 million tonnes has been extracted since
- The asphalt was used for road surfacing in Europe and the USA but was eventually replaced by bitumen from oil refineries
- Production peaked at about 200 000 tonnes in the 1960s but then declined considerably
- Exports have been quite variable over the years
- Currently the asphalt is processed to make automobile under-coating and similar weather-proof coatings
- Today the Pitch Lake is a major tourist attraction with up to 20 000 visitors a year

The extraordinary Pitch Lake at La Brea was mined for asphalt for many years. Today it is a major tourist attraction.

Maracas Bay is a popular weekend beach resort for residents of Port of Spain. It is also a fishing village and features the classic pirogue boats, usually fitted with an outboard motor.

Rainfall

Average annual rainfall

	more than 3000 mm
	2500 – 3000 mm
	2000 – 2500 mm
	1500 – 2000 mm
	1000 – 1500 mm
	less than 1000 mm

→ Normal direction of the wind

● Climate station

Scale 1 : 1 500 000

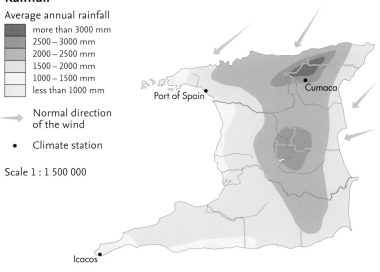

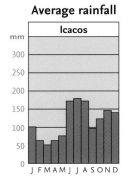

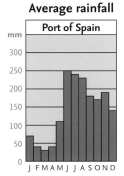

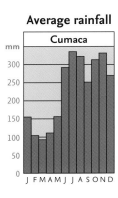

Mud volcanoes

- Mud volcanoes are a mixture of gas, mud and hot water
- The gas most associated with Trinidad's mud volcanoes is methane
- They are mainly found in the southern half of Trinidad near oil reserves
- There is no eruption of lava but the volcanoes bubble most of the time and generally form a cone of mud and clay
- The volcano near Piparo, in south-central Trinidad, erupted in 1997, covering the village in a layer of mud

● Mud volcanoes

Scale 1 : 1 500 000

Devil's Woodyard mud volcano has been active for over 150 years and is a major tourist attraction. It is surrounded by a number of smaller mud volcanoes.

Caroni Swamp

- Caroni Swamp is located on the west coast of Trinidad where the Caroni river enters the Gulf of Paria
- The wetland consists of marshes, mangrove swamp and tidal mudflats giving a rich variety of habitats for both marine and freshwater plants and animals
- From the 1920s rice and sugar cane cultivation gradually encroached on the swamp affecting the water quality
- As agricultural activity gradually declined in the 1960s, salt water moved further inland and the coverage of mangrove forest steadily increased
- The swamp is constantly threatened by flood-control measures, industrial pollution from nearby factories and the development of housing and roads for Trinidad's growing population

This large protected swampland is laced with many navigable channels and is a major attraction for ecotourists.

Within the swamp is the Caroni Bird Sanctuary. Of the many nesting birds, the scarlet ibis is the most notable and is the national bird of Trinidad.

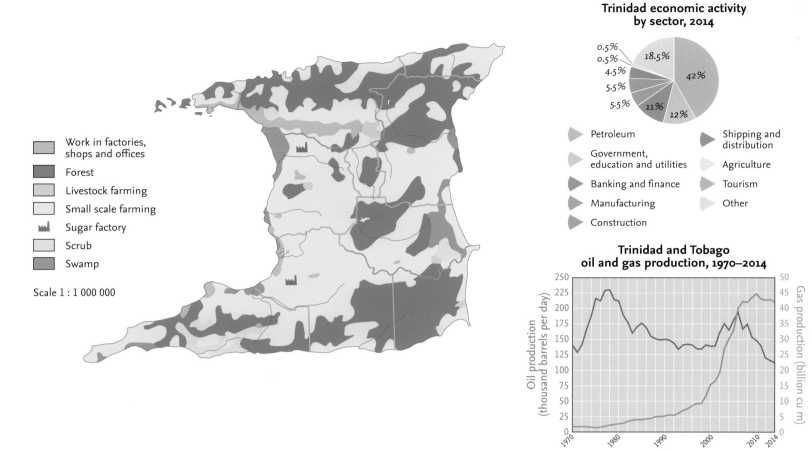

Trinidad economic activity by sector, 2014

0.5%
0.5%
4.5%
5.5%
5.5%
18.5%
42%
11%
12%

- Petroleum
- Government, education and utilities
- Banking and finance
- Manufacturing
- Construction
- Shipping and distribution
- Agriculture
- Tourism
- Other

Work in factories, shops and offices
Forest
Livestock farming
Small scale farming
Sugar factory
Scrub
Swamp

Scale 1 : 1 000 000

Trinidad and Tobago oil and gas production, 1970–2014

Oil production (thousand barrels per day)

Gas production (billion cu m)

Year

Mining and manufacturing

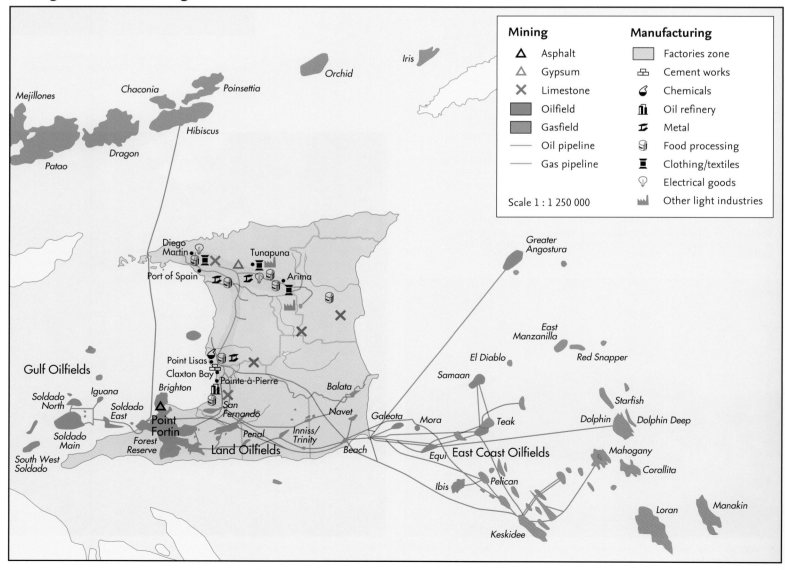

Mining
- △ Asphalt
- △ Gypsum
- ✕ Limestone
- Oilfield
- Gasfield
- Oil pipeline
- Gas pipeline

Scale 1 : 1 250 000

Manufacturing
- Factories zone
- Cement works
- Chemicals
- Oil refinery
- Metal
- Food processing
- Clothing/textiles
- Electrical goods
- Other light industries

History

- Before European settlement Trinidad was inhabited by indigenous Arawaks then Caribs
- Christopher Columbus explored the islands on his third voyage in **1498**
- Trinidad remained under Spanish rule until **1797** when it passed to the British, but was mainly colonised by French settlers
- From the late **17th** century the British, French, Dutch and Courlanders fought to control Tobago with the island eventually ending up under British rule
- In the late **18th** century African slaves were brought in to work on the sugar and cotton plantations
- When slavery was abolished in **1838** there were not enough freed Africans to work the plantations. After **1845** contract labourers were hired from India, China, and Madeira, and these were supplemented by freed slaves from many of the nearby Caribbean islands
- In **1889** the two islands became a single British crown colony
- Trinidad and Tobago gained independence from the British in **1962** and became a republic in **1976**

Carnival

- Carnival originated with the French celebration of Lent in the 1700s
- The African slaves matched this with a festival celebrating the harvesting of the sugar cane
- After emancipation, and despite opposition from the colonial rulers, Carnival (known locally as 'Mas') went on to develop into the massive and spectacular event it is today
- The Trinidad carnival is one of the biggest in the world held annually on the Monday and Tuesday before Ash Wednesday
- As well as being the main social and cultural event of the year, Carnival now has great economic significance, currently attracting about an additional 10 000 visitors from all over the world
- The tourist industry benefits by over US$100 million each year from both domestic and foreign tourist expenditure

Migration to Trinidad and Tobago

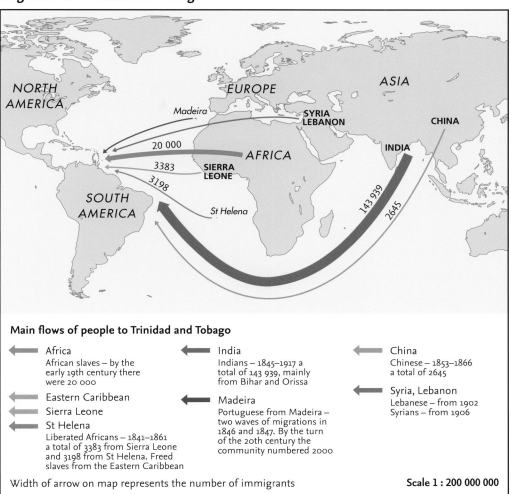

Main flows of people to Trinidad and Tobago

Africa — African slaves – by the early 19th century there were 20 000

Eastern Caribbean

Sierra Leone

St Helena — Liberated Africans – 1841–1861 a total of 3383 from Sierra Leone and 3198 from St Helena. Freed slaves from the Eastern Caribbean

India — Indians – 1845–1917 a total of 143 939, mainly from Bihar and Orissa

Madeira — Portuguese from Madeira – two waves of migrations in 1846 and 1847. By the turn of the 20th century the community numbered 2000

China — Chinese – 1853–1866 a total of 2645

Syria, Lebanon — Lebanese – from 1902 Syrians – from 1906

Width of arrow on map represents the number of immigrants

Scale 1 : 200 000 000

A performer at the Carnival celebrations on 11 February 2012, in Port of Spain.

A steelband plays for the judges at a competition in St Clair, Trinidad, in 2011.

Tourism

Stop-over visitor arrivals, 1995–2014

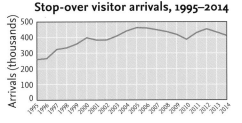

Stop-over visitor arrivals by month, 2014

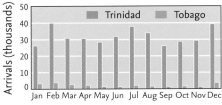

Stop-over visitor arrivals by country of origin, 2014

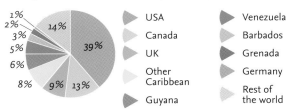

USA 39%, UK 13%, Canada 9%, Other Caribbean 8%, Guyana 6%, Venezuela 5%, Barbados 3%, Grenada 2%, Germany 1%, Rest of the world 14%

Stop-over visitor arrivals by purpose of visit, 2010

Leisure/beach vacation 45%, Visiting friends and relatives 25%, Business/convention 18%, Wedding/honeymoon 9%, Study 2%, Other 1%

Cruise passenger arrivals, 2001–2014

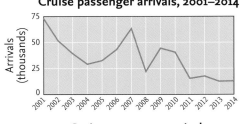

Cruise passenger arrivals by month, 2014

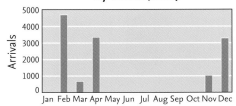

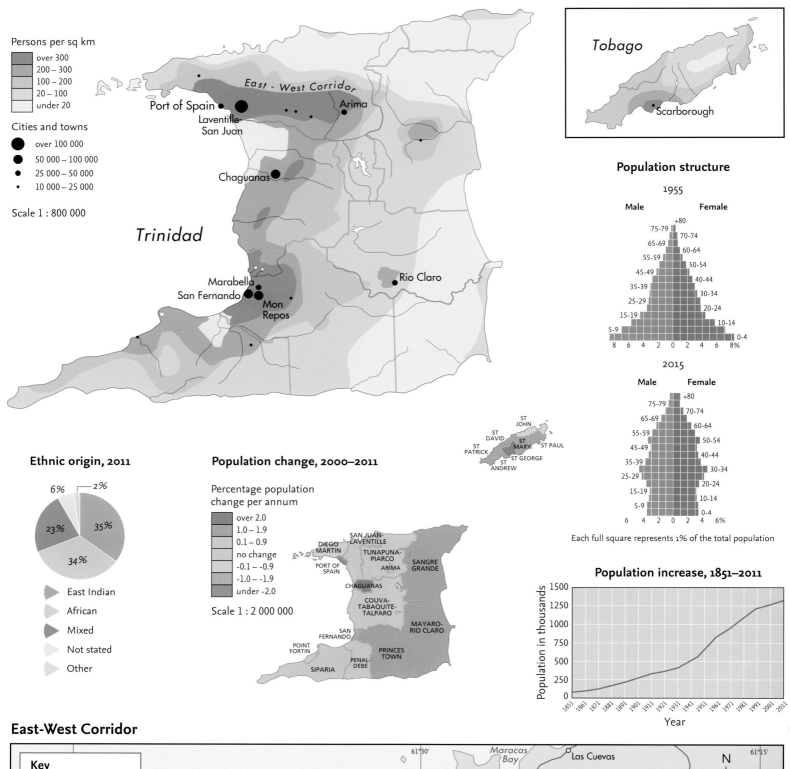

Persons per sq km

- over 300
- 200 – 300
- 100 – 200
- 20 – 100
- under 20

Cities and towns

- over 100 000
- 50 000 – 100 000
- 25 000 – 50 000
- 10 000 – 25 000

Scale 1 : 800 000

Trinidad

Port of Spain
Laventille-San Juan
Arima
East - West Corridor
Chaguanas
Marabella
San Fernando
Mon Repos
Rio Claro

Tobago

Scarborough

Population structure

1955

Male | Female
+80
75-79 | 70-74
65-69 | 60-64
55-59 | 50-54
45-49 | 40-44
35-39 | 30-34
25-29 | 20-24
15-19 | 10-14
5-9 | 0-4
8 6 4 2 0 2 4 6 8%

2015

Male | Female
+80
75-79 | 70-74
65-69 | 60-64
55-59 | 50-54
45-49 | 40-44
35-39 | 30-34
25-29 | 20-24
15-19 | 10-14
5-9 | 0-4
6 4 2 0 2 4 6%

Each full square represents 1% of the total population

Ethnic origin, 2011

6% | 2%
23% | 35%
34%

- East Indian
- African
- Mixed
- Not stated
- Other

Population change, 2000–2011

Percentage population change per annum

- over 2.0
- 1.0 – 1.9
- 0.1 – 0.9
- no change
- -0.1 – -0.9
- -1.0 – -1.9
- under -2.0

Scale 1 : 2 000 000

ST JOHN
ST DAVID
ST MARY
ST PATRICK
ST GEORGE
ST ANDREW
ST PAUL

SAN JUAN-LAVENTILLE
DIEGO MARTIN
PORT OF SPAIN
TUNAPUNA-PIARCO
ARIMA
SANGRE GRANDE
CHAGUANAS
COUVA-TABAQUITE-TALPARO
MAYARO-RIO CLARO
SAN FERNANDO
POINT FORTIN
PRINCES TOWN
PENAL-DEBE
SIPARIA

Population increase, 1851–2011

Population in thousands
1500
1250
1000
750
500
250
0
1851 1861 1871 1881 1891 1901 1911 1921 1931 1941 1951 1961 1971 1981 1991 2001 2011
Year

East-West Corridor

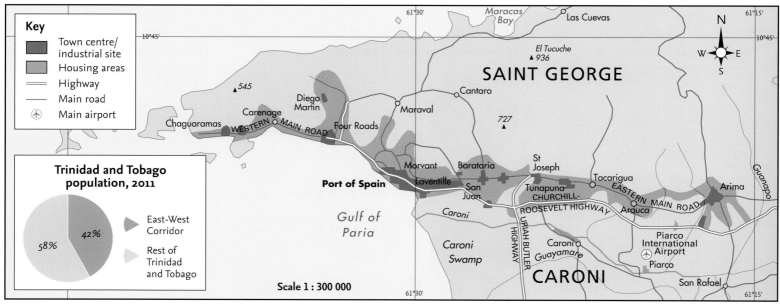

Key

- Town centre/industrial site
- Housing areas
- Highway
- Main road
- Main airport

Maracas Bay
Las Cuevas
El Tucuche ▲ 936
SAINT GEORGE
Cantaro
▲545
Diego Martin
Maraval
727 ▲
Chaguaramas
Carenage
WESTERN O MAIN ROAD
Four Roads
Morvant
Barataria
St Joseph
Tacarigua
EASTERN MAIN ROAD
Arima
Port of Spain
Laventille
San Juan
Tunapuna
CHURCHILL-ROOSEVELT HIGHWAY
Arouca
Guanapo
Gulf of Paria
Caroni
URIAH BUTLER HIGHWAY
Caroni
Piarco International Airport
Caroni Swamp
Guayamare
Piarco
CARONI
San Rafael
Scale 1 : 300 000

Trinidad and Tobago population, 2011

58% | 42%

- East-West Corridor
- Rest of Trinidad and Tobago

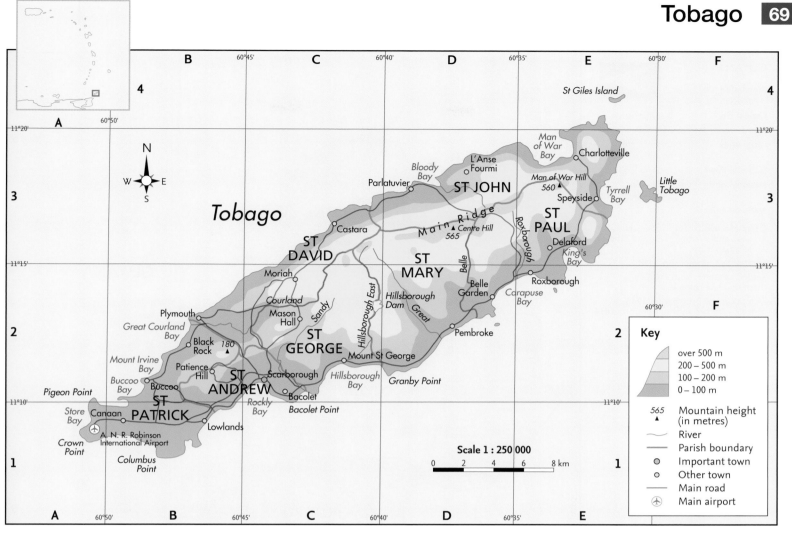

Key

	over 500 m
	200 – 500 m
	100 – 200 m
	0 – 100 m
565 ▲	Mountain height (in metres)
	River
	Parish boundary
⊙	Important town
○	Other town
	Main road
⊕	Main airport

Scale 1 : 250 000

0   2   4   6   8 km

Features

- ● Forest reserve
- ★ Point of interest
- □ Major resort
- ⊕ Main airport
- ⊕ Port
- 🚢 Cruise ships
- ⚓ Major marina
- 🐟 Fishing port

Pirate's Bay
Fort Campbleton
Hummingbird Gallery
Englishman's Bay
Tobago Forest Reserve
Little Tobago Bird Sanctuary
King's Bay Waterfall
Argyle Waterfalls
Arnos Farm and Nature Reserve
Arnos Vale Waterwheel and Nature Park
Tobago Cocoa Estate
Fort James
Highland Waterfall
Richmond Great House
Fort Bennett
Grafton Caledonia Wildlife Sanctuary
Mount Irvine Beach
Genesis Nature Park
Buccoo Reef nd Nylon Pool
Kimme Museum
Store Bay
Pigeon Point Heritage Park
Fort Milford
Fort Granby

Scarborough:
Tobago House of Assembly
Fort King George and Tobago Museum
Botanical Gardens

Scale 1 : 350 000

Resources

- Work in factories, shops and offices
- Forest
- Crop farming

Scale 1 : 500 000

Rainfall

Average annual rainfall

- more than 2000 mm
- 1000 – 2000 mm
- less than 1000 mm

Scale 1 : 700 000

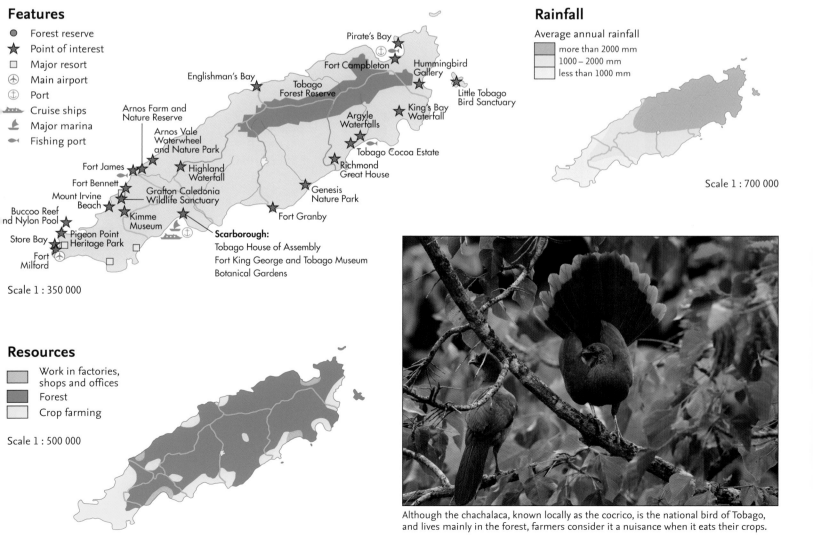

Although the chachalaca, known locally as the cocrico, is the national bird of Tobago, and lives mainly in the forest, farmers consider it a nuisance when it eats their crops.

GUYANA

Population (2012)	
747 884	
Capital city	Georgetown
Area	214 969 sq km
Languages	English, creole, Amerindian
National flower	Victoria Regia Lily
National bird	Hoatzin or Canje Pheasant
National animal	Jaguar

Original inhabitants included coastal Arawaks and inland Caribs, and other Amerindian tribes

Sighted by Columbus in **1498**

Settled by Dutch from **1616** in three separate colonies

Also settled by British from **1746**, and ceded by Netherlands to Britain in **1814**

Became a British colony named British Guiana in **1831**

Became independent on 26 May **1966** and renamed Guyana

Declared a Cooperative Republic on 23 February **1970**

Economic activity

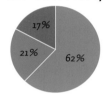

- 17%
- 21%
- 62%

▶ Services
▶ Agriculture, fishing and forestry
▶ Manufacturing

Average rainfall

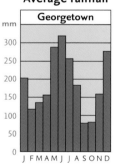

Georgetown

mm
300
250
200
150
100
50
0
J F M A M J J A S O N D

Provinces

ESSEQUIBO
DEMERARA
BERBICE

Scale 1 : 14 000 000

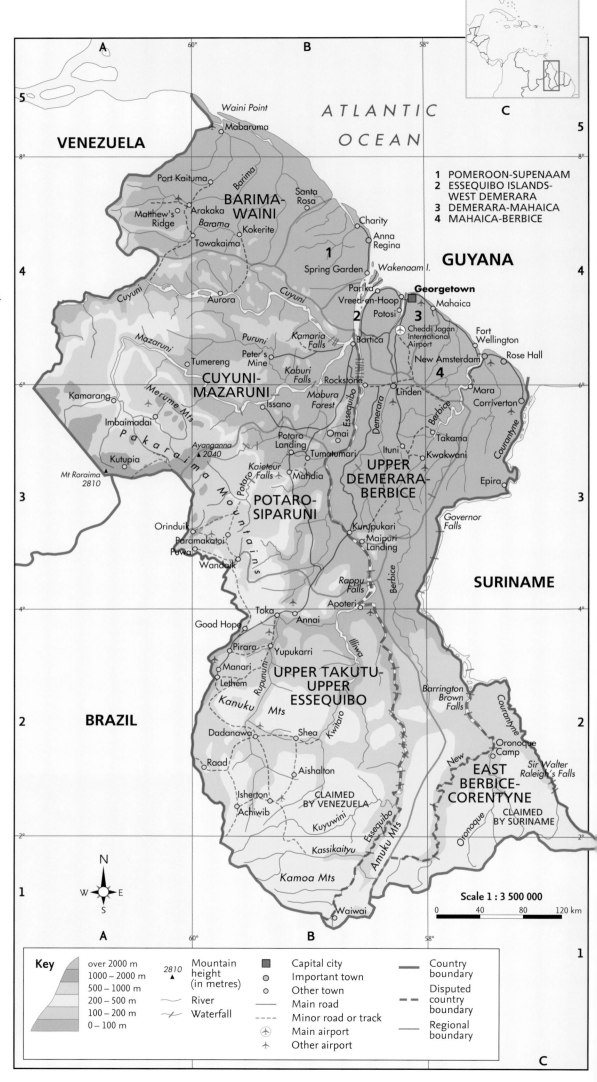

VENEZUELA

ATLANTIC OCEAN

Waini Point
Mabaruma

Port Kaituma
Barima
Santa Rosa

BARIMA-WAINI

Matthew's Ridge
Arakaka
Barama
Kokerite
Charity
Anna Regina

Towakaima

Spring Garden
Wakenaam I.

GUYANA

1

1 POMEROON-SUPENAAM
2 ESSEQUIBO ISLANDS-WEST DEMERARA
3 DEMERARA-MAHAICA
4 MAHAICA-BERBICE

Cuyuni
Aurora
Cuyuni
Parika
2 Vreed-en-Hoop
Potosi

Georgetown
3 Mahaica

Cheddi Jagan International Airport

Fort Wellington
Rose Hall

Puruni
Kamaria Falls
Bartica

New Amsterdam

Peter's Mine
Tumereng
Kaburi Falls

CUYUNI-MAZARUNI

Mabura Forest
Rockstone

Berbice
Linden
4
Mara
Corriverton

Kamarang
Mazaruni
Issano

Omai
Essequibo
Demerara
Takama

Imbaimadai
Potaro Landing

Ituni
Kwakwani

Ayanganna
▲2040
Kaieteur Falls
Mahdia
Tumatumari

UPPER DEMERARA-BERBICE

Kutupia
Merume Mts
Pakaraima

Mt Roraima
2810

Orinduik
Paramakatoi
Puwa

POTARO-SIPARUNI

Kurupukari
Maipuri Landing

Governor Falls

Wandaik

Rappu Falls
Berbice

SURINAME

Toka
Annai
Apoteri

Good Hope
Illiwa

Pirara
Yupukarri

Manari
Lethem
Rupununi

UPPER TAKUTU-UPPER ESSEQUIBO

Barrington Brown Falls

Courantyne

Kanuku
Mts

Dadanawa
Shea
Kwitaro

BRAZIL

Oronoque Camp

Sir Walter Raleigh's Falls

Raad
Aishalton

New

EAST BERBICE-CORENTYNE

Isherton
Achiwib

CLAIMED BY VENEZUELA

Kuyuwini

Essequibo
Amuku Mts

CLAIMED BY SURINAME

Oronoque

Kassikaityu

Kamoa Mts

Waiwai

N
W E
S

Scale 1 : 3 500 000
0   40   80   120 km

Key

over 2000 m	**2810** ▲	Mountain height (in metres)
1000 – 2000 m		
500 – 1000 m	◎	Capital city
200 – 500 m	⊚	Important town
100 – 200 m	○	Other town
0 – 100 m	―	River
	⤳	Waterfall
	―	Main road
	- - -	Minor road or track
	✈	Main airport
	✈	Other airport
	―	Country boundary
	- - -	Disputed country boundary
	―	Regional boundary

Features

- ● National park
- ★ Point of interest
- □ Major resort
- ✈ Main airport
- ⊕ Port
- 🚢 Cruise ships
- 🐟 Fishing port

Georgetown:
St George's Cathedral
National Museum
Promenade Gardens
Parliament Building
Guyana Zoo and Botanical Gardens
Walter Roth Museum of Anthropology
Museum of African Heritage
International Conference Centre
Providence Cricket Stadium

Shell Beach
Saxacalli Beach
Salto Oshi (King George VI Falls)
Kamarang Meru (Great Falls)
Amaila Falls
King Edward VIII Falls
Kumaka Falls
Kaieteur Falls
Kaieteur National Park
Orinduik Falls
Iwokrama Forest Reserve
Barrington Brown Falls
King George V Falls

Scale 1 : 7 000 000

Minerals

- □ Bauxite
- ■ Diamonds
- ■ Oil
- ● Gold
- ● Manganese
- ● Clay

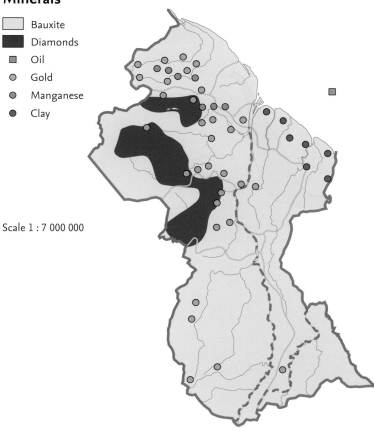

Scale 1 : 7 000 000

Bauxite mining in Guyana

- Guyana has the oldest bauxite industry in the Caribbean, started in 1916 south of Georgetown
- A settlement named Mackenzie grew up and the workers excavated the bauxite (aluminium ore) by hand, and later with steam-powered machinery
- The ore was loaded into barges and sent down the Demerara River where it was transferred to ships at Georgetown
- The ore then travelled to smelters in Canada for refining into metal. Guyana (then British Guiana) did not have the energy to run smelters, but Canada had developed very cheap HEP on its large rivers
- Over the years more companies came to Guyana and bauxite is still the country's main export

Mashramani, often abbreviated to 'Mash', takes place on 23 February each year to celebrate Republic Day when Guyana gained independence. There are float parades, spectacular costumes and masquerade bands and dancing in the streets.

Gold and diamond mining is widespread in the interior of Guyana. Unfortunately the widely-used system of alluvial mining (panning, or sifting the river sediment) is very destructive.

BELIZE

Population (2010)	312 971
Capital city	Belmopan
Area	22 965 sq km
Languages	English, Spanish, Mayan, creole
National flower	Black Orchid
National bird	Keel-billed Toucan
National animal	Baird's Tapir

Occupied by the Mayans until conquest and settlement

Progressively conquered and partially occupied by the Spanish from **1544** onwards

From the early **1600s** British settlers cut and exported logwood, and later mahogany

In **1787** some 2000 British refugees from the Mosquito Coast of Nicaragua settled in Belize, and by **1854** the British had total possession

In **1862** the British declared Belize a colony which it named British Honduras

The name was changed to Belize in **1973**, and Belize became independent on 21 September **1981**

Features

- ● National park
- ★ Point of interest
- ▢ Major resort
- ✈ Main airport
- ⚓ Port
- ⛴ Cruise ships
- 🐟 Fishing port

Belize City:
Museum of Belize
Maritime Museum
Baron Bliss Lighthouse

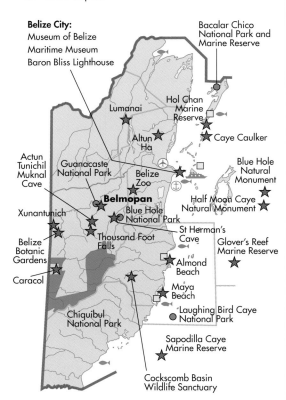

Scale 1 : 3 000 000

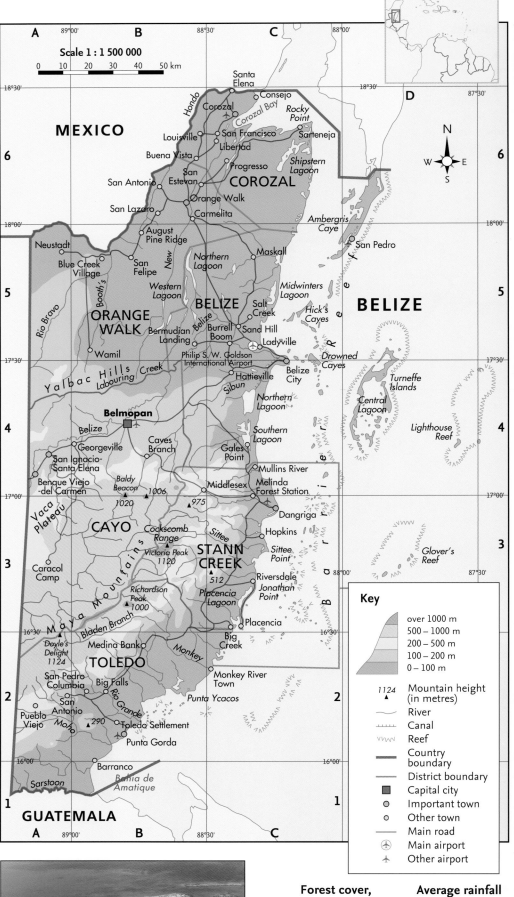

Scale 1 : 1 500 000

0 10 20 30 40 50 km

Key

over 1000 m
500 – 1000 m
200 – 500 m
100 – 200 m
0 – 100 m

- ▲ 1124 Mountain height (in metres)
- River
- Canal
- Reef
- Country boundary
- District boundary
- ▢ Capital city
- ◉ Important town
- ○ Other town
- Main road
- ✈ Main airport
- ✈ Other airport

Chewing gum

- Chewing gum was originally made from chicle, the sap of the sapodilla tree
- The sapodilla tree is common throughout the Caribbean, commonly called the 'Dilly' tree. It is widespread in Belize
- In the 1880s American companies, including Wrigley's and Beechnut, bought large amounts from local sap collectors, known as 'chicleros'
- In the 1960s chewing gum began to be made from a cheaper chemical product related to synthetic rubber, and the chicle industry collapsed
- Chewing gum is a worldwide pollution agent (it is banned in Singapore). It cannot be cleaned up easily as it does not dissolve in water

The Great Blue Hole is a large solution hole (315 m wide and 124 m deep), now flooded since sea level rose after the ice ages. It is surrounded by coral reefs which are a World Heritage site popular with tourists.

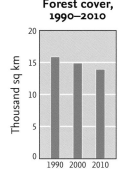

Forest cover, 1990–2010

Thousand sq km

1990 2000 2010

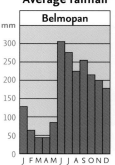

Average rainfall

mm

Belmopan

J F M A M J J A S O N D

Map 1 (Political)

NORTH AMERICA

Bahía de Campeche

GUATEMALA
- Guatemala City
- Flores
- Santa Ana

BELIZE
- Belmopan

Gulf of Honduras

Caribbean Sea

- San Pedro Sula

HONDURAS
- Tegucigalpa

EL SALVADOR
- San Salvador

NICARAGUA
- León
- Managua
- Puerto Cabezas

- Liberia

COSTA RICA
- San José

PANAMA
- Panama City
- David

SOUTH AMERICA

PACIFIC OCEAN

Facts about Central America

Population (2015)
45 723 000

Largest country
Nicaragua 130 000 sq km

Country with most people (2015)
Guatemala 16 343 000

Largest city (2015)
San Salvador 1 740 000

Key

— Country boundary
■ Capital city
○ Important city / town

Scale 1 : 11 000 000

0   100   200   300   400 km

Map 2 (Physical)

Bahía de Campeche

Yucatán

Laguna de Términos

Sierra Madre de Chiapas

Volcán de Tajamulco 4210

Maya Mts

Hondo

Belize
Ambergris Caye
Turneffe Is

Islas del Cisne

Grand Cayman

Jamaica

Caribbean Sea

Lago de Izabal
Motagua
Cerro Las Minas 2850
Ulúa
Aguan
Patuca
Coco
Grande

Gulf of Honduras

Islas de la Bahía

Laguna de Caratasca

Mosquitia

Cord. Isabelia

Costa de Mosquitos

Cayos Miskitos

I. de Providencia

I. de San Andrés

Golfo de Fonseca
L. Managua
L. Nicaragua
S. Juan
Punta de Perlas
Is del Maíz

C. Sta Elena

Golfo de Nicoya
Chirripó 3819
Istmus of Panama
Barú 3475
Bahía de Coronado
Pen. de Osa
Golfo de Chiriquí
I. de Coiba
Pen. de Azuero
Punta Mala
Golfo de los Mosquitos
Panama Canal
Isla del Rey
Golfo de Panamá

Cristóbal Colón 5775

Golfo de Morrosquillo

Golfo del Darién

Sa de Perija

Cauca

Golfo de Cupica

PACIFIC OCEAN

Facts about Central America

Area
523 166 sq km

Highest peak
Volcán de Tajamulco 4210 m

Longest river
Coco 750 km

Largest lake
Lake Nicaragua 8150 sq km

Key

over 5000 m
3000 – 5000 m
2000 – 3000 m
1000 – 2000 m
500 – 1000 m
200 – 500 m
0 – 200 m

▲ 4210 Mountain height (in metres)

Scale 1 : 11 000 000

0   100   200   300   400 km

Lambert Conformal Conic projection

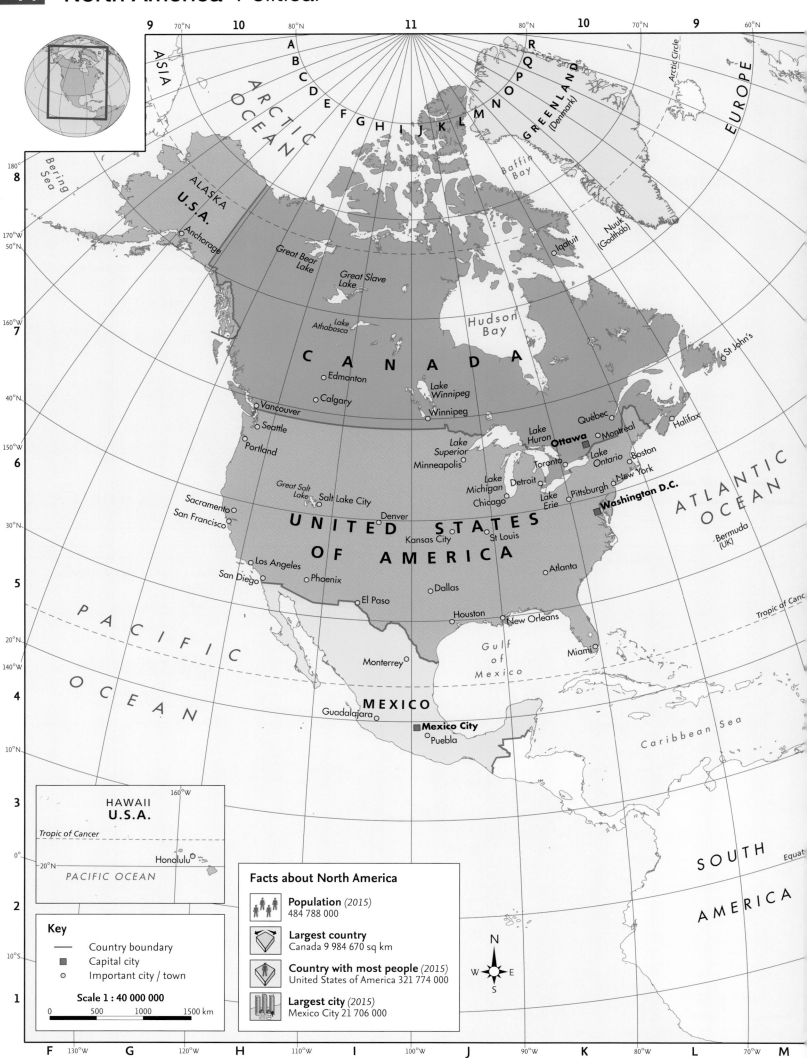

Facts about North America

Population *(2015)*
484 788 000

Largest country
Canada 9 984 670 sq km

Country with most people *(2015)*
United States of America 321 774 000

Largest city *(2015)*
Mexico City 21 706 000

Key
— Country boundary
■ Capital city
○ Important city / town

Scale 1 : 40 000 000
0   500   1000   1500 km

HAWAII
U.S.A.
Tropic of Cancer
Honolulu
PACIFIC OCEAN

Lambert Azimuthal Equal Area projection

Lambert Azimuthal Equal Area projection

Key

- over 5000 m
- 3000 – 5000 m
- 2000 – 3000 m
- 1000 – 2000 m
- 500 – 1000 m
- 200 – 500 m
- 0 – 200 m
- land below sea level

Ice cap

▲ 6190 Mountain height (in metres)

Scale 1 : 40 000 000

0   500   1000   1500 km

Facts about North America

Area
24 680 331 sq km

Highest peak
Denali 6190 m

Lowest point
Death Valley -86 m

Longest river
Mississippi-Missouri 5969 km

Largest lake
Lake Superior 82 100 sq km

Key

	over 5000 m
	3000 – 4000 m
	2000 – 3000 m
	1000 – 2000 m
	500 – 1000 m
	200 – 500 m
	0 – 200 m
	land below sea level
▲ 4418	Mountain height (in metres)
	River
	Seasonal river
	Canal
	Lake
	Seasonal lake
	Country boundary
	Regional boundary
	Road
	Railway
✈	Airport
■	Capital city
◉	Important city / town
○	Other city / town

Scale 1 : 12 000 000

0   100   200   300   400   500 km

1 VERMONT
2 NEW HAMPSHIRE
3 MASSACHUSETTS
4 CONNECTICUT
5 RHODE ISLAND

Lambert Conformal Conic projection

Caribbean Sea

ATLANTIC OCEAN

NORTH AMERICA

Tropic of Cancer

I. de Coco (Costa Rica)

I. de Malpelo (Colombia)

Barranquilla
Cartagena
Maracaibo
Cabimas
Valencia
Caracas
Maracay
Barquisimeto
Cúcuta
San Cristóbal
Ciudad Bolívar
Ciudad Guayana
Georgetown
Paramaribo
Cayenne
Medellín
Bucaramanga
VENEZUELA
GUYANA
SURINAME
FRENCH GUIANA
Manizales
Bogotá
Buenaventura
COLOMBIA
Cali
Quito
ECUADOR
Guayaquil
Iquitos

Islas Galapagos (Ecuador)

P E R U

Chiclayo
Trujillo

Rio Branco
Pôrto Velho
B R A Z I L
Manaus
Santarém
Belém
São Luís
Fernando de Noronha (Brazil)
Teresina
Fortaleza
Natal
Campina Grande
João Pessoa
Recife
Maceió
Aracaju
Salvador

Lima
Callao
Huancayo
Cusco

Arequipa
Arica
Iquique

BOLIVIA
La Paz
Cochabamba
Santa Cruz
Sucre
Corumbá
Cuiabá
Brasília
Goiânia

Campo Grande
Ribeirão Prêto
Belo Horizonte
Nova Iguaçu
Vitória
Campos
I. da Trindade (Brazil)
Is Martin Vaz (Brazil)

PACIFIC OCEAN

Antofagasta
PARAGUAY
Asunción
Campinas
São Paulo
Curitiba
Santos
Rio de Janeiro
Tropic of Capricorn

Salta
San Miguel de Tucumán
Corrientes
Joinville
Florianopolis

Islas Desventuradas (Chile)

Porto Alegre

Archipiélago Juan Fernández (Chile)
Córdoba
Santa Fé
Paraná
Pelotas
Valparaíso
Mendoza
Rosario
URUGUAY
Santiago
C H I L E
A R G E N T I N A
Buenos Aires
La Plata
Montevideo

Talcahuano
Concepción
Mar del Plata
Bahía Blanca

Puerto Montt
Comodoro Rivadavia

ATLANTIC OCEAN

Falkland Islands (UK)
Stanley
Claimed by Argentina

Punta Arenas

South Georgia and South Sandwich Islands (UK)
Claimed by Argentina

Lambert Azimuthal Equal Area projection

Facts about South America

Population (2015)
418 449 000

Largest country
Brazil 8 514 879 sq km

Country with most people
Brazil 207 848 000 (2015)

Largest city (2015)
São Paulo 21 028 000

Key

— Country boundary
--- Disputed boundary
■ Capital city
○ Important city / town

Scale 1 : 35 000 000

0   400   800   1200 km

Gulf of Mexico
Yucatan Channel
Yucatán
G. of Honduras
Sierra Madre
I. de Coco
I. de Malpelo
Islas Galapagos
G. de Guayaquil
Pta Negra

Andros
Bahamas
Cuba
Greater Antilles
Jamaica
Hispaniala
Puerto Rico
Leeward Is
Caribbean Sea
Lesser Antilles
Windward Is
Trinidad
Punta Gallinas
Lake Nicaragua
Isthmus of Panama
Golfo del Darién
L. Maracaibo
Orinoco
Orinoco Delta
Mouths of the Amazon

Tropic of Cancer
9
ATLANTIC OCEAN
10°N
Equator
Fernando de Noronha
C. de São Roque

Llanos
Cordillera Occidental
Cordillera Central
Cordillera Oriental
Meta
Guaviare
Caquetá
Volcán Cotopaxi 5896
6310 Chimborazo
Marañón
Nevado de Huascarán 6768

Mt Roraima 2810
Guiana Highlands
Essequibo
Pico da Neblina 3014
Japurá
Amazon
Negro
Amazon
Juruá
Purus
Madeira
Selvas
Tapajós
Xingu
Araguaia
Tocantins
Parnaíba

8
G
H
7
6
São Francisco
Brazilian Highlands

Cordillera Central
Cordillera Oriental
Andes
Cordillera Occidental
Altiplano
L. Titicaca
Lago de Poopó
Atacama Desert
6908 Nevado Ojos del Salado
6961 Cerro Aconcagua
Gran Chaco
Paraguay
Paraná
Uruguay
Paraná
Mato Grosso Plateau
Agulhas Negras 2797

10°S
I. da Trindade
Is Martin Vaz
Tropic of Capricorn
20°S
5
4

PACIFIC
OCEAN

Islas Desventuradas (Chile)
Archipiélago Juan Fernández

Pampas
Patagonia
Rio de la Plata
Golfo San Matías
Isla de Chiloé
Laguna del Carbón
Bahía Grande
Str. of Magellan
Falkland Islands
Isla Grande de Tierra del Fuego
Cape Horn
South Georgia
South Sandwich Islands

ATLANTIC
OCEAN
30°S
40°S
3
2
1

N
W   E
S

Key

	over 5000 m
	3000 – 5000 m
	2000 – 3000 m
	1000 – 2000 m
	500 – 1000 m
	200 – 500 m
	0 – 200 m
	land below sea level

Ice cap

▲ 6961 Mountain height (in metres)

Scale 1 : 35 000 000

0   400   800   1200 km

Facts about South America

	Area 17 815 420 sq km
	Highest peak Cerro Aconcagua 6961 m
	Lowest point Laguna del Carbón -105 m
	Longest river Amazon 6516 km
	Largest lake Lake Titicaca 8340 sq km

Lambert Azimuthal Equal Area projection

A 90°W B 80°W C 70°W D 60°W E 50°W F 40°W

110°W 100°W A 90°W B 80°W C 70°W D 60°W E 50°W F 40°W G 30°W H 20°W 10°W 50°W

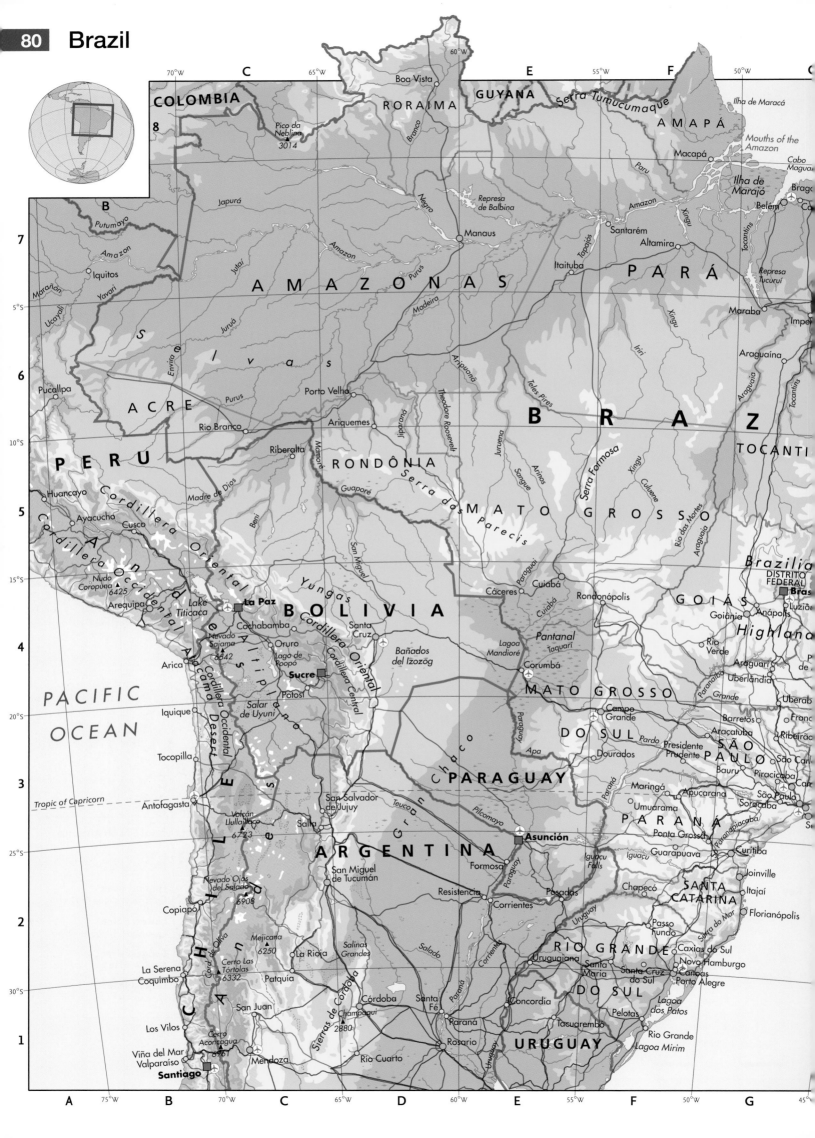

COLOMBIA

GUYANA

Boa Vista

RORAIMA

Serra Tumucumaque

AMAPÁ

Ilha de Maracá

Macapá

Mouths of the Amazon

Cabo Magua

Pico da Neblina 3014

Ilha de Marajó

Braga

Branco

Negro

Represa de Balbina

Manaus

Belém

Japurá

Paru

Amazon

Santarém

Tapajós

Xingu

Altamira

PARÁ

Iquitos

Amazon

Yavari

Jutaí

Purus

Marañón

Itaituba

Juruá

A M A Z O N A S

Madeira

Ucayali

Maraba

Imper

Pucallpa

Purus

Porto Velho

Aripuanã

Theodore Roosevelt

Telles Pires

Xingu

Iriri

Araguaína

Tocantins

ACRE

Ariquemes

B R A Z

Rio Branco

RONDÔNIA

Juruena

Serra Formosa

Xingu

Culuene

Rio das Mortes

TOCANTI

PERU

Riberalta

Serra dos Parecis

M A T O

G R O S S O

Araguaia

Huancayo

Madre de Dios

Guaporé

San Miguel

Sangue

Arinos

Brazília

Ayacucha

Beni

Paraguai

Cáceres

Cuiabá

Rondonópolis

GOIÁS

Bras

DISTRITO FEDERAL

Cusco

Nudo Coropuna ▲ 6425

Lake Titicaca

La Paz

B O L I V I A

Cuiabá

Goiânia

Anápolis

Luziâ

Arequipa

Cochabamba

Santa Cruz

Lagoa Mandioré

Pantanal

Taquari

Highlana

Nevado Sajama ▲ 6542

Oruro

Lago de Poopó

Cordillera Oriental

Bañados del Izozóg

Corumbá

M A T O   G R O S S O

Rio Verde

Araguari

Uberlândia

Arica

Sucre

Potosí

Cordillera Central

Grande

Uberab

PACIFIC

Iquique

Salar de Uyuni

Campo Grande

Paraguay

DO SUL

Pardo

Barretos

Franc

OCEAN

Paraguay

Dourados

Presidente Prudente

Araçatuba

SÃO

Ribeirão

Tocopilla

Apa

PARAGUAY

Paraná

Maringá

Bauru

PAULO

São

Uberab

Tropic of Capricorn

Antofagasta

San Salvador de Jujuy

Teuco

Pilcomayo

Paraná

Apucarana

São Paula

Piracicaba

Cai

Volcán Llullaillaco ▲ 6723

Salta

Asunción

PARANÁ

Sorocaba

S

Umuarama

Guarapuava

Curitiba

ARGENTINA

Formosa

Iguaçu Falls

Ponta Grossa

Paranapiacaba

Se

San Miguel de Tucumán

Iguaçu

Joinville

SANTA

CATARINA

Nevado Ojos del Salado ▲ 6908

Resistencia

Posadas

Chapecó

Itajaí

Copiapó

Corrientes

Uruguay

Florianópolis

Mejicana ▲ 6250

Salinas Grandes

Salado

RIO GRANDE

Caxias do Sul

Cerro Las Tórtolas ▲ 6332

La Rioja

Corrientes

Uruguaiana

Passo Fundo

Santa do Sul

La Serena

Patquía

Paraná

Santa Maria

Novo Hamburgo

Canoas

Coquimbo

Concordia

DO SUL

Porto Alegre

Córdoba

Santa Fé

Lagoa dos Patos

Sierras de Córdoba

Champaquí ▲ 2880

Paraná

Pelotas

Tacuarembó

Los Vilos

Cerro Aconcagua ▲ 6961

San Juan

Rosario

URUGUAY

Rio Grande

Lagoa Mirim

Viña del Mar

Valparaíso

Mendoza

Río Cuarto

Santiago

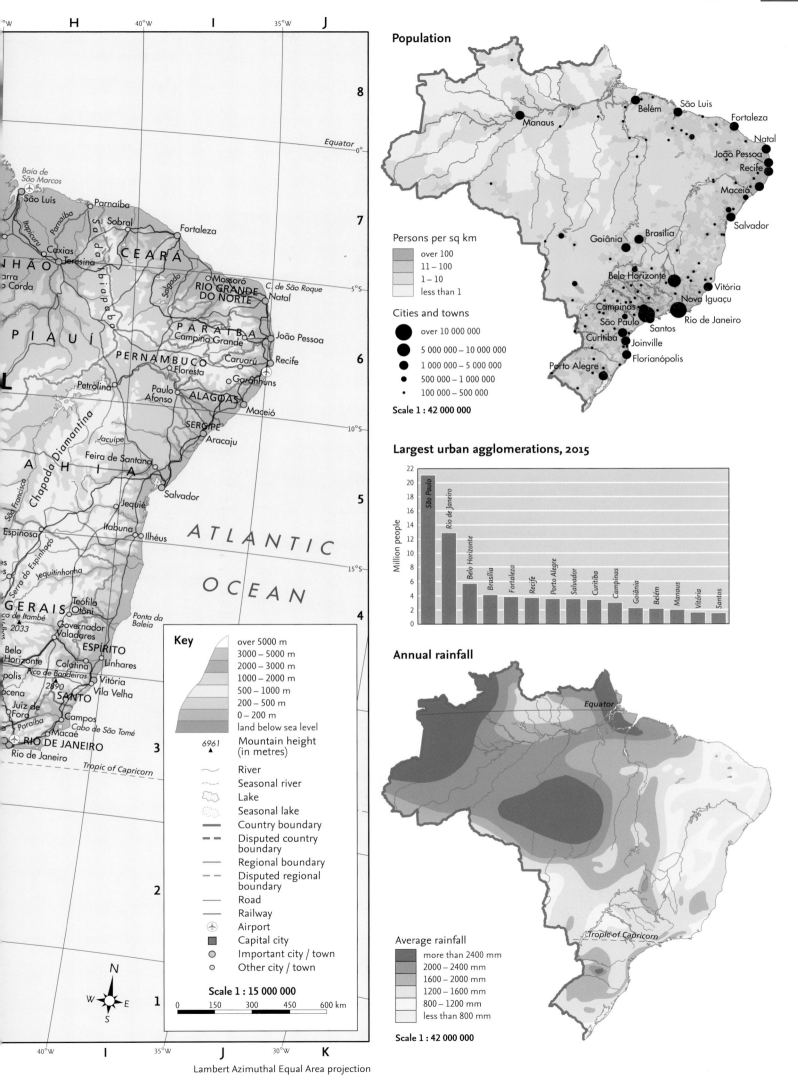

Population

Persons per sq km
over 100
11 – 100
1 – 10
less than 1

Cities and towns
over 10 000 000
5 000 000 – 10 000 000
1 000 000 – 5 000 000
500 000 – 1 000 000
100 000 – 500 000

Scale 1 : 42 000 000

Largest urban agglomerations, 2015

Annual rainfall

Average rainfall
more than 2400 mm
2000 – 2400 mm
1600 – 2000 mm
1200 – 1600 mm
800 – 1200 mm
less than 800 mm

Scale 1 : 42 000 000

Key
over 5000 m
3000 – 5000 m
2000 – 3000 m
1000 – 2000 m
500 – 1000 m
200 – 500 m
0 – 200 m
land below sea level
6961 Mountain height (in metres)
River
Seasonal river
Lake
Seasonal lake
Country boundary
Disputed country boundary
Regional boundary
Disputed regional boundary
Road
Railway
Airport
Capital city
Important city / town
Other city / town

Scale 1 : 15 000 000
0   150   300   450   600 km

Lambert Azimuthal Equal Area projection

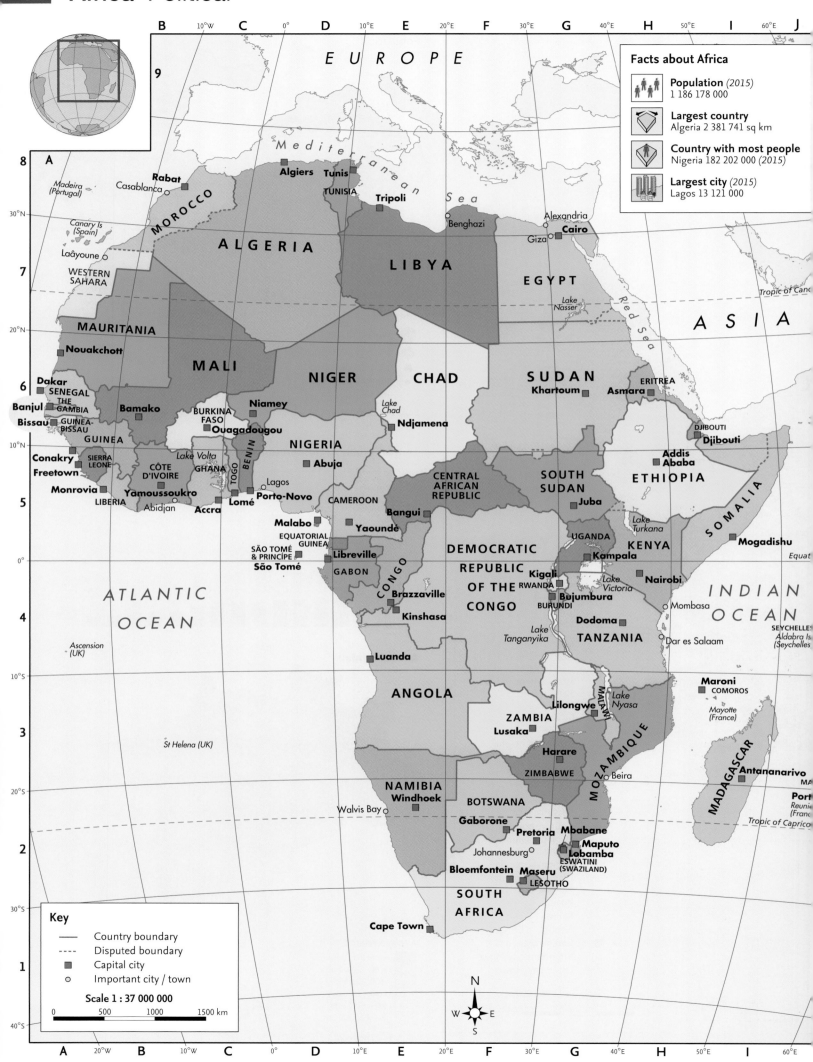

Facts about Africa

Population (2015)
1 186 178 000

Largest country
Algeria 2 381 741 sq km

Country with most people
Nigeria 182 202 000 (2015)

Largest city (2015)
Lagos 13 121 000

EUROPE

Mediterranean Sea

MOROCCO
Rabat
Casablanca
Algiers
Tunis
TUNISIA
Tripoli
Benghazi
Alexandria
Cairo
Giza

Madeira
(Portugal)

Canary Is
(Spain)

Laâyoune

WESTERN
SAHARA

ALGERIA

LIBYA

EGYPT

Lake Nasser

Red Sea

Tropic of Canc

ASIA

MAURITANIA

Nouakchott

MALI

NIGER

CHAD

SUDAN

Khartoum

ERITREA
Asmara

Dakar
SENEGAL
THE GAMBIA
Banjul
Bissau
GUINEA-BISSAU

Bamako

BURKINA
FASO
Niamey

Ouagadougou

Ndjamena

Lake Chad

DJIBOUTI
Djibouti

Conakry
Freetown
SIERRA
LEONE

GUINEA

CÔTE
D'IVOIRE

GHANA

Lake Volta

BENIN
TOGO

NIGERIA

Abuja

CENTRAL
AFRICAN
REPUBLIC

SOUTH
SUDAN

Juba

Addis
Ababa

ETHIOPIA

Monrovia

LIBERIA

Yamoussoukro

Abidjan

Accra
Lomé
Porto-Novo

Lagos

CAMEROON

Bangui

SOMALIA

Malabo

Yaoundé

Mogadishu

EQUATORIAL
GUINEA
SÃO TOMÉ
& PRINCÍPE
São Tomé

Libreville

GABON

CONGO

DEMOCRATIC

REPUBLIC

OF THE

CONGO

UGANDA

Kampala

Kigali
RWANDA
Bujumbura
BURUNDI

KENYA

Lake Victoria

Nairobi

Equat

INDIAN
OCEAN

Brazzaville

Kinshasa

Lake Turkana

Mombasa

SEYCHELLE
Aldabra Is
(Seychelles)

ATLANTIC

OCEAN

Luanda

ANGOLA

Dodoma

TANZANIA

Dar es Salaam

Lake Tanganyika

Ascension
(UK)

St Helena (UK)

Lilongwe

MALAWI

Lake Nyasa

ZAMBIA

Lusaka

Maroni
COMOROS

Mayotte
(France)

Harare

ZIMBABWE

MOZAMBIQUE

MADAGASCAR

Antananarivo
MA

NAMIBIA
Windhoek

BOTSWANA

Beira

Walvis Bay

Gaborone

Pretoria

Johannesburg

Mbabane
Maputo
Lobamba
ESWATINI
(SWAZILAND)

Port
Reunie
(Franc

Tropic of Caprico

Bloemfontein

Maseru
LESOTHO

SOUTH

AFRICA

Cape Town

Key

—— Country boundary

----- Disputed boundary

■ Capital city

○ Important city / town

Scale 1 : 37 000 000

0   500   1000   1500 km

N
W E
S

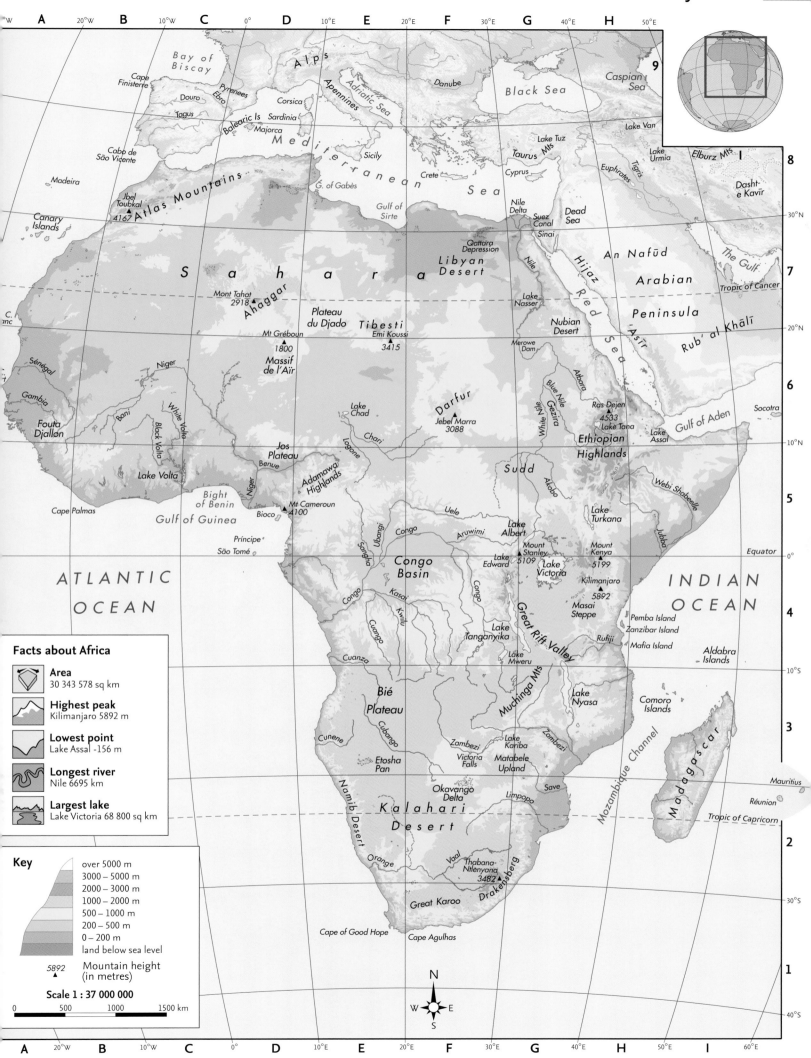

Facts about Africa

Area
30 343 578 sq km

Highest peak
Kilimanjaro 5892 m

Lowest point
Lake Assal -156 m

Longest river
Nile 6695 km

Largest lake
Lake Victoria 68 800 sq km

Key

over 5000 m
3000 – 5000 m
2000 – 3000 m
1000 – 2000 m
500 – 1000 m
200 – 500 m
0 – 200 m
land below sea level

5892 ▲ Mountain height
(in metres)

Scale 1 : 37 000 000

0   500   1000   1500 km

Lambert Azimuthal Equal Area projection

INDIAN OCEAN

ATLANTIC OCEAN

Mediterranean Sea

Black Sea

Red Sea

The Gulf

Gulf of Aden

Gulf of Guinea

Countries and regions

IRAN
IRAQ
KUWAIT
SAUDI ARABIA
YEMEN
SOMALILAND
SOMALIA
DJIBOUTI
ERITREA
ETHIOPIA
SUDAN
SOUTH SUDAN
KENYA
UGANDA
TANZANIA
RWANDA
BURUNDI
DEMOCRATIC REPUBLIC OF THE CONGO
CONGO
GABON
EQUATORIAL GUINEA
SÃO TOMÉ AND PRÍNCIPE
CAMEROON
CENTRAL AFRICAN REPUBLIC
CHAD
NIGERIA
NIGER
BENIN
TOGO
GHANA
BURKINA FASO
CÔTE D'IVOIRE
LIBERIA
SIERRA LEONE
GUINEA
GUINEA-BISSAU
SENEGAL
THE GAMBIA
MAURITANIA
MALI
WESTERN SAHARA
MOROCCO
ALGERIA
LIBYA
TUNISIA
EGYPT
ANGOLA

GEORGIA
ARMENIA
AZERBAIJAN
TURKEY
SYRIA
LEBANON
ISRAEL
JORDAN
CYPRUS
GREECE
BULGARIA
MACEDONIA
KOSOVO
MONTENEGRO
ALBANIA
ITALY
MALTA
SPAIN
PORTUGAL
ANDORRA

Cities

Eşfahān
Tabriz
Baghdād
Basra
Kuwait
Riyadh
Mecca
Jeddah
Sana
Aden
Berbera
Hargeisa
Djibouti
Asmara
Addis Ababa
Khartoum
Omdurman
Wad Medani
Juba
Wau
Kampala
Nairobi
Mombasa
Dodoma
Dar es Salaam
Zanzibar
Kigali
Bujumbura
Bukavu
Kinshasa
Brazzaville
Pointe-Noire
Libreville
Francevill
Malabo
Yaoundé
Douala
Ndjamena
Bangui
Abuja
Lagos
Ibadan
Kano
Porto-Novo
Lomé
Accra
Ouagadougou
Yamoussoukro
Abidjan
Monrovia
Freetown
Conakry
Bissau
Banjul
Dakar
Nouakchott
Nouâdhibou
Bamako
Niamey
Zinder
Maiduguri
Tripoli
Benghazi
Tunis
Sfax
Algiers
Oran
Constantine
Béchar
Rabat
Casablanca
Marrakesh
Tangier
Agadir
Laâyoune
Cairo
Giza
Alexandria
Aswān
Port Sudan
Mogadishu
Kismayo

Rome
Naples
Palermo
Madrid
Barcelona
Valencia
Seville
Lisbon
Oporto
Athens
Thessaloniki
Sofia
Skopje
Ankara
Istanbul
Izmir
Adana
Aleppo
Damascus
Beirut
Jerusalem
Amman
Nicosia
Tbilisi
Yerevan

Physical features

Zagros Mts
Taurus Mountains
Atlas Mountains
Jbel Toubkal 4167
Ahaggar
Mont Tahat 2918
Massif de l'Aïr
Tibesti
Emi Koussi 3415
Plateau du Djado
Tropic of Cancer
An Nafūd
Rub' al Khali
'Asir
Nile
Blue Nile
White Nile
Lake Nasser
Lake Tana
Lake Turkana
Lake Victoria
Lake Albert
Lake Edward
Lake Tanganyika
Lake Chad
Lake Volta
Congo Basin
Darfur
Jebel Marra 3088
Ras Dejen 4533
Ethiopian Highlands
Mount Kenya 5199
Kilimanjaro 5895
Mount Stanley 5109
Sinai
Suez Canal
Qattara Depression
Libyan Desert
Nubian Desert
Sahara
Sudd
Equator

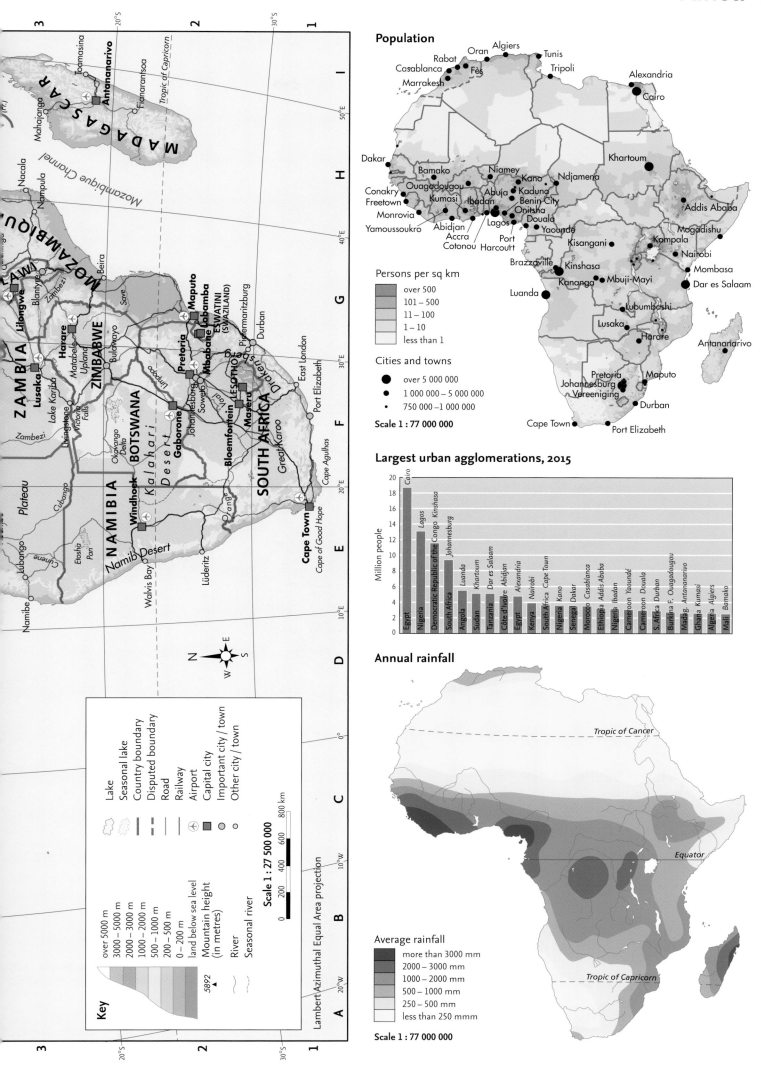

Population

Persons per sq km

- over 500
- 101 – 500
- 11 – 100
- 1 – 10
- less than 1

Cities and towns

- over 5 000 000
- 1 000 000 – 5 000 000
- 750 000 – 1 000 000

Scale 1 : 77 000 000

Algiers, Tunis, Tripoli, Oran, Rabat, Fès, Casablanca, Marrakesh, Alexandria, Cairo, Dakar, Khartoum, Bamako, Niamey, Kano, Ndjamena, Conakry, Ouagadougou, Kaduna, Freetown, Kumasi, Abuja, Benin City, Ibadan, Onitsha, Douala, Monrovia, Lagos, Yaoundé, Yamoussoukro, Abidjan, Accra, Cotonou, Port Harcourt, Addis Ababa, Mogadishu, Kampala, Nairobi, Kisangani, Brazzaville, Kinshasa, Mombasa, Kananga, Mbuji-Mayi, Dar es Salaam, Luanda, Lubumbashi, Lusaka, Harare, Antananarivo, Pretoria, Johannesburg, Vereeniging, Maputo, Durban, Cape Town, Port Elizabeth

Largest urban agglomerations, 2015

Million people

20, 18, 16, 14, 12, 10, 8, 6, 4, 2, 0

Cairo	Egypt
Lagos	Nigeria
Kinshasa	Democratic Republic of the Congo
Johannesburg	South Africa
Luanda	Angola
Khartoum	Sudan
Dar es Salaam	Tanzania
Abidjan	Côte d'Ivoire
Alexandria	Egypt
Nairobi	Kenya
Cape Town	South Africa
Kano	Nigeria
Dakar	Senegal
Casablanca	Morocco
Addis Ababa	Ethiopia
Ibadan	Nigeria
Yaoundé	Cameroon
Douala	Cameroon
Durban	S. Africa
Ouagadougou	Burkina F.
Antananarivo	Madag.
Kumasi	Ghana
Algiers	Algeria
Bamako	Mali

Annual rainfall

Tropic of Cancer

Equator

Tropic of Capricorn

Average rainfall

- more than 3000 mm
- 2000 – 3000 mm
- 1000 – 2000 mm
- 500 – 1000 mm
- 250 – 500 mm
- less than 250 mm

Scale 1 : 77 000 000

MADAGASCAR, Toamasina, Antananarivo, Fianarantsoa, Mahajanga, Mozambique Channel, Nacala, Nampula, Namibe, MOZAMBIQUE, Beira, MALAWI, Lilongwe, Blantyre, Zambezi, Zimbabwe, Harare, Matabele Upland, Bulawayo, ZAMBIA, Lusaka, Lake Kariba, Livingstone, Victoria Falls, Zambezi, Plateau, Cubango, Cuando, Okavango Delta, Kalahari Desert, BOTSWANA, Gaborone, Maputo, EWATINI (SWAZILAND), Mbabane, Lobamba, Pretoria, Johannesburg, Soweto, Vereeniging, Pietermaritzburg, Durban, LESOTHO, Maseru, Bloemfontein, Drakensberg, SOUTH AFRICA, East London, Port Elizabeth, Great Karoo, Orange, Cape of Good Hope, Cape Agulhas, NAMIBIA, Windhoek, Namib Desert, Walvis Bay, Lüderitz, Etosha Pan, Cunene, Cubango, Cuando

N W E S

Scale 1 : 27 500 000

0 200 400 600 800 km

Lambert Azimuthal Equal Area projection

Key

land height (in metres)
- over 5000 m
- 3000 – 5000 m
- 2000 – 3000 m
- 1000 – 2000 m
- 500 – 1000 m
- 200 – 500 m
- 0 – 200 m
- land below sea level

5892 ▲ Mountain height (in metres)

- River
- Seasonal river
- Lake
- Seasonal lake
- Country boundary
- Disputed boundary
- Road
- Railway
- ✈ Airport
- ■ Capital city
- ● Important city / town
- ○ Other city / town

ATLANTIC OCEAN

Barents Sea

Norwegian Sea

Arctic Circle

Reykjavik ICELAND

Faroe Islands (Denmark)

North Sea

Oslo NORWAY SWEDEN FINLAND

Helsinki St Petersburg RUSSIA

Stockholm

Tallinn ESTONIA

Edinburgh

Belfast

IRELAND UNITED KINGDOM

Dublin

Cardiff **London** The Hague NETH. DENMARK **Copenhagen**

Amsterdam **Berlin**

LATVIA **Riga**

Moscow

LITHUANIA **Vilnius**

RUSSIA

Minsk BELARUS

Brussels BEL. GERMANY POLAND

Luxembourg LUX. **Prague** **Warsaw**

Paris CZECHIA

FRANCE Munich SLOVAKIA **Kyiv**

Volgograd

UKRAINE

Bern SW. L. **Vienna** **Bratislava**

Lyon AUSTRIA **Budapest** MOLDOVA

HUNGARY **Chișinău** Odesa

Ljubljana SL. **Zagreb** ROMANIA

Milan CROATIA **Belgrade** **Bucharest**

MONACO SAN MARINO B.H. SERBIA

Crimea Administered by Russia

Andorra la Vella A. **Sarajevo**

ITALY MO. **Pristina** BULGARIA

Black Sea

PORTUGAL V.C. **Podgorica** K. **Sofia**

Lisbon **Madrid** **Rome** **Skopje** Istanbul

SPAIN **Tirana** N.M.

Barcelona ALBANIA TURKEY

Gibraltar (UK)

Mediterranean Sea

GREECE

ASIA

Athens

Caspian Sea

Valletta

MALTA

AFRICA

Bay of Biscay

Conic Equidistant projection

Facts about Europe (excluding Russia)

Population (2015)
594 823 000

Largest country
Ukraine 603 700 sq km

Country with most people (2015)
Germany 80 689 000

Largest city (2015)
Istanbul 12 459 000

Key

- over 5000 m
- 3000 – 5000 m
- 2000 – 3000 m
- 1000 – 2000 m
- 500 – 1000 m
- 200 – 500 m
- 0 – 200 m
- land below sea level

Ice cap

5642 ▲ Mountain height (in metres)

Scale 1 : 25 000 000

0   250   500   750   1000 km

Facts about Europe

Area
9 908 599 sq km

Highest peak
Mount Elbrus 5642 m

Lowest point
Caspian Sea -28 m

Longest river
Volga 3688 km

Largest lake
Caspian Sea 371 000 sq km

Conic Equidistant projection

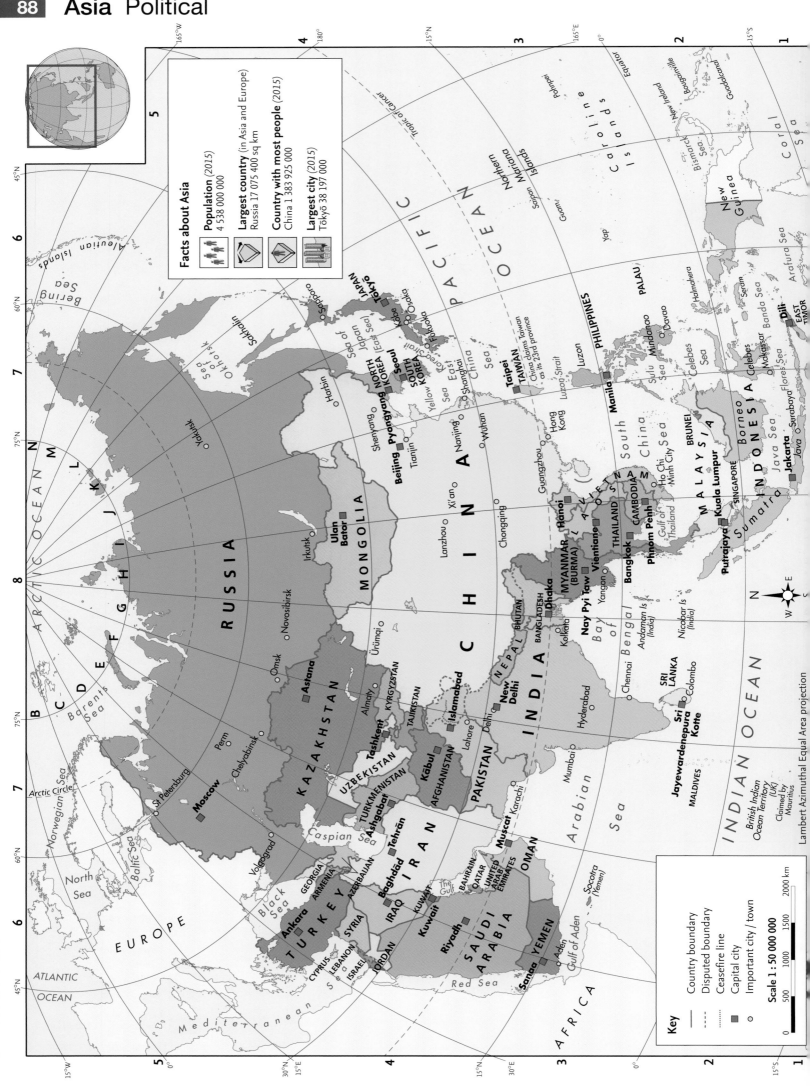

Facts about Asia

Population (2015)
4 538 000 000

Largest country (in Asia and Europe)
Russia 17 075 400 sq km

Country with most people (2015)
China 1 383 925 000

Largest city (2015)
Tōkyō 38 197 000

Key
— Country boundary
--- Disputed boundary
······· Ceasefire line
■ Capital city
○ Important city / town

Scale 1:50 000 000

Lambert Azimuthal Equal Area projection

Facts about Asia

Area
45 036 492 sq km

Highest peak
Mt Everest 8849 m

Lowest point
Dead Sea -426 m

Longest river
Chang Jiang 6380 km

Largest lake
Caspian Sea 371 000 sq km

Key

Mountain height (in metres)	
over 5000 m	
3000 – 5000 m	
2000 – 3000 m	
1000 – 2000 m	
500 – 1000 m	
200 – 500 m	
0 – 200 m	
land below sea level	

Ice cap

8849 ▲ Mountain height (in metres)

Scale 1 : 50 000 000

Lambert Azimuthal Equal Area projection

0   500   1000   1500   2000 km

PACIFIC OCEAN

INDIAN OCEAN

ATLANTIC OCEAN

Bering Sea
Aleutian Islands
Sea of Okhotsk
Kamchatka Peninsula
Mys Lopatka
Khrebet Kolymskiy
Sakhalin
Kuril Islands
Hokkaido
Honshu
Shikoku
Kyushu
Sea of Japan (East Sea)
Korea Strait
Yellow Sea
East China Sea
Okinawa
Ryukyu Islands
Taiwan
Luzon Strait
Luzon
Philippines
Samar
Mindanao
Palawan
South China Sea
Sulu Sea
Celebes Sea
Celebes
Borneo
Hainan
Nan Ling
Xi Jiang
Chang Jiang
Mekong
Gulf of Thailand
Peninsular Malaysia
Strait of Malacca
Sumatra
Kepulauan Mentawai
Java Sea
Java
Bali
Flores
Flores Sea
Lombok
Bali

Northern Mariana Islands
Saipan
Guam
Yap
Palau Islands
Halmahera
Seram
Buru
Banda Sea
Arafura Sea
Timor
Timor Sea
New Guinea
Puncak Jaya 4884 ▲
Cape York
Gulf of Carpentaria
Bismarck Sea
New Ireland
New Britain
Bougainville Island
Pohnpei
Caroline Islands
Equator

Verkhoyanskiy Khrebet
Khrebet Dzhugdzhur
Stanovoy Khrebet
Sikhote-Alin
Amur
Argun
Da Hinggan Ling
Manchuria
Huang He
North China Plain
Huang He
Hai He
Gobi Desert
Yablonovyy Khrebet
Lena
Lake Baikal
Selenga
Angara
Nizhnyaya Tunguska
Podkamennaya Tunguska
Central Siberian Plateau
Taymyr Peninsula
Yenisey
Yenisey
SIBERIA
Severnaya Zemlya
Novaya Zemlya
Barents Sea
Franz Josef Land
Spitsbergen
Arctic Circle
Wrangel Island
New Siberia Islands
Laptev Sea
ARCTIC OCEAN
Kara Sea
Gora Narodnaya 1894 ▲
Ob'
Irtysh
West Siberian Plain
Ural Mountains
Ob'
Lake Zaysan
Altai Mountains
Tien Shan
Turpan Pendi
Lop Nur
Taklimakan Desert
Kunlun Shan
Gongga Shan 7514
Plateau of Tibet
Himalaya
Mount Everest 8849 ▲
Annapurna 8091 ▲
Dhaulagiri 8167 ▲
K2 8611 ▲
Karakoram Ra.
Hindu Kush
Pamir
Aral Sea
Syr Darya
Amu Darya
Lake Balkhash
Ganges
Brahmaputra
Mouths of the Ganges
Bay of Bengal
Yamuna
Godavari
Narmada
Deccan
Eastern Ghats
Western Ghats
Cape Comorin
Sri Lanka
Andaman Islands
Nicobar Islands
Andaman Sea
Arakan Yoma
Irrawaddy
Salween
Mouths of the Irrawaddy
Laccadive Islands
Maldives
Chagos Archipelago

Thar Desert
Indus
Sutlej
Salt Range
Sulaiman Range
Helmand
Dasht-e Kavir
Dasht-e Lut
Iranian Plateau
Makran
Gulf of Oman
Jaziret Masirah
The Gulf
Zagros Mts
Elburz Mts
Caspian Sea
Tigris
Euphrates
Arabian Peninsula
Rub' al Khali
An Nafud
Hijaz
'Asir
Arabian Sea
Gulf of Aden
Socotra
Red Sea
Nubian Desert
Eastern Desert
Western Desert
Ethiopian Highlands
Caucasus
Elbrus 5642 ▲
Mount Ararat 5165 ▲
Taurus Mts
Cyprus
Mediterranean Sea
Black Sea
Don
Dnieper
Volga
Ural
Kama
Northern Dvina
White Sea
Kola Peninsula
North Cape
Norwegian Sea
Lake Onega
Lake Ladoga
Central Russian Upland
North European Plain
Baltic Sea
Vistula
Carpathian Mts
Danube
Rhine
Alps
Pyrenees
Bay of Biscay
North Sea
Novaya Zemlya

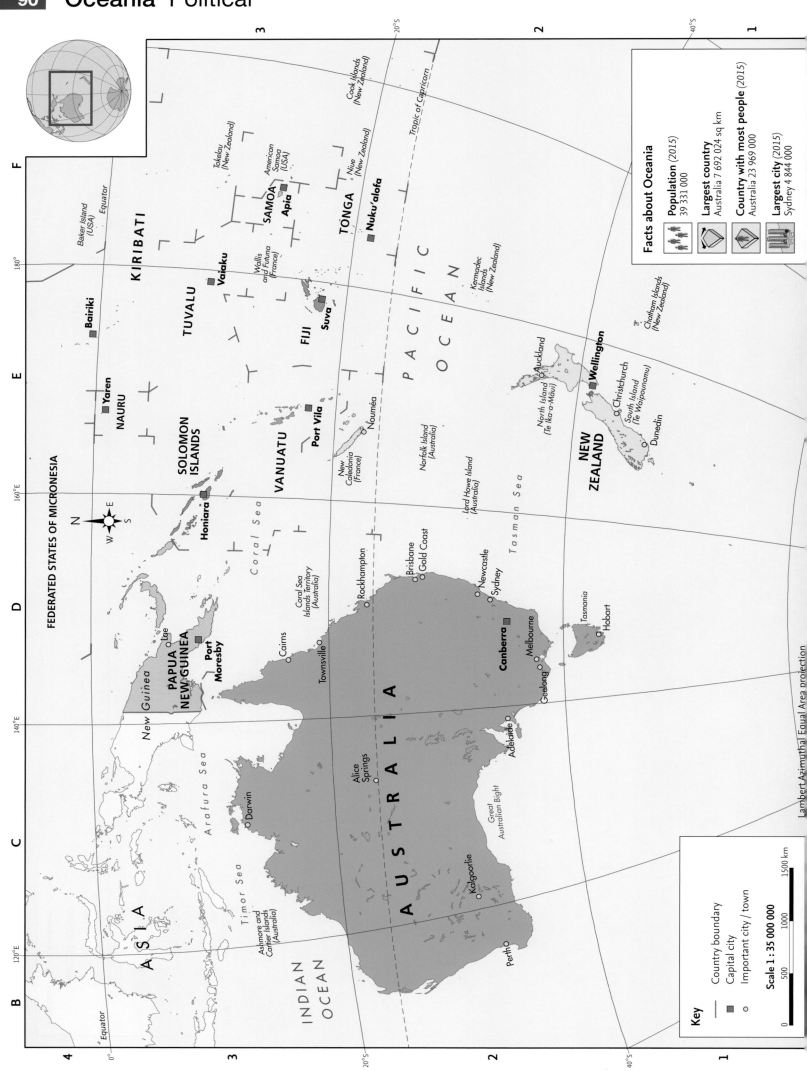

Facts about Oceania

Population (2015)
39 331 000

Largest country
Australia 7 692 024 sq km

Country with most people (2015)
Australia 23 969 000

Largest city (2015)
Sydney 4 844 000

Key

— Country boundary
■ Capital city
○ Important city / town

Scale 1 : 35 000 000

0   500   1000   1500 km

PACIFIC OCEAN

INDIAN OCEAN

ASIA

AUSTRALIA

NEW ZEALAND

PAPUA NEW GUINEA

FEDERATED STATES OF MICRONESIA

KIRIBATI

TUVALU

NAURU

SOLOMON ISLANDS

VANUATU

FIJI

SAMOA

TONGA

Baker Island (USA)
Equator
Tokelau (New Zealand)
American Samoa (USA)
Niue (New Zealand)
Cook Islands (New Zealand)
Tropic of Capricorn
Wallis and Futuna (France)
Kermadec Islands (New Zealand)
Chatham Islands (New Zealand)
New Caledonia (France)
Norfolk Island (Australia)
Lord Howe Island (Australia)
Coral Sea Islands Territory (Australia)
Ashmore and Cartier Islands (Australia)

Bairiki
Yaren
Vaiaku
Apia
Nuku'alofa
Suva
Honiara
Port Vila
Nouméa
Port Moresby
Lae

Wellington
Auckland
Christchurch
Dunedin
North Island (Te Ika-a-Māui)
South Island (Te Waipounamu)
Tasmania

Canberra
Sydney
Newcastle
Brisbane
Gold Coast
Rockhampton
Townsville
Cairns
Darwin
Alice Springs
Perth
Kalgoorlie
Adelaide
Melbourne
Geelong
Hobart

Coral Sea
Tasman Sea
Arafura Sea
Timor Sea
Great Australian Bight
New Guinea

N
W E
S

Lambert Azimuthal Equal Area projection

Facts about Oceania

Area
8 844 516 sq km

Highest peak
Puncak Jaya 4884 m

Lowest point
Kati Thanda-Lake Eyre -16 m

Longest river
Murray-Darling 3672 km

Largest lake
Kati Thanda-Lake Eyre 0–8900 sq km

Key

- over 5000 m
- 3000 – 5000 m
- 2000 – 3000 m
- 1000 – 2000 m
- 500 – 1000 m
- 200 – 500 m
- 0 – 200 m
- land below sea level

4884 ▲ Mountain height (in metres)

Scale 1 : 35 000 000

0   500   1000   1500 km

Lambert Azimuthal Equal Area projection

ASIA

INDIAN OCEAN

PACIFIC OCEAN

Tasman Sea

Coral Sea

Arafura Sea

Timor Sea

Bismarck Sea

Tropic of Capricorn

Equator

Admiralty Islands
New Ireland
New Britain
Bougainville Island
Solomon Islands
Guadalcanal
Mount Wilhelm 4509 ▲
Puncak Jaya 4884 ▲
Gulf of Papua
Cape York
Torres Strait
Melville Island
Arnhem Land
Gulf of Carpentaria
Cape York Peninsula
Great Barrier Reef
Kimberley Plateau
Pilbara
North West Cape
Mount Bruce 1235
Cape Leeuwin
Great Sandy Desert
Lake Mackay
Lake Disappointment
Gibson Desert
Macdonnell Ranges
Uluru / Ayers Rock 863 ▲
Musgrave Ranges
Great Victoria Desert
Nullarbor Plain
Great Australian Bight
Barkly Tableland
Great Dividing Range
Grey Range
Kati Thanda-Lake Eyre
Lake Torrens
Lake Gairdner
Spencer Gulf
Kangaroo Island
Darling
Murray
Lachlan
Darling Downs
Blue Mts
Mount Kosciuszko 2229 ▲
Cape Howe
Flinders Island
Bass Str.
Mount Ossa 1617 ▲
Tasmania
South East Cape

Nauru
Gilbert Islands
Santa Cruz Islands
Espírito Santo
Loyalty Islands
New Caledonia
Vanua Levu
Fiji
Viti Levu
Tomanivi 1323 ▲
Samoa
Niue
Tonga
Chatham Islands
East Cape
North Cape
Cook Strait
Aoraki / Mount Cook 3724 ▲
Southern Alps
Stewart Island
Auckland Islands

N
W E
S

- ■ Capital city
- ○ Other town/city

A B C D E F G H

9

GREENLAND
(Denmark)

Arctic Circle
RUSSIA
U.S.A.
Nuuk
(Godthåb)

80°N 160°W 140°W 120°W 100°W 80°W 60°W 40°W 20°W

Anchorage

C A N A D A

60°N

Edmonton

8

Vancouver Winnipeg

Seattle Ottawa Montreal

Toronto Boston

40°N Chicago Detroit

San Francisco Pittsburgh New York

UNITED Washington Philadelphia
STATES D.C.

Los Angeles **OF AMERICA** Azores
(Port.) Rab

7 MOR

Phoenix

Dallas Laâyoune
Tropic of Cancer **WESTERN**
SAHARA

20°N Houston

Monterrey Miami

MEXICO **THE BAHAMAS** **MAURITANI**

Havana Nassau Nouakchott

Guadalajara **CUBA** **CAPE VERDE** **SENEGAL**

Mexico City Kingston DOMINICAN San Juan THE GAMBIA Dakar
Belmopan BELIZE REP. Bissau
GUATEMALA HAITI PUERTO GUINEA-BISSAU GUINEA

6 Guatemala City HONDURAS JAMAICA RICO Conakry
EL SALVADOR (USA) Freetown
Managua **NICARAGUA** Caracas TRINIDAD & TOBAGO SIERRA LEONE Monrovia
COSTA RICA Panama Port of Spain LIBERIA
San José City **VENEZUELA**
PANAMA Georgetown Paramaribo

Bogotá GUY Cayenne
COLOMBIA SUR. FR. G.

Quito

Galapagos Is **ECUADOR**

PACIFIC (Ec.) ATLANT

Equator 0°

OCEAN B R A Z I L OCEAN

KIRIBATI Recife

Marquesas
Is P
(Fr.) E Lima
French R
5 Polynesia U La Paz Brasília
SAMOA (Fr.) Society Is Tuamoto Is **BOLIVIA**
(Fr.) Sucre Belo Horizonte
Cook Tahiti Rio de Janeiro
Islands **PARAGUAY**
(NZ) 20°S São Paulo
TONGA Asunción
Tropic of Capricorn Pitcairn Easter I.
Island (UK) (Chile) C

4 H **ARGENTINA** **URUGUAY**
I Santiago Montevideo
L Buenos
E Aires

40°S

3 Falkland Islands South Georgia
(UK) and South
Sandwich Islands
(UK)

Antarctic Circle

ATLANTIC
OCEAN 60°S

140°W 120°W 100°W 80°W 60°W 40°W 20°W

Santiago 2

HAITI
Port-au- Santo San British
Prince Domingo Juan Virgin Is Anguilla
US (UK) (UK)
DOMINICAN Virgin Is St-Martin (Fr.)
REPUBLIC Mayagüez (USA) St-Barthélemy (Fr.)
Sint Maarten
PUERTO RICO (Neth.)
(USA) St Eustatius Basseterre **ANTIGUA AND**
(Neth.) **BARBUDA**
ST KITTS AND NEVIS St John's
Montserrat *Guadeloupe*
(UK) (Fr.)
Basse-Terre

C a r i b b e a n **DOMINICA** Roseau

S e a Martinique Fort-de-France
(Fr.)

Scale 1 : 15 000 000 **ST LUCIA** Castries

Aruba Curaçao Bonaire **ST VINCENT AND** **BARBADOS**
(Neth.) (Neth.) (Neth.) **THE GRENADINES** Kingstown
Bridgetown
Willemstad **GRENADA**
St George's

Scarborough

Port of Spain **TRINIDAD**
AND TOBAGO

SOUTH AMERICA

Mona Passage

World facts

Population (2015)
7 349 472 000

Largest country
Russia 17 075 400 sq km

Country with most people (2015)
China 1 383 925 000

Largest city (2015)
Tōkyō 38 197 000

International boundaries in the sea shown on this map indicate ownership
of islands and island groups only. They do not infer the alignment of legal
maritime boundaries.
Not all countries are named on the map.

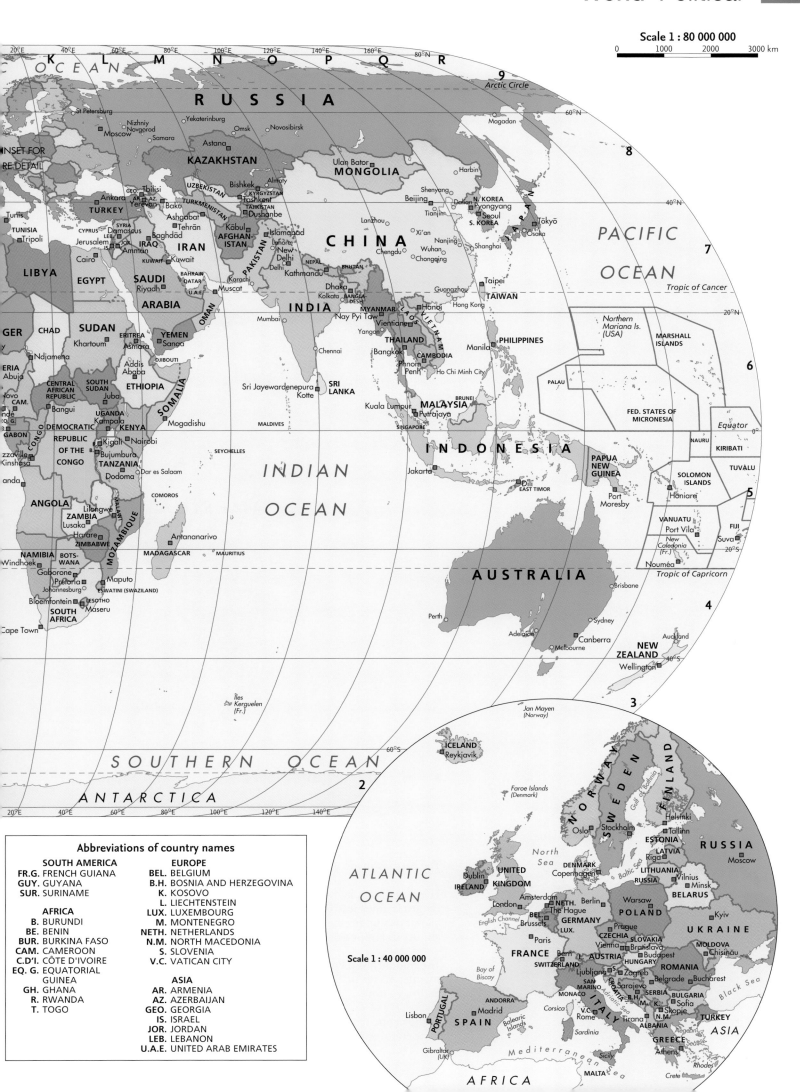

Scale 1 : 80 000 000

0 1000 2000 3000 km

OCEAN

RUSSIA

Arctic Circle

St Petersburg
Nizhniy Novgorod   Yekaterinburg   Omsk   Novosibirsk
Moscow   Samara
Astana
KAZAKHSTAN   **MONGOLIA**   Ulan Bator   Harbin
INSET FOR
RE DETAIL
GEO. Tbilisi   Bishkek   Almaty   Shenyang
Ankara   AR. AZ. Yerevan   **UZBEKISTAN**   **KYRGYZSTAN**   Beijing   N. KOREA   Pyongyang
TURKEY   Baku   **TURKMENISTAN**   Tashkent   **TAJIKISTAN**   Tianjin   Dalian   Seoul
SYRIA   Damascus   Ashgabat   Dushanbe   Lanzhou   **CHINA**   Xi'an   Nanjing   Shanghai   Osaka   Tōkyō
CYPRUS   LEB.   Baghdad   Tehrān   Kābul   **AFGHAN-   ISTAN**   Islamabad   Lahore   Delhi   Chengdu   Wuhan   Chongqing
Jerusalem   IS.   JOR.   **IRAQ**   **IRAN**   New   Delhi   **NEPAL**   Kathmandu   **BHUTAN**   Guangzhou   Taipei
Amman   KUWAIT   Kuwait   Karachi   Dhaka   **BANGLA-   DESH**   Hong Kong   **TAIWAN**
Cairo   BAHRAIN   QATAR   Riyadh   U.A.E.   **INDIA**   Hanoi   **MYANMAR**   **LAOS**

LIBYA   **EGYPT**   **SAUDI   ARABIA**   Muscat   **VIETNAM**
PACIFIC   OCEAN
Tropic of Cancer

GER   **CHAD**   **SUDAN**   **YEMEN**   Sanaa   Mumbai   Nay Pyi Taw   Vientiane   **THAILAND**   Manila   **PHILIPPINES**
Khartoum   ERITREA   Asmara   DJIBOUTI   Yangon   Bangkok   **CAMBODIA**   Northern   Mariana Is.   (USA)   **MARSHALL   ISLANDS**
Ndjamena   **CENTRAL   AFRICAN   REPUBLIC**   **SOUTH   SUDAN**   **ETHIOPIA**   Chennai   Phnom   Penh   Ho Chi Minh City   **PALAU**
ERIA   Abuja   Addis   Ababa   Sri Jayewardenepura   Kotte   **SRI   LANKA**   **MALAYSIA**   **BRUNEI**   **FED. STATES OF   MICRONESIA**   Equator
ovo   CAM.   Juba   **SOMALIA**   **MALDIVES**   Kuala Lumpur   Putrajaya   **NAURU**   **KIRIBATI**
nde   Bangui   **UGANDA**   **KENYA**   Mogadishu   SINGAPORE   **TUVALU**
GABON   **DEMOCRATIC**   Kampala   **SEYCHELLES**   **INDONESIA**   **SOLOMON   ISLANDS**
zzaville   Kinshasa   **REPUBLIC   OF THE   CONGO**   Kigali   Nairobi   Jakarta   **PAPUA   NEW   GUINEA**   Honiara
anda   B.   Bujumbura   **TANZANIA**   Dar es Salaam   Dili   **EAST TIMOR**   Port   Moresby   **VANUATU**   Port Vila
Dodoma   **INDIAN   OCEAN**   New   Caledonia   (Fr.)   **FIJI**   Suva
ANGOLA   **ZAMBIA**   MALAWI   COMOROS   Nouméa
Lilongwe   **AUSTRALIA**   Tropic of Capricorn
Lusaka   Antananarivo
Harare   Brisbane
NAMIBIA   **BOTS-   WANA**   **ZIMBABWE**   **MOZAMBIQUE**   **MADAGASCAR**   **MAURITIUS**
Windhoek   Perth   Sydney
Gaborone   Pretoria   Maputo   Adelaide   Canberra
Johannesburg   Maseru   LESOTHO   Auckland
Bloemfontein   ESWATINI (SWAZILAND)   Melbourne   **NEW   ZEALAND**
Cape Town   **SOUTH   AFRICA**   Wellington

Îles   Kerguelen   (Fr.)

SOUTHERN   OCEAN

ANTARCTICA

Abbreviations of country names

SOUTH AMERICA		EUROPE	
FR.G.	FRENCH GUIANA	BEL.	BELGIUM
GUY.	GUYANA	B.H.	BOSNIA AND HERZEGOVINA
SUR.	SURINAME	K.	KOSOVO
		L.	LIECHTENSTEIN
AFRICA		LUX.	LUXEMBOURG
B.	BURUNDI	M.	MONTENEGRO
BE.	BENIN	NETH.	NETHERLANDS
BUR.	BURKINA FASO	N.M.	NORTH MACEDONIA
CAM.	CAMEROON	S.	SLOVENIA
C.D'I.	CÔTE D'IVOIRE	V.C.	VATICAN CITY
EQ. G.	EQUATORIAL GUINEA		
GH.	GHANA	**ASIA**	
R.	RWANDA	AR.	ARMENIA
T.	TOGO	AZ.	AZERBAIJAN
		GEO.	GEORGIA
		IS.	ISRAEL
		JOR.	JORDAN
		LEB.	LEBANON
		U.A.E.	UNITED ARAB EMIRATES

Jan Mayen   (Norway)

ICELAND   Reykjavík

Faroe Islands   (Denmark)

ATLANTIC   OCEAN

NORWAY   **SWEDEN**   **FINLAND**
Oslo   Stockholm   Helsinki
North   Sea   **ESTONIA**   Tallinn   **RUSSIA**
DENMARK   Riga   **LATVIA**   Moscow
Dublin   **UNITED   KINGDOM**   Copenhagen   **LITHUANIA**
IRELAND   Amsterdam   Vilnius   Minsk
London   **NETH.**   Berlin   Warsaw   **BELARUS**
Brussels   **GERMANY**   **POLAND**   Kyiv
English Channel   BEL.   LUX.   Prague   **UKRAINE**
Paris   **CZECHIA**   **SLOVAKIA**   **MOLDOVA**   Chişinău
Vienna   Bratislava   Budapest
FRANCE   Bern   **AUSTRIA**   **HUNGARY**   **ROMANIA**
SWITZERLAND   L   Ljubljana   S   Zagreb   Belgrade   Bucharest
Bay of   Biscay   **MONACO**   SAN   MARINO   CROATIA   B.H.   **SERBIA**   **BULGARIA**   Sofia   Black Sea
ANDORRA   V.C.   **ITALY**   Sarajevo   M.   Skopje   N.M.
Lisbon   Madrid   Rome   Tirana   **ALBANIA**   **TURKEY**
PORTUGAL   **SPAIN**   Corsica   Adriatic Sea   **GREECE**   Aegean   Sea
Balearic   Islands   Sardinia   **ASIA**   Athens
Gibraltar   (UK)   Mediterranean   Sea   Sicily   **MALTA**   Crete   Rhodes

AFRICA

Scale 1 : 40 000 000

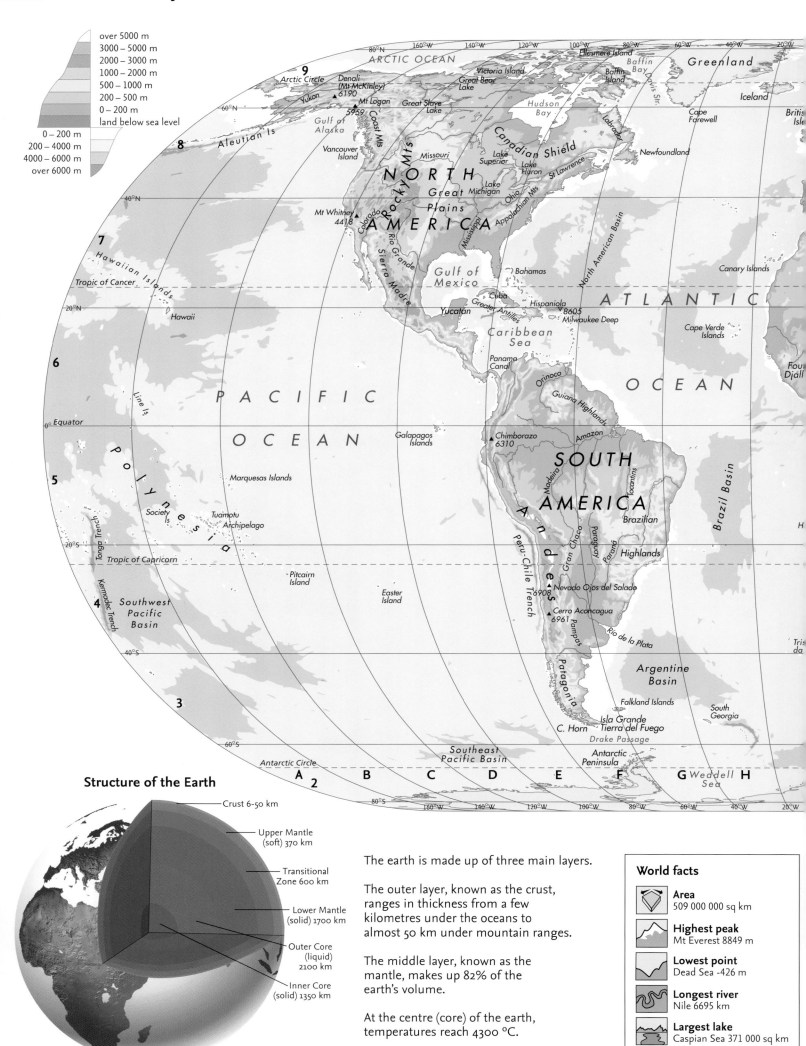

over 5000 m
3000 – 5000 m
2000 – 3000 m
1000 – 2000 m
500 – 1000 m
200 – 500 m
0 – 200 m
land below sea level

0 – 200 m
200 – 4000 m
4000 – 6000 m
over 6000 m

ARCTIC OCEAN

Arctic Circle
Denali (Mt McKinley) ▲6190
Yukon
Mt Logan ▲5959
Gulf of Alaska
Aleutian Is
Vancouver Island
Missouri
Victoria Island
Great Bear Lake
Great Slave Lake
Hudson Bay
Ellesmere Island
Baffin Bay
Baffin Island
Davis Str.
Greenland
Iceland
Cape Farewell
British Isle

NORTH AMERICA
Rocky Mts
Coast Mts
Great Plains
Mt Whitney ▲4418
Colorado
Rio Grande
Sierra Madre
Lake Superior
Lake Huron
Lake Michigan
Ohio
Mississippi
Appalachian Mts
Canadian Shield
St Lawrence
Newfoundland
Labrador
North American Basin
Canary Islands
Cape Verde Islands

Hawaiian Islands
Tropic of Cancer
Hawaii
Gulf of Mexico
Bahamas
Cuba
Yucatan
Greater Antilles
Hispaniola
▽8605
Milwaukee Deep
Caribbean Sea

ATLANTIC OCEAN

Four Djall

PACIFIC OCEAN
Line Is
Galapagos Islands
Panama Canal
Orinoco
Guiana Highlands
Amazon
Equator

Marquesas Islands
Chimborazo ▲6310
SOUTH AMERICA

Polynesia
Society Is
Tuamotu Archipelago
Madeira
Brazilian
Brazil Basin
Tonga Trench
Tropic of Capricorn
Pitcairn Island
Easter Island
Peru-Chile Trench
Andes
Gran Chaco
Paraguay
Paraná
Highlands
Tocantins

Kermadec Trench
Southwest Pacific Basin
▲6908
Nevado Ojos del Salado
Cerro Aconcagua ▲6961
Pampas
Rio de la Plata
Argentine Basin
Falkland Islands
South Georgia
Patagonia
Isla Grande Tierra del Fuego
C. Horn
Drake Passage
Southeast Pacific Basin
Antarctic Peninsula
Weddell Sea
Antarctic Circle

Structure of the Earth

Crust 6-50 km
Upper Mantle (soft) 370 km
Transitional Zone 600 km
Lower Mantle (solid) 1700 km
Outer Core (liquid) 2100 km
Inner Core (solid) 1350 km

The earth is made up of three main layers.

The outer layer, known as the crust, ranges in thickness from a few kilometres under the oceans to almost 50 km under mountain ranges.

The middle layer, known as the mantle, makes up 82% of the earth's volume.

At the centre (core) of the earth, temperatures reach 4300 °C.

World facts

Area
509 000 000 sq km

Highest peak
Mt Everest 8849 m

Lowest point
Dead Sea -426 m

Longest river
Nile 6695 km

Largest lake
Caspian Sea 371 000 sq km

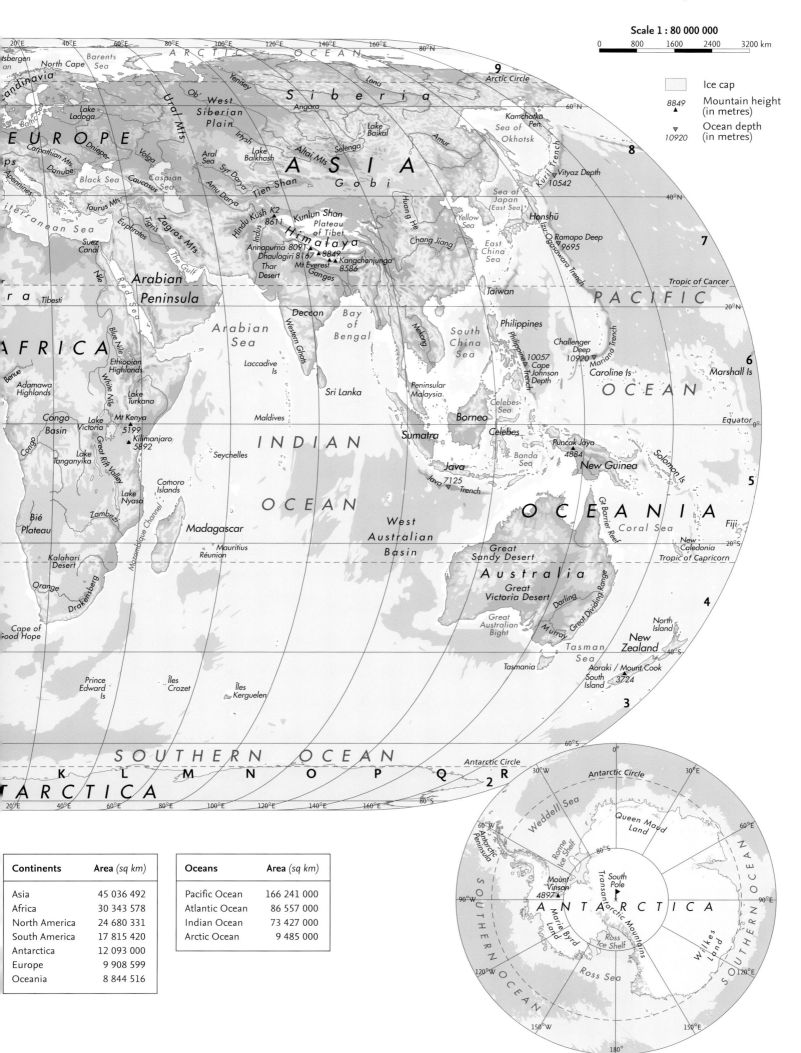

Continents	Area (sq km)
Asia	45 036 492
Africa	30 343 578
North America	24 680 331
South America	17 815 420
Antarctica	12 093 000
Europe	9 908 599
Oceania	8 844 516

Oceans	Area (sq km)
Pacific Ocean	166 241 000
Atlantic Ocean	86 557 000
Indian Ocean	73 427 000
Arctic Ocean	9 485 000

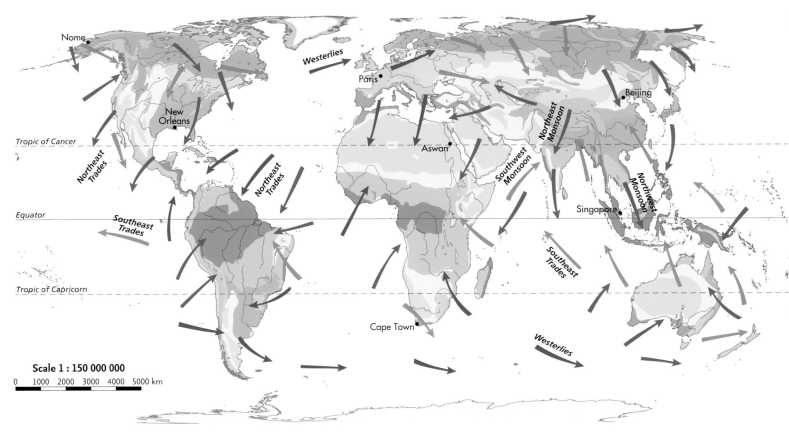

Climate types

Ice cap	**Continental**	**Subtropical**
Very cold and dry	Rainy climate, cold winters, mild summers	Wet warm winters, hot summers
Tundra and mountain	**Continental**	**Mediterranean**
Very cold winters, altitude affects climate	Rainy climate, cold winters, warm summers	Rainy mild winters, dry hot summers
Subarctic	**Temperate**	**Semi-arid**
Rainy climate with long cold winters	Rainy climate, mild winters, warm summers	Hot and dry with rainy season

Desert	• Climate station
Very hot and dry all year	
	→ Wind direction (January)
Tropical	
Hot with wet and dry seasons	→ Wind direction (July)
Tropical	→ Wind direction (all year)
Hot and wet all year	

Rainfall

Average annual rainfall

- more than 3000 mm
- 2000 – 3000 mm
- 1000 – 2000 mm
- 500 – 1000 mm
- 250 – 500 mm
- less than 250 mm

• Climate station

Scale 1 : 250 000 000

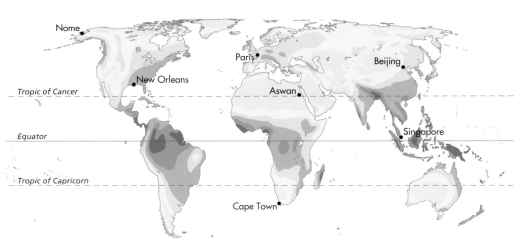

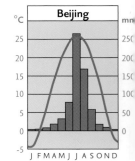

Climate graphs

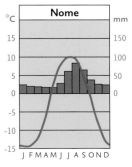

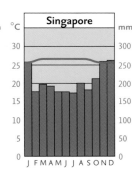

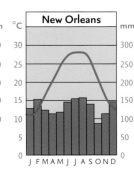

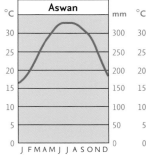

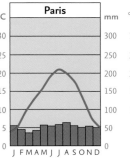

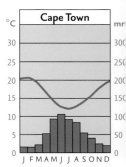

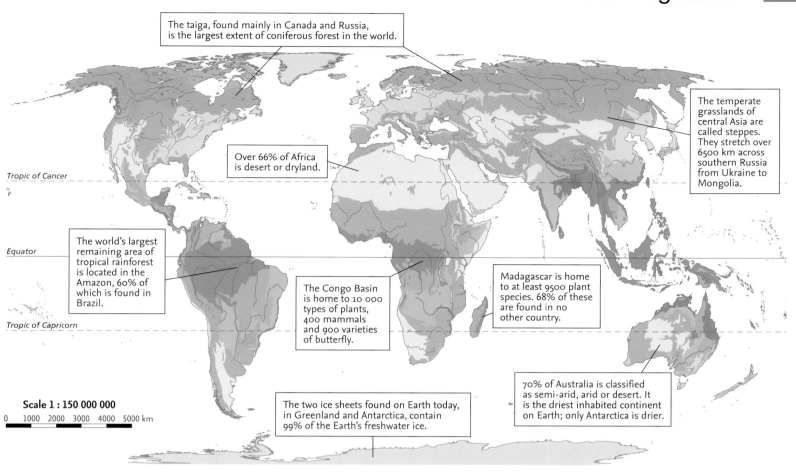

The taiga, found mainly in Canada and Russia, is the largest extent of coniferous forest in the world.

The temperate grasslands of central Asia are called steppes. They stretch over 6500 km across southern Russia from Ukraine to Mongolia.

Over 66% of Africa is desert or dryland.

Tropic of Cancer

The world's largest remaining area of tropical rainforest is located in the Amazon, 60% of which is found in Brazil.

Equator

The Congo Basin is home to 10 000 types of plants, 400 mammals and 900 varieties of butterfly.

Madagascar is home to at least 9500 plant species. 68% of these are found in no other country.

Tropic of Capricorn

70% of Australia is classified as semi-arid, arid or desert. It is the driest inhabited continent on Earth; only Antarctica is drier.

The two ice sheets found on Earth today, in Greenland and Antarctica, contain 99% of the Earth's freshwater ice.

Scale 1 : 150 000 000

0 1000 2000 3000 4000 5000 km

Types of vegetation

Ice cap and ice shelf
Extremely cold.
No vegetation.

Arctic tundra
Very cold climate.
Simple vegetation such as mosses, lichens, grasses and flowering herbs.

Mountain/Alpine
Very low night-time temperatures. Only a few dwarf trees and small leafed shrubs can grow.

Mediterranean
Mild winters and dry summers. Vegetation is mixed shrubs and herbaceous plants.

Savanna grassland
Warm or hot climate.
Tropical grasslands with scattered thorn bushes or trees.

Temperate grassland
Grassland is the main vegetation. Summers are hot and winters cold.

Desert
Hot with little rainfall.
Very sparse vegetation except cacti and grasses adapted to the harsh conditions.

Boreal/Taiga forest
Found between 50° and 70°N. Low temperatures.
Cold-tolerant evergreen conifers.

Coniferous forest
Dense forests of pine, spruce and larch.

Mixed forest
Broadleaf and coniferous forests.

Tropical forest
Dense rainforest found in areas of high rainfall near the equator.

Dry tropical forest
Semi deciduous trees with low shrubs and bushes.

Sub tropical forest
Rainfall is seasonal. Mainly hard leaf evergreen forest.

Monsoon forest
Areas which experience Monsoon rain. All trees are deciduous.

Arctic tundra in Alaska.

Taiga forest in Siberia, Russia.

Savanna grassland in Tanzania, Africa.

The Sahara desert in Morocco, Africa.

Earthquakes and volcanoes

- ● Earthquake
- ▲ Volcano
- —— Plate boundary
- ←→ Direction of movement

Floods

- ⌇ Rivers that experience major flooding
- ▨ Country affected annually by severe flooding
- 💧 Severe floods causing over 1000 deaths in 1 year (1985–2015)
- 💧 Severe floods causing 500–1000 deaths in 1 year (1985–2015)

Plates

The earth's crust is broken into huge plates which fit together like parts of a giant jigsaw. These float on the semi-molten rock below. The boundaries of the plates are marked by lines of volcanoes and earthquake activity.

Diverging plates

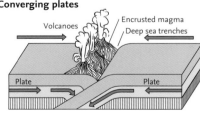

Diverging convection currents

Converging plates

Converging convection currents

Shearing plates

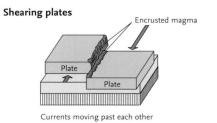

Currents moving past each other

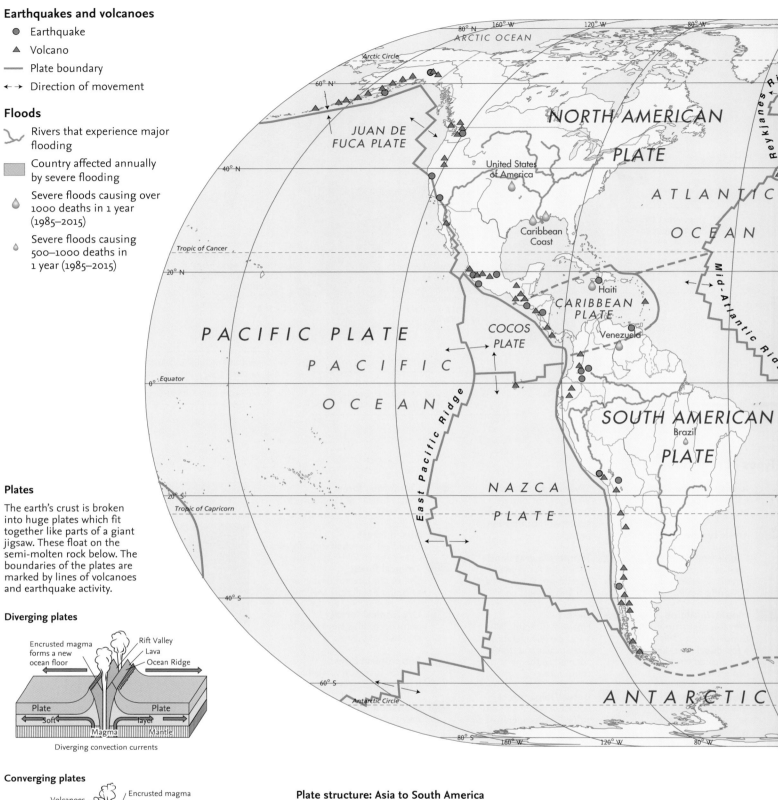

Plate structure: Asia to South America

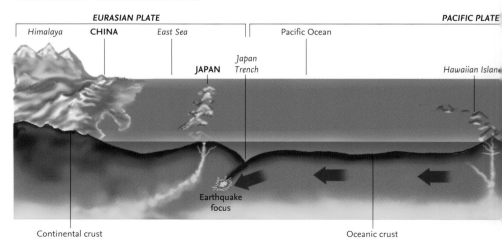

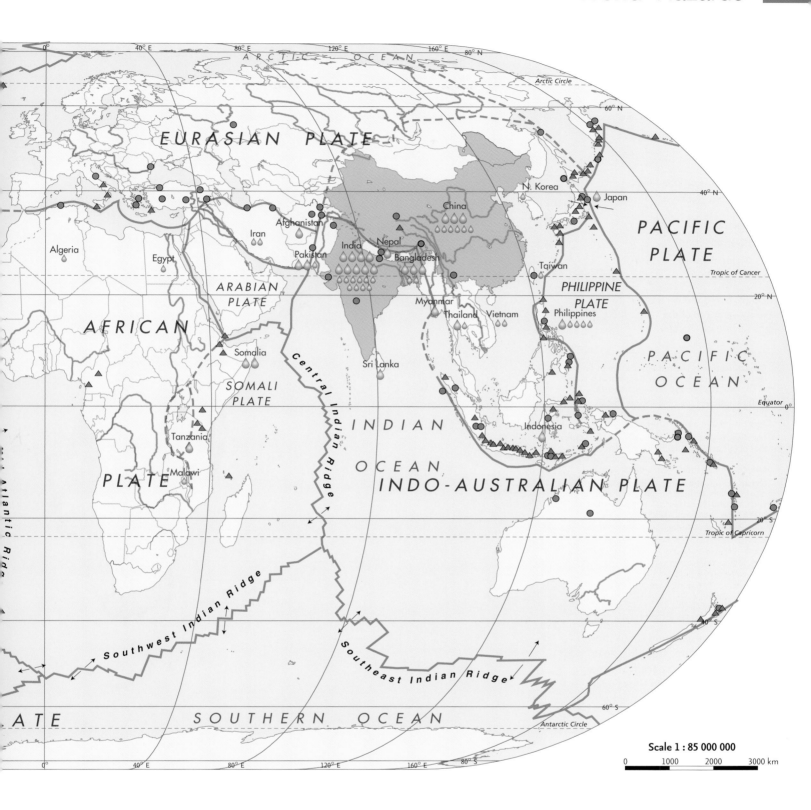

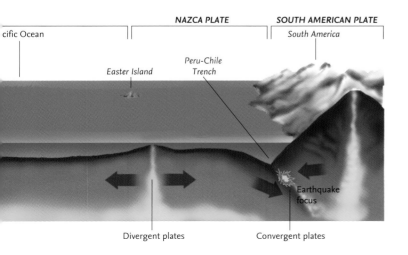

Divergent plates   Convergent plates

Earthquakes

Earthquakes occur most frequently along the junction of plates which make up the earth's crust.
They are caused by the release of stress which builds up at the plate edges. When shock waves from these movements reach the surface they are felt as earthquakes which may result in severe damage to property or loss of lives.

Volcanoes

The greatest number of volcanoes are located in the Pacific 'Ring of Fire'. Violent eruptions often occur when two plates collide and the heat generated forces molten rock (magma) upwards through weaknesses in the earth's crust.

See pages 16–17 for more on earthquakes and volcanoes in the Caribbean.

Desertification

- Existing deserts
- Areas at risk of desertification

Deforestation

- Existing tropical forests
- Forests cleared since 1940

Forest fires

- Recent major forest fires

Pollution

- Coastal pollution
- River pollution
- Major city with air pollution

The pink-boxed text on the map shows some of the signs of climate change.

Desertification is the transformation of fertile land into an arid or semi-arid region as a result of climatic change and human activities.

Deforestation is the clearance of forests so that the land can be used for other purposes – usually agriculture, but also urban expansion.

Forests are also lost through repeated **forest fires** that occur accidentally. These are also called wildfires or bushfires, and occur most often in forested regions that have a dry season.

Ocean acidification, due to increasing carbon dioxide levels, reduces the ability of marine life, such as coral, to extract calcium carbonate to make their shells and skeletons.

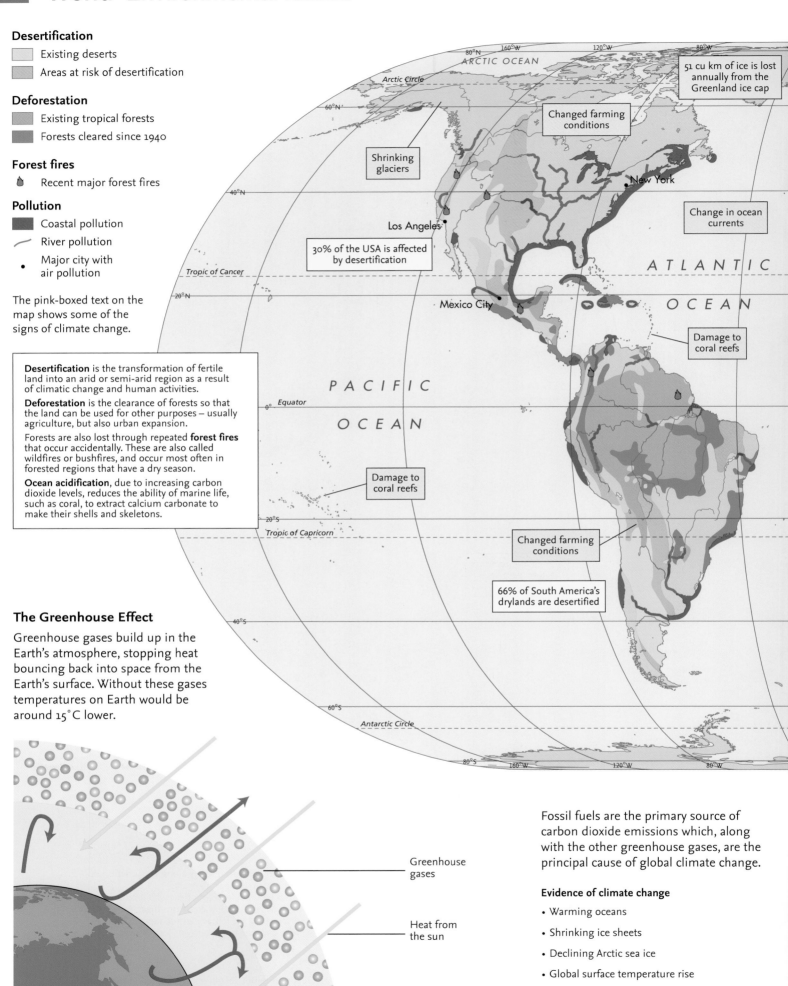

51 cu km of ice is lost annually from the Greenland ice cap

Changed farming conditions

Shrinking glaciers

New York

Change in ocean currents

Los Angeles

30% of the USA is affected by desertification

Mexico City

Damage to coral reefs

PACIFIC OCEAN

ATLANTIC OCEAN

Damage to coral reefs

Changed farming conditions

66% of South America's drylands are desertified

The Greenhouse Effect

Greenhouse gases build up in the Earth's atmosphere, stopping heat bouncing back into space from the Earth's surface. Without these gases temperatures on Earth would be around 15°C lower.

Greenhouse gases

Heat from the sun

Heat from the Earth

Fossil fuels are the primary source of carbon dioxide emissions which, along with the other greenhouse gases, are the principal cause of global climate change.

Evidence of climate change

- Warming oceans
- Shrinking ice sheets
- Declining Arctic sea ice
- Global surface temperature rise
- Sea level rise
- Retreating glaciers
- Ocean acidification
- Extreme events

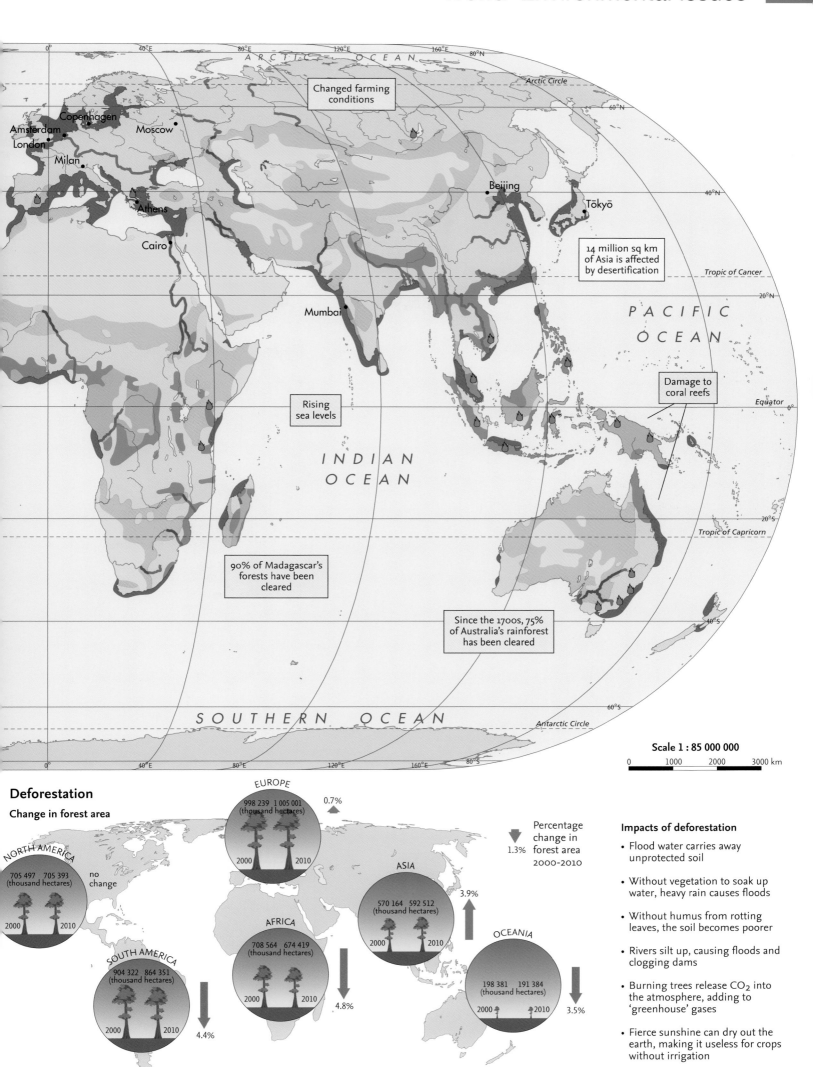

Changed farming
conditions

14 million sq km
of Asia is affected
by desertification

Damage to
coral reefs

Rising
sea levels

90% of Madagascar's
forests have been
cleared

Since the 1700s, 75%
of Australia's rainforest
has been cleared

Scale 1 : 85 000 000

0   1000   2000   3000 km

Deforestation

Change in forest area

EUROPE
998 239   1 005 001
(thousand hectares)
0.7%
2000   2010

Percentage
change in
forest area
1.3% 2000-2010

ASIA
570 164   592 512
(thousand hectares)
3.9%
2000   2010

NORTH AMERICA
705 497   705 393
(thousand hectares)
no
change
2000   2010

AFRICA
708 564   674 419
(thousand hectares)
2000   2010
4.8%

OCEANIA
198 381   191 384
(thousand hectares)
2000   2010
3.5%

SOUTH AMERICA
904 322   864 351
(thousand hectares)
2000   2010
4.4%

Impacts of deforestation

- Flood water carries away
  unprotected soil

- Without vegetation to soak up
  water, heavy rain causes floods

- Without humus from rotting
  leaves, the soil becomes poorer

- Rivers silt up, causing floods and
  clogging dams

- Burning trees release CO_2 into
  the atmosphere, adding to
  'greenhouse' gases

- Fierce sunshine can dry out the
  earth, making it useless for crops
  without irrigation

City populations (2015)

- ● over 15 000 000
- ● 10 000 000 – 15 000 000
- ● 5 000 000 – 10 000 000
- · 1 000 000 – 5 000 000

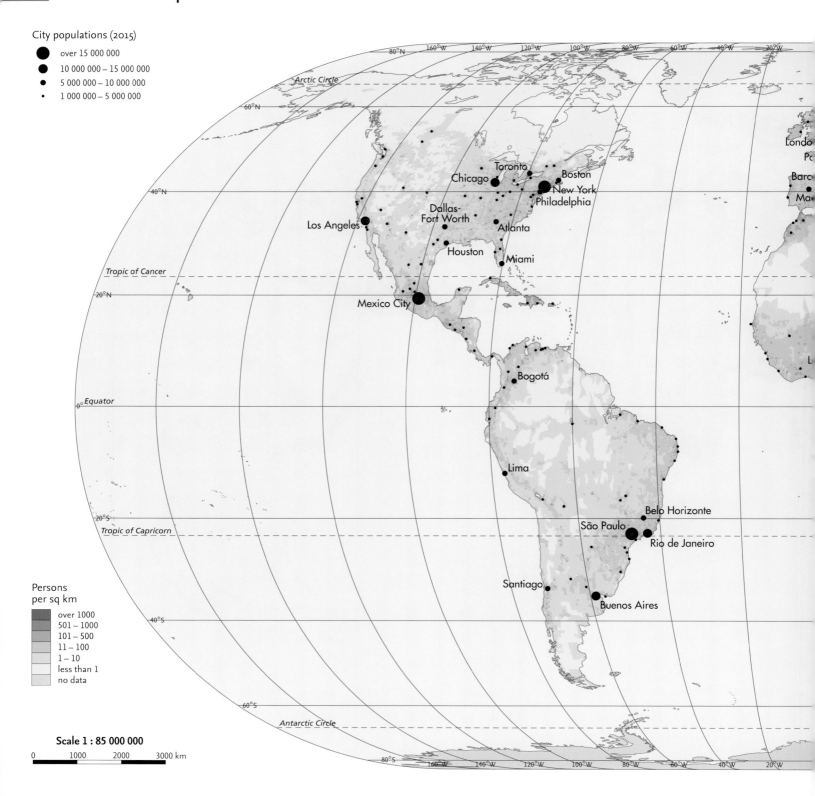

Persons
per sq km

- over 1000
- 501 – 1000
- 101 – 500
- 11 – 100
- 1 – 10
- less than 1
- no data

Scale 1 : 85 000 000

0   1000   2000   3000 km

World population distribution by continent

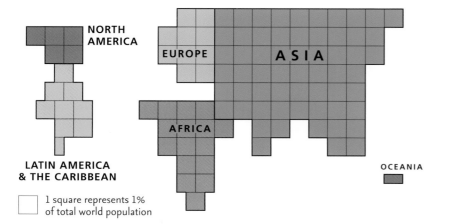

NORTH
AMERICA

EUROPE

A S I A

AFRICA

LATIN AMERICA
& THE CARIBBEAN

OCEANIA

☐ 1 square represents 1%
of total world population

Facts about world population

World population, 2015	7 349 472 000
World population, 2050*	9 725 148 000
Population 60 years and over, 2015	14.0%
Population 60 years and over, 2050*	26.0%
Population under 15 years, 2015	26.1%
Population under 15 years, 2050*	21.3%
Life expectancy, 2015-2020*	72
Male life expectancy, 2015-2020*	69
Female life expectancy, 2015-2020*	74

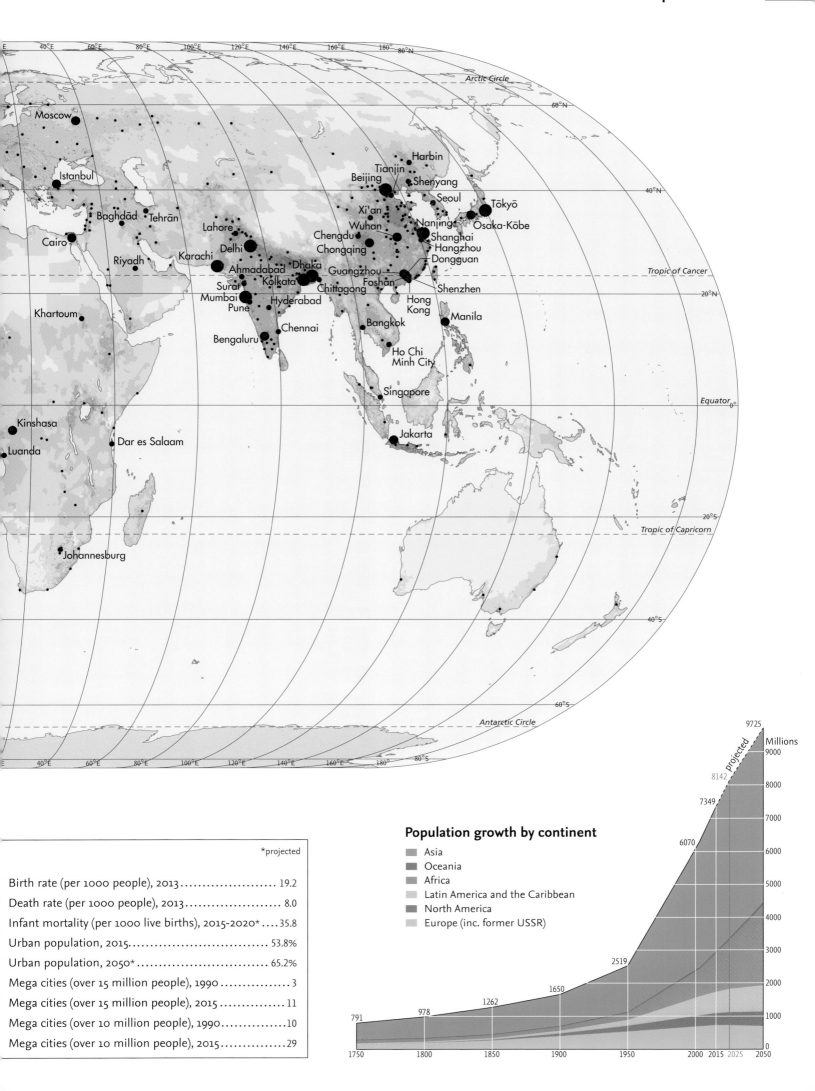

Moscow
Istanbul
Baghdād · Tehrān
Cairo
Riyadh
Khartoum
Kinshasa
Luanda
Dar es Salaam
Johannesburg

Harbin
Tianjin
Beijing · Shenyang
Seoul
Tōkyō
Xi'an
Wuhan
Nanjing
Ōsaka-Kōbe
Chengdu
Shanghai
Chongqing
Hangzhou
Dongguan
Lahore
Guangzhou
Delhi
Ahmadabad · Dhaka
Foshan
Shenzhen
Surat · Kolkata
Chittagong
Mumbai
Hyderabad
Hong Kong
Pune
Manila
Chennai
Bangkok
Bengaluru
Ho Chi Minh City
Singapore
Jakarta
Karachi

Arctic Circle
60°N
40°N
Tropic of Cancer
20°N
Equator 0°
20°S
Tropic of Capricorn
40°S
60°S
Antarctic Circle

40°E 60°E 80°E 100°E 120°E 140°E 160°E 180° 80°N

	*projected
Birth rate (per 1000 people), 2013	19.2
Death rate (per 1000 people), 2013	8.0
Infant mortality (per 1000 live births), 2015-2020*	35.8
Urban population, 2015	53.8%
Urban population, 2050*	65.2%
Mega cities (over 15 million people), 1990	3
Mega cities (over 15 million people), 2015	11
Mega cities (over 10 million people), 1990	10
Mega cities (over 10 million people), 2015	29

Population growth by continent

- Asia
- Oceania
- Africa
- Latin America and the Caribbean
- North America
- Europe (inc. former USSR)

9725
projected
8142
7349
6070
2519
1650
1262
978
791

Millions
9000
8000
7000
6000
5000
4000
3000
2000
1000
0

1750 1800 1850 1900 1950 2000 2015 2025 2050

Flag	Country	Capital city	Area sq km	Total population 2015[†]
	Afghanistan	Kābul	652 225	32 527 000
	Albania	Tirana	28 748	2 897 000
	Algeria	Algiers	2 381 741	39 667 000
	Andorra	Andorra la Vella	465	70 000
	Angola	Luanda	1 246 700	25 022 000
	Antigua & Barbuda	St John's	442	81 799
	Argentina	Buenos Aires	2 766 889	43 417 000
	Armenia	Yerevan	29 800	3 018 000
	Australia	Canberra	7 692 024	23 969 000
	Austria	Vienna	83 855	8 545 000
	Azerbaijan	Baku	86 600	9 754 000
	Bahamas, The	Nassau	13 939	353 658
	Bahrain	Manama	691	1 377 000
	Bangladesh	Dhaka	143 998	160 996 000
	Barbados	Bridgetown	430	277 821
	Belarus	Minsk	207 600	9 496 000
	Belgium	Brussels	30 520	11 299 000
	Belize	Belmopan	22 965	312 971
	Benin	Porto-Novo	112 620	10 880 000
	Bhutan	Thimphu	46 620	775 000
	Bolivia	La Paz/Sucre	1 098 581	10 725 000
	Bosnia and Herzegovina	Sarajevo	51 130	3 810 000
	Botswana	Gaborone	581 370	2 262 000
	Brazil	Brasília	8 514 879	207 848 000
	Brunei	Bandar Seri Begawan	5 765	423 000
	Bulgaria	Sofia	110 994	7 150 000
	Burkina Faso	Ouagadougou	274 200	18 106 000
	Burundi	Bujumbura	27 835	11 179 000
	Cambodia	Phnom Penh	181 035	15 578 000
	Cameroon	Yaoundé	475 442	23 344 000
	Canada	Ottawa	9 984 670	35 940 000
	Cape Verde	Praia	4 033	521 000
	Central African Republic	Bangui	622 436	4 900 000
	Chad	Ndjamena	1 284 000	14 037 000
	Chile	Santiago	756 945	17 948 000
	China	Beijing	9 606 802	1 383 925 000
	Colombia	Bogotá	1 141 748	48 229 000
	Comoros	Moroni	1 862	788 000
	Congo	Brazzaville	342 000	4 620 000
	Congo, Dem. Rep. of the	Kinshasa	2 345 410	77 267 000
	Costa Rica	San José	51 100	4 808 000
	Côte d'Ivoire	Yamoussoukro	322 463	22 702 000
	Croatia	Zagreb	56 538	4 240 000
	Cuba	Havana	110 860	11 167 325
	Cyprus	Nicosia	9 251	1 165 000
	Czechia	Prague	78 864	10 543 000
	Denmark	Copenhagen	43 075	5 669 000
	Djibouti	Djibouti	23 200	888 000
	Dominica	Roseau	750	71 293

[†] or latest data available

Flag	Country	Capital city	Area sq km	Total population 2015
	Dominican Republic	Santo Domingo	48 442	9 445
	East Timor	Dili	14 874	1 185
	Ecuador	Quito	272 045	16 144
	Egypt	Cairo	1 001 450	91 508
	El Salvador	San Salvador	21 041	6 127
	Equatorial Guinea	Malabo	28 051	845
	Eritrea	Asmara	117 400	5 228
	Estonia	Tallinn	45 200	1 313
	Eswatini (Swaziland)	Mbabane/Lobamba	17 364	1 287
	Ethiopia	Addis Ababa	1 133 880	99 391
	Fiji	Suva	18 330	892
	Finland	Helsinki	338 145	5 503
	France	Paris	543 965	64 395
	French Guiana	Cayenne	90 000	269
	Gabon	Libreville	267 667	1 725
	Gambia, The	Banjul	11 295	1 991
	Georgia	Tbilisi	69 700	4 000
	Germany	Berlin	357 022	80 689
	Ghana	Accra	238 537	27 410
	Greece	Athens	131 957	10 955
	Grenada	St George's	348	103
	Guatemala	Guatemala City	108 890	16 343
	Guinea	Conakry	245 857	12 609
	Guinea-Bissau	Bissau	36 125	1 844
	Guyana	Georgetown	214 969	747
	Haiti	Port-au-Prince	27 750	10 320
	Honduras	Tegucigalpa	112 088	8 075
	Hungary	Budapest	93 030	9 855
	Iceland	Reykjavík	102 820	329
	India	New Delhi	3 166 620	1 311 051
	Indonesia	Jakarta	1 919 445	257 564
	Iran	Tehrān	1 648 000	79 109
	Iraq	Baghdād	438 317	36 423
	Ireland	Dublin	70 282	4 688
	Israel	Jerusalem*	22 072	8 064
	Italy	Rome	301 245	59 798
	Jamaica	Kingston	10 991	2 730
	Japan	Tōkyō	377 727	126 573
	Jordan	'Ammān	89 206	7 595
	Kazakhstan	Astana	2 717 300	17 625
	Kenya	Nairobi	582 646	46 050
	Kiribati	Bairiki	717	112
	Kosovo	Pristina	10 908	1 805
	Kuwait	Kuwait	17 818	3 892
	Kyrgyzstan	Bishkek	198 500	5 940
	Laos	Vientiane	236 800	6 802
	Latvia	Rīga	64 589	1 971
	Lebanon	Beirut	10 452	5 851
	Lesotho	Maseru	30 355	2 135

* disputed cap

Flag	Country	Capital city	Area sq km	Total population 2015[†]
	Liberia	Monrovia	111 369	4 503 000
	Libya	Tripoli	1 759 540	6 278 000
	Liechtenstein	Vaduz	160	38 000
	Lithuania	Vilnius	65 200	2 878 000
	Luxembourg	Luxembourg	2 586	567 000
	Madagascar	Antananarivo	587 041	24 235 000
	Malawi	Lilongwe	118 484	17 215 000
	Malaysia	Kuala Lumpur/Putrajaya	332 965	30 331 000
	Maldives	Male	298	364 000
	Mali	Bamako	1 240 140	17 600 000
	Malta	Valletta	316	419 000
	Marshall Islands	Dalap-Uliga-Darrit	181	53 000
	Mauritania	Nouakchott	1 030 700	4 068 000
	Mauritius	Port Louis	2 040	1 273 000
	Mexico	Mexico City	1 972 545	127 017 000
	Micronesia, Fed. States of	Palikir	701	526 000
	Moldova	Chişinău	33 700	4 069 000
	Mongolia	Ulan Bator	1 565 000	2 959 000
	Montenegro	Podgorica	13 812	626 000
	Morocco	Rabat	446 550	34 378 000
	Mozambique	Maputo	799 380	27 978 000
	Myanmar	Nay Pyi Taw	676 577	53 897 000
	Namibia	Windhoek	824 292	2 459 000
	Nauru	Yaren	21	10 000
	Nepal	Kathmandu	147 181	28 514 000
	Netherlands	Amsterdam/The Hague	41 526	16 925 000
	New Zealand	Wellington	270 534	4 529 000
	Nicaragua	Managua	130 000	6 082 000
	Niger	Niamey	1 267 000	19 899 000
	Nigeria	Abuja	923 768	182 202 000
	North Korea	Pyongyang	120 538	25 155 000
	North Macedonia	Skopje	25 713	2 078 000
	Norway	Oslo	323 878	5 211 000
	Oman	Muscat	309 500	4 491 000
	Pakistan	Islamabad	881 888	188 925 000
	Palau	Ngerulmud	497	21 000
	Panama	Panama City	77 082	3 929 000
	Papua New Guinea	Port Moresby	462 840	7 619 000
	Paraguay	Asunción	406 752	6 639 000
	Peru	Lima	1 285 216	31 377 000
	Philippines	Manila	300 000	100 699 000
	Poland	Warsaw	312 683	38 612 000
	Portugal	Lisbon	88 940	10 350 000
	Puerto Rico	San Juan	9 104	3 725 789
	Qatar	Doha	11 437	2 235 000
	Romania	Bucharest	237 500	19 511 000
	Russia	Moscow	17 075 400	143 457 000
	Rwanda	Kigali	26 338	11 610 000
	St Kitts & Nevis	Basseterre	261	54 940

Flag	Country	Capital city	Area sq km	Total population 2015[†]
	St Lucia	Castries	617	173 765
	St Vincent & the Grenadines	Kingstown	389	109 991
	Samoa	Apia	2 831	193 000
	San Marino	San Marino	61	32 000
	São Tomé & Príncipe	São Tomé	964	190 000
	Saudi Arabia	Riyadh	2 200 000	31 540 000
	Senegal	Dakar	196 720	15 129 000
	Serbia	Belgrade	77 453	7 046 000
	Seychelles	Victoria	455	96 000
	Sierra Leone	Freetown	71 740	6 453 000
	Singapore	Singapore	639	5 604 000
	Slovakia	Bratislava	49 035	5 426 000
	Slovenia	Ljubljana	20 251	2 068 000
	Solomon Islands	Honiara	28 370	584 000
	Somalia	Mogadishu	637 657	10 787 000
	South Africa	Pretoria/Cape Town/Bloemfontein	1 219 090	54 490 000
	South Korea	Seoul	99 274	50 293 000
	South Sudan	Juba	644 329	12 340 000
	Spain	Madrid	504 782	46 122 000
	Sri Lanka	Sri Jayewardenepura Kotte	65 610	20 715 000
	Sudan	Khartoum	1 861 484	40 235 000
	Suriname	Paramaribo	163 820	543 000
	Sweden	Stockholm	449 964	9 779 000
	Switzerland	Bern	41 293	8 299 000
	Syria	Damascus	184 026	18 502 000
	Taiwan	Taipei	36 179	23 462 000
	Tajikistan	Dushanbe	143 100	8 482 000
	Tanzania	Dodoma	945 087	53 470 000
	Thailand	Bangkok	513 115	67 959 000
	Togo	Lomé	56 785	7 305 000
	Tonga	Nuku'alofa	748	106 000
	Trinidad & Tobago	Port of Spain	5 128	1 328 019
	Tunisia	Tunis	164 150	11 254 000
	Turkey	Ankara	779 452	78 666 000
	Turkmenistan	Ashgabat	488 100	5 374 000
	Tuvalu	Vaiaku	25	10 000
	Uganda	Kampala	241 038	39 032 000
	Ukraine	Kyiv	603 700	44 824 000
	United Arab Emirates	Abu Dhabi	77 700	9 157 000
	United Kingdom	London	243 609	64 716 000
	United States of America	Washington D.C.	9 826 635	321 774 000
	Uruguay	Montevideo	176 215	3 432 000
	Uzbekistan	Tashkent	447 400	29 893 000
	Vanuatu	Port Vila	12 190	265 000
	Venezuela	Caracas	912 050	31 108 000
	Vietnam	Hanoi	329 565	93 448 000
	Yemen	Sanaa	527 968	26 832 000
	Zambia	Lusaka	752 614	16 212 000
	Zimbabwe	Harare	390 759	15 603 000

The important names on the maps in the atlas are found in the index. The names are listed in alphabetical order. Each entry gives the country or region of the world in which the name is located followed by the page number, its grid reference and then its co-ordinates of latitude and longitude. Names of very large areas may have these co-ordinates omitted. Area names which are included in the index are referenced to the centre of the feature. In the case of rivers, the mouth or confluence is taken as the point of reference. It is therefore necessary to follow the river upstream from this point to find its name on the map.

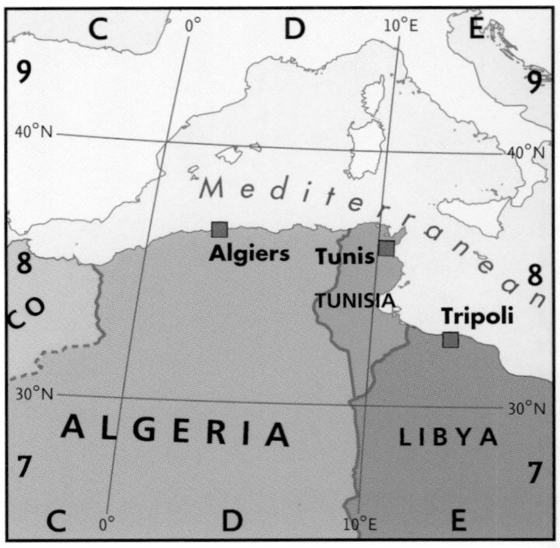

On the map of part of Africa to the right, Algiers is found in grid square D8 at latitude 36°50'N, longitude 3°00'E. This appears in the index as **Algiers** Algeria **82 D8** 36.50N 3.00E

The chart below explains all the elements listed for each entry:

Algiers	Algeria	82	D8	36.50N	3.00E
Name of the feature to be located.	Name of the country in which the feature is situated.	Page in the atlas where the feature is shown.	Grid square where the feature is found.	Degrees and minutes north or south of the equator.	Degrees and minutes east or west of Greenwich meridian.

Some abbreviations have been used in the index; these are listed below:

A&B	Antigua and Barbuda	Is.	Islands	r.	river
Austa.	Australasia	Jam.	Jamaica	*resr.*	reservoir
b.	bay	*l.*	lake	S. Africa	South Africa
c.	cape	*mtn.*	mountain	S. America	South America
C. America	Central America	*mts.*	mountains	StK&N	St Kitts and Nevis
cy.	county	N. America	North America	StV&G	St Vincent and the Grenadines
des.	desert	Oc.	Ocean	*str.*	strait
Dom. Rep.	Dominican Republic	*p.*	parish	T&C Is.	Turks and Caicos Islands
f.	physical feature e.g. valley, plain	*pen.*	peninsula	T&T	Trinidad and Tobago
g.	gulf	P.N.G.	Papua New Guinea	U.K.	United Kingdom
i.	island	*pt.*	point	U.S.A.	United States of America

Parishes of Jamaica:

AN	S Ann	KN	Kingston
AW	St Andrew	MR	Manchester
CE	St Catherine	MY	St Mary
CN	Clarendon	PD	Portland
EH	St Elizabeth	TS	St Thomas
HR	Hanover	TY	Trelawny
JS	St James	WD	Westmoreland

A

Aberdeen EH Jam. **29 D2** 18.12N 77.42W
Abidjan Côte d'Ivoire **82 C5** 5.19N 4.01W
Above Rocks *town* CE Jam. **30 C3** 18.06N 76.52W
Abuja Nigeria **82 D5** 9.12N 7.11E
Accompong EH Jam. **29 C2** 18.14N 77.45W
Accra Ghana **82 C5** 5.33N 0.15W
Acklins Island The Bahamas **46 G3** 22.26N 73.52W
Aconcagua, Cerro *mtn.* Argentina **79 C3** 32.37S 70.00W
Addis Ababa Ethiopia **82 G5** 9.03N 38.42E
Adelaide Australia **90 C2** 34.56S 138.36E
Adelphi JS Jam. **28 C3** 18.27N 77.48W
Adriatic Sea Europe **87 F4** 44.19N 13.24E
Aenon Town CN Jam. **29 E2** 18.13N 77.24W
Afghanistan Asia **88 F5** 33.00N 65.30E
Africa 82-83
Aguadilla Puerto Rico **51 A2** 18.27N 67.10W
Agulhas, Cape S. Africa **83 F1** 34.50S 20.03E
Ahaggar *f.* Algeria **83 D7** 23.10N 4.23E
Airy Castle *town* TS Jam. **31 E2** 17.55N 76.21W
Aishalton Guyana **70 B2** 2.32N 59.07W
Albania Europe **86 F4** 41.00N 20.00E
Albany MY Jam. **30 C4** 18.18N 76.51W
Albany WD Jam. **28 B3** 18.16N 78.13W
Albert Town TY Jam. **29 D3** 18.18N 77.33W
Albion AN Jam. **30 B4** 18.19N 77.13W
Albion MR Jam. **29 E2** 18.00N 77.30W
Albion TS Jam. **31 D2** 17.53N 76.36W
Albion *hill* AN Jam. **30 B4** 18.20N 77.14W
Aldabra Islands Seychelles **83 H4** 9.16S 46.30E
Alexandria Egypt **82 F8** 31.13N 29.55E
Alexandria AN Jam. **29 E3** 18.18N 77.21W
Alexandria HR Jam. **28 B3** 18.21N 78.01W
Algeria Africa **82 D7** 28.00N 2.00E
Algiers Algeria **82 D8** 36.50N 3.00E
Alice Springs Australia **90 C2** 23.42S 133.52E
Alligator Church PD Jam. **31 E3** 18.05N 76.27W
Alligator Pond *town* MR Jam. **29 D1** 17.52N 77.34W
Alligator Pond Bay MR/EH Jam. **29 D1** 17.51N 77.34W
All Saints A&B **54 B2** 17.04N 61.46W
Alma WD Jam. **28 B3** 18.18N 78.12W
Almaty Kazakhstan **88 G5** 43.16N 77.01E
Alps *mts.* Europe **87 E4** 46.00N 7.30E
Alston CN Jam. **29 E2** 18.11N 77.26W
Altai Mountains Mongolia **89 G6** 46.30N 90.00E
Altiplano *f.* Bolivia **79 D5** 16.24S 68.39W
Alva AN Jam. **29 E3** 18.18N 77.19W
Amazon *r.* Brazil **79 E6** 2.00S 50.00W
Amazon, Mouths of the Brazil **79 F7** 0.41N 49.28W
Ambergris Caye *i.* Belize **72 D6** 18.02N 87.58W
Amity Cross WD Jam. **28 B3** 18.15N 78.06W
Amity Hall JS Jam. **28 C3** 18.24N 77.49W
Amity Hall TS Jam. **31 E2** 17.57N 76.15W
Amman Jordan **93 K7** 31.57N 35.56E
Amsterdam Netherlands **86 E5** 52.22N 4.54E
Amuku Mountains Guyana **70 B1** 1.50N 58.20W
Amur *r.* Russia **89 K6** 53.17N 140.37E
Anchovy JS Jam. **28 C3** 18.25N 77.56W
Andes *mts.* S. America **79 C5** 15.00S 74.00W
Andorra Europe **86 E4** 42.30N 1.32E
Andorra la Vella Andorra **86 E4** 42.31N 1.32E
Andros *is.* The Bahamas **46 B5** 24.38N 78.00W
Anegada *i.* British Virgin Is. **52 C3** 18.45N 64.22W
Angels CE Jam. **30 C3** 18.01N 76.58W
Angola Africa **82 E3** 12.00S 18.00E
Anguilla *i.* **52 F2** 18.13N 63.02W
Ankara Turkey **88 D5** 39.55N 32.50E
Annapurna *mtn.* Nepal **89 G4** 28.34N 83.49E
Anna Regina Guyana **70 B4** 7.15N 58.27W
Annotto Bay MY Jam. **30 C4** 18.17N 76.47W
Annotto Bay *town* MY Jam. **30 C4** 18.16N 76.46W
Anse De Mai Dominica **56 A5** 15.35N 61.23W
Anse-la-Raye St Lucia **57 A2** 13.56N 61.03W
Antananarivo Madagascar **82 H3** 18.52S 47.30E
Antarctica 95
Antigua and Barbuda 54
Apennines *mts.* Italy **87 F4** 44.37N 10.47E
Apia Samoa **90 F3** 13.50S 171.44W
Appalachian Mountains U.S.A. **75 L6** 39.30N 78.00W
Appleton EH Jam. **29 D2** 18.10N 77.44W
Arabian Peninsula Asia **89 D4** 24.00N 45.00E
Arabian Sea Asia **89 F4** 19.00N 65.00E
Arafura Sea Australia/Indonesia **91 C3** 9.04S 132.58E
Aral Sea Kazakhstan/Uzbekistan **89 F6** 45.07N 60.05E
Arctic Ocean 94 B9 78.00N 145.00W
Arecibo Puerto Rico **51 B2** 18.29N 66.44W
Argentina S. America **78 D3** 35.00S 65.00W
Arima T&T **63 C3** 10.38N 61.17W
Aripo, Mount T&T **63 D3** 10.43N 61.15W
Armenia Asia **88 D5** 40.00N 45.00E
Arnhem Land *f.* Australia **91 C3** 13.26S 133.57E
Arntully TS Jam. **31 D3** 18.01N 76.36W
Arouca T&T **63 C3** 10.38N 61.20W
Arthurs Seat CN Jam. **30 B3** 18.08N 77.13W
Aruba *i.* **62 B2** 12.30N 69.58W
Ashgabat Turkmenistan **88 E5** 37.53N 58.21E
Asia 88-89
Askenish HR Jam. **28 B3** 18.23N 78.09W
Asmara Eritrea **82 G6** 15.20N 38.58E
Astana Kazakhstan **88 F6** 51.09N 71.27E
Asunción Paraguay **78 E4** 25.15S 57.40W
Atacama Desert Chile **79 D4** 26.13S 69.39W
Athens Greece **86 G3** 37.59N 23.42E
Atlantic Ocean 94 G7
Atlas Mountains Africa **83 C8** 33.00N 4.00W
Auchindown WD Jam. **28 C2** 18.07N 77.59W
Auchtembeddie MR Jam. **29 D2** 18.13N 77.37W
Auckland New Zealand **90 E2** 36.52S 174.45E
Augier St Lucia **57 B1** 13.46N 60.59W
August Town AW Jam. **31 D2** 18.00N 76.44W
Aurora Guyana **70 B4** 6.46N 59.45W
Australia Austa. **90 C2** 25.00S 135.00E
Austria Europe **86 F4** 47.30N 14.00E
Axe And Adze HR Jam. **28 B3** 18.22N 78.02W
Azerbaijan Asia **88 E5** 40.10N 47.50E

B

Bachelors Hall TS Jam. **31 E2** 17.57N 76.19W
Back Rio Grande *r.* PD Jam. **31 E3** 18.07N 76.28W
Baffin Bay *sea* Canada/Greenland **75 M10** 72.51N 66.20W
Baffin Island Canada **75 L9** 68.50N 70.00W
Baghdād Iraq **88 D5** 33.20N 44.26E
Bahrain Asia **88 E4** 26.00N 50.35E
Baikal, Lake Russia **89 I6** 53.30N 108.00E
Baileys Vale *town* MY Jam. **30 C4** 18.21N 76.55W
Bairiki Kiribati **90 E4** 1.21N 172.57E
Baku Azerbaijan **93 L8** 40.22N 49.53E
Balaclava EH Jam. **29 D2** 18.10N 77.39W
Baldwins *r.* CN Jam. **29 E1** 17.54N 77.20W
Balkan Mountains Bulgaria/Serbia **87 G4** 43.23N 22.47E
Balkhash, Lake Kazakhstan **89 F6** 46.51N 75.00E
Ballards Valley *town* EH Jam. **29 D1** 17.54N 77.37W
Baltic Sea *g.* Europe **87 F5** 55.28N 16.46E
Bamako Mali **82 C6** 12.40N 7.59W
Bamboo AN Jam. **29 E3** 18.23N 77.16W
Banana Ground MR Jam. **29 E2** 18.05N 77.26W
Banbury WD Jam. **28 B3** 18.16N 78.07W
Bangkok Thailand **88 H3** 13.45N 100.35E
Bangladesh Asia **88 G4** 24.00N 90.00E
Bangui Central African Republic **82 E5** 4.23N 18.37E
Banjul The Gambia **82 B6** 13.27N 16.36W
Banks CN Jam. **29 E1** 17.50N 77.19W
Bannister CE Jam. **30 B2** 17.58N 77.07W
Baptist EH Jam. **28 C2** 18.05N 77.51W
Baracoa Cuba **48 F2** 20.23N 74.31W
Barama *r.* Guyana **70 B4** 7.40N 59.15W
Barbados 60
Barbecue Bottom TY Jam. **29 D3** 18.22N 77.33W
Barcelona Spain **86 E4** 41.25N 2.10E
Barents Sea Arctic Oc. **87 H7** 73.00N 40.00E
Barima *r.* Guyana **70 B5** 8.16N 59.43W
Barkly Tableland *f.* Australia **91 C3** 18.06S 135.25E
Barranquilla Venezuela **78 C8** 11.00N 74.50W
Barrett Town JS Jam. **28 C4** 18.31N 77.48W
Barrouallie StV&G **58 A2** 13.14N 61.16W
Bartica Guyana **70 B4** 6.22N 58.37W
Bartons CE Jam. **30 B3** 18.02N 77.08W
Basse-Terre *i.* Guadeloupe **55 A2** 16.10N 61.43W
Basse-Terre *town* Guadeloupe **55 A1** 16.00N 61.45W
Basseterre StK&N **53 B4** 17.17N 62.43W
Bass Strait Australia **91 D2** 39.43S 146.11E
Bath TS Jam. **31 E2** 17.57N 76.21W
Bayamo Cuba **48 E2** 20.23N 76.39W
Bayamón Puerto Rico **51 B2** 18.24N 66.10W
Bay Road WD Jam. **28 B2** 18.14N 78.12W
Beckford Kraal CN Jam. **29 E2** 18.05N 77.19W
Beecher Town AN Jam. **30 B4** 18.22N 77.07W
Beeston Spring *town* WD Jam. **28 C2** 18.09N 77.58W
Beijing China **88 I5** 39.55N 116.25E
Belair Barbados **60 B2** 13.09N 59.33W
Belarus Europe **86 G5** 53.00N 28.00E
Belfast U.K. **86 D5** 54.36N 5.57W
Belfield MY Jam. **30 C4** 18.16N 76.51W
Belgium Europe **86 E5** 51.00N 4.30E
Belgrade Serbia **86 G4** 44.49N 20.28E
Belize 72
Belize *r.* Belize **72 C5** 17.30N 88.12W
Belize City Belize **72 C4** 17.30N 88.12W
Bellas Gate CE Jam. **30 B3** 18.03N 77.09W
Bellefield MR Jam. **29 E2** 18.05N 77.27W
Belleplaine Barbados **60 B3** 13.14N 59.33W
Bellevue EH Jam. **29 D1** 17.54N 77.40W
Belmont WD Jam. **28 B2** 18.09N 78.02W
Belmont Point WD Jam. **28 B2** 18.09N 78.02W
Belmopan Belize **72 B4** 17.15N 88.46W
Belo Horizonte Brazil **78 F4** 19.45S 43.53W
Belvedere PD Jam. **31 D3** 18.13N 76.42W
Belvedere TS Jam. **31 E2** 17.53N 76.26W
Belvedere Point TS Jam. **31 E2** 17.52N 76.26W
Benbow CE Jam. **30 B3** 18.14N 77.01W
Bengal, Bay of Indian Oc. **89 G4** 17.00N 89.00E
Benin Africa **82 D5** 9.00N 2.30E
Benin, Bight of *g.* Africa **83 D5** 5.17N 3.27E
Bensonton AN Jam. **30 B3** 18.15N 77.13W
Benue *r.* Nigeria **83 D5** 7.49N 6.48E
Bequia *i.* StV&G **58 D5** 13.00N 61.17W
Berbice *r.* Guyana **70 C4** 6.17N 57.30W
Berekua Dominica **56 B3** 15.14N 61.19W
Bering Sea N. America/Asia **89 N6** 60.00N 170.00W
Berkshire MR Jam. **29 D1** 17.58N 77.33W
Berlin Germany **86 F5** 52.32N 13.25E
Bermaddy CE Jam. **30 B3** 18.12N 77.03W
Bermuda *i.* Atlantic Oc. **74 M6** 32.18N 65.00W
Bern Switzerland **86 E4** 46.57N 7.26E
Bernard Lodge CE Jam. **30 C2** 17.58N 76.56W
Berridale PD Jam. **31 E3** 18.09N 76.29W
Bethel Gap TS Jam. **31 D2** 17.59N 76.35W
Bethel Town WD Jam. **28 C3** 18.18N 77.57W
Bhutan Asia **88 G4** 27.25N 90.00E
Bickersteth JS Jam. **28 C3** 18.21N 77.55W
Bideford EH Jam. **29 D1** 17.57N 77.42W
Big Creek *town* Belize **72 C3** 16.31N 88.24W
Billy Bay *town* EH Jam. **29 C1** 17.54N 77.47W
Bimini Islands The Bahamas **46 A6** 25.43N 79.13W
Birches Hill HR Jam. **28 B3** 18.23N 78.06W
Biscay, Bay of *sea* France/Spain **87 D4** 45.40N 5.07W
Bishkek Kyrgyzstan **93 M8** 42.54N 74.32E
Bismarck Sea P.N.G. **91 D3** 4.01S 149.01E
Bissau Guinea Bissau **82 B6** 11.52N 15.39W
Bito AW Jam. **31 D2** 17.58N 76.40W

Published by Collins
An imprint of HarperCollins Publishers
Westerhill Road, Bishopbriggs, Glasgow G64 2QT
www.harpercollins.co.uk

HarperCollins Publishers
Macken House, 39/40 Mayor Street Upper, Dublin 1, D01 C9W8, Ireland

First edition 2018

© HarperCollins Publishers 2018
Maps © Collins Bartholomew Ltd and Mona Informatix Limited 2018

Collins ® is a registered trademark of HarperCollins Publishers Ltd

This book contains FSC™ certified paper and other controlled sources to ensure responsible forest management.

For more information visit: www.harpercollins.co.uk/green

ISBN 978-0-00-829867-8

20 19 18 17 16 15 14 13 12 11 10

Printed in Bosnia and Herzogovina

All mapping in this atlas is generated from Collins Bartholomew digital databases. Collins Bartholomew, the UK's leading independent geographical information supplier, can provide a digital, custom, and premium mapping service to a variety of markets. For further information, e-mail: collinsbartholomew@harpercollins.co.uk or visit our website at www.collinsbartholomew.com

If you would like to comment on any aspect of this book, please contact us at the above address or online.
www.collins.co.uk
e-mail: collinsmaps@harpercollins.co.uk

Photo credits

cover Photo Spirit/SS (Blue Mountains), Danita Delmont/SS (bird); **p8-9** Antony McAulay/SS; **p9** xfox01/SS (sun); **p12** Vilainecrevette/SS; **p13** Vyshnivskyy/SS; **p15** NASA Earth Observatory (satellite image), THONY BELIZAIRE/AFP/Getty Images (Red Cross); **p16** Jonathan Torgovnik/Getty Images; **p17** Christopher Pillitz/Getty Images; **p20** Jeremy Beeler/SS (Xunantunich), Everett Historical/SS (Columbus); **p21** NICOLAS DERNE/AFP/Getty Images (Syrian), ALBERTO PIZZOLI/AFP/Getty Images (Patricia Scotland); **p22-23** Planet Observer/Getty Images; **p22** Broadbelt/SS (Climate change), Ethan Daniels/SS (Waste), Sven Creutzmann/Mambo photo/Getty Images (Mining damage), Robin Moore/Getty Images (Deforestation); **p23** Gillian Holliday/SS (cane toad), Pierre-Yves Babelon/SS (casuarina), Frolova_Elena/SS (lionfish), Ethan Daniels/SS (Endangered species), Steve Photography/SS (Wind power), Wild Horizon/Getty Images (Coral reef damage), Altin Osmanaj/SS (Carbon dioxide emissions); **p24** Asma Samoh/SS (coat of arms), Danita Delmont/SS (bird), graphicsbuzz.com (tree), songsak/SS (flower), twiggyjamaica/SS (fruit); **p25** Robert S. Patton/Getty Images (Cockpit Country), mikolajn/SS (Falmouth), Photo Spirit/SS (Blue Mountains), KKulikov/SS (mangrove), Craig F Scott/SS (Rio Minho), Education Images/Getty Images (Kingston); **p27** UniversalImagesGroup/Getty Images, **p28** jiawangkun/SS (Falmouth Courthouse), KGPA Ltd/Alamy Stock Photo (ginger); **p31** Jan Schneckenhaus/SS (Dunns River Falls), delaflow/SS (Kingston); **p32** travel.gypsy.photography/SS (Lucea), CO Leong/SS (cruise ship), Lucky-photographer/SS (lighthouse), KKulikov/SS (Nassau Mountains); **p33** Westend61 GmbH/Alamy Stock Photo (church), Kavon McKenzie/SS (Turtle Bay), Craig F Scott/SS (distillery), Photo Spirit/SS (Rodney memorial), Eye Ubiquitous/Alamy Stock Photo (banana plantation); **p34** Arina Grin/SS; **p35** Taku/SS (Stevenson screen), Darren Pullman/SS (thermometer), dotini/SS (rain gauge), pixfly/SS (anemometer & wind vane), Ramilon Stockphoto/SS (barometer), Neil Cooper/Alamy Stock Photo (Ivan), Stocktrek Images, Inc./Alamy Stock

Photo (Gustav); **p36** Art Directors & TRIP/Alamy Stock Photo (deforestation), Penny Tweedie/Alamy Stock Photo (mining damage), Robert Fried/Alamy Stock Photo (water pollution), National Geographic Creative/Alamy Stock Photo (iguana); **p37** Ian Cumming/Getty Images (coffee), National Geographic Creative/Alamy Stock Photo (fishing); **p38** Education Images/Getty Images (Port Kaiser), Michael Dwyer/Alamy Stock Photo (distillery); **p39** Craig F Scott/SS; **p41** Sean Sprague/Alamy Stock Photo; **p43** Georgios Kollidas/SS (Bogle), Hulton Deutsch/Getty Images (Bustamante), MPI/Stringer/Getty Images (Garvey), Georgios Kollidas/SS (Gordon), Keystone Pictures USA/Alamy Stock Photo (Manley), unknown (Queen Nanny), Georgios Kollidas/SS (Sharpe), Roger Sedres/Alamy Stock Photo (Bolt), Aspen Photo/SS (Fraser-Pryce), Ian Dickson/Getty Images (Marley), Gary Doak/Alamy Stock Photo (James); **p44** CREATISTA/SS (rafting), Ruth Peterkin/SS (Ocho Rios); **p46** NASA Earth Observatory; **p47** jo Crebbin/SS; **p48** Wikimedia Commons (both); **p49** Frontpage/SS; **p50** glenda/SS (Haiti), hessbeck/SS (Santo Domingo); **p51** Sean Pavone/SS; **p52** R.A.R. de Bruijn Holding BV/SS; **p54** PlusONE/SS; **p55** OkFoto/SS; **p56** T photography/SS; **p57** Paul Wishart/SS; **p58** Salim October/SS; **p59** Qin Xie/SS; **p60** NASA Earth Observatory; **p61** CJG - Caribbean/Alamy Stock Photo (fish market), LOOK Die Bildagentur der Fotografen GmbH/Alamy Stock Photo (Crop Over); **p62** timsimages/SS; **p64** lidian Neeleman/SS (Port of Spain), Anton_Ivanov/SS (Pitch Lake), John de la Bastide/SS (Maracas Bay); **p65** Chad Mohammed (mud volcano), John de la Bastide/SS (Caroni Swamp), Martin Mecnarowski/SS (scarlet ibis); **p67** Salim October/SS (Carnival), John de la Bastide/SS (steelband); **p69** Martin Mecnarowski/SS; **p71** ZUMA Press, Inc./Alamy Stock Photo (Mash), Nature Picture Library/Alamy Stock Photo (mining); **p72** Tami Freed/SS; **p97** George Burba/SS (tundra), Serg Zastavkin/SS (taiga), Oleg Znamenskiy/SS (savanna), oleandra/SS (Sahara). [SS = Shutterstock]

Acknowledgements

p19 (population map) Global Rural-Urban Mapping Project, Version 1 (GRUMPv1): Population Density Grid. Palisades, NY: NASA Socioeconomic Data and Applications Center (SEDAC);

p34 (seasonal rainfall maps) Meteorological Service of Jamaica; **p36** (land cover map) MODIS data from NASA EOSDIS Land Processes DAAC, USGS Earth Resources Observation and Science (EROS) Center, Sioux Falls, South Dakota (https://lpdaac.usgs.gov); **p37** (fishing grounds) NRCA Data unit.

Many thanks to the following for their contributions to the atlas: Kevin Facey, Kevin Thompson, Farah Christian, Neil Sealey, and the team at the Mona GeoInformatics Institute, Jamaica.